Route 42

A Novel way to Cut Costs, Change Culture and Create Competitiveness

Dr Richard Russill

Cambridge
Academic

Imprints include:
Liverpool Academic Press
Liverpool Business Publishing
Tudor Educational

ISBN 10: 1903-499-96-8
ISBN 13: 978-1903-499-96-2

Printed and bound in the United Kingdom by 4edge Ltd, 7a Eldon Way Industrial Estate, Hockley, Essex, SS5 4AD.

About this book... and the people who helped to write it.

THIS BOOK IS primarily about people. These are the practitioners, valued colleagues when I was in the oil business, consulting partners and clients, and executives in all sorts of companies and at all levels with whom I have worked. I respect all these inspirational people and celebrate what they have boldly achieved by trying new approaches ... in the process challenging the general view in business about procurement's role in it. In doing so they have not only made positive impacts in their companies but have discovered new capabilities in themselves and the fulfilment that goes with it. Two factors have brought all our minds together. One is the belief that business success comes through people, not despite them. And secondly, that procurement is not a mechanistic function but an intensely human commercial activity. Procurement's story needs to be told in a different way. This novel does that, informed as it is by real life and real people. Too many to name, I thank you all.

Other folk have helped enormously in different ways. Tony Shephard, long-standing friend and author himself, showed me how to add colour and a sense of place to my writing, without which he said it looked like the minutes of a business meeting! Going further back, Lora Western (then in the media business in Hong Kong and latterly with *The Wall Street Journal*) showed me how to write in the first place, saying in a few words what initially took many. Huge thanks to you, Lora, and also to Nicki Copeland (copy editing) and Jacqueline Dabromeit (cover design, using Nick Russill's photo) who contributed so much to the quality of the prose and the book's appearance. Thank you Prof Mike Leenders for your friendship and encouragement over the years, and for reviewing *'Route 42'* ... and Andrew Young at Cambridge Academic for enthusiastically gaining commitment to publish it.

Then there are the friends and business contacts who have dipped into the story or consumed it completely prior to publishing. Their encouraging reactions have meant so much, especially coming from folk who aren't necessarily interested in a business narrative, let alone a procurement one. Especial thanks go to my wife Sue who not only endured my absences whilst away on business or at home with the writing, but also read the finished product. Her conclusion that the book 'is enjoyable and strangely compelling' means all the more given that she can be a stern critic!

Richard Russill
Pembrokeshire, Wales, UK

'Route 42' is dedicated to Megan, Elin, Lilia, Mia, Thomas and Benjamin as they set out on life's journey, inspiring others with their fresh takes on life and their hopes for it.

42

Chapter One

A Wednesday in August – California

SCOTT MEETS ME at the front of the hotel and we start a journey punctuated by several exclamations along the lines of 'shit we need a U-turn.' Tyres squeal on sun-baked tarmac as we hurtle east into the late summer Californian afternoon. If he was trying to shake off the cops he'd have succeeded, though probably losing all sense of direction. But this doesn't happen and we arrive at Gullmech Corporation's offices one hour inland from Los Angeles, where Scott is Supply Manager. He joined Gullmech at the beginning of the year, having worked for a food and drinks company beforehand.

Gullmech's office building is what you'd expect of a high-tech aerospace company. Lots of glass and stainless steel set into a long, single-storey building, faced in state-of-the-art composite cladding under a raised-seam metal roof. Hard angles and reflective glass are softened by palm trees and well-watered lawns fronting the building. Although they can't be seen, I assume the engineering workshops and factory area stretch away from the rear of the offices. A gleaming Hummer SUV dominates the parking lot. With winches, anchor points, spotlights and enormous tyres, it looks every muscle-bound inch ready for interplanetary warfare rather than terrestrial travel. We park next to it. Scott reveals that the vehicle belongs to the company's new VP and General Manager.

First thing is to meet him. Ed Bradbury turns out to be a friendly, business-like, 'can-do' sort of guy. Tall and slim, he listens and talks well, has excellent business experience and has clearly done his homework on me. My first impression, formed outside by the Hummer's testosterone-charged presence, was incorrect. He hasn't got an ego problem. Ed has that magic mix of make-it-happen energy and people-handling skill. He won't suffer fools gladly or tolerate management waffle but will encourage candour and inspire people, adding value to their efforts rather than just measuring whatever results from it. He'll be a real force for change – organic, sustained change and not here-today gone-tomorrow flashes in the pan.

Ed's office exhibits the usual US-executive array of sports trophies and business textbooks. Politely, he asks if he can finish an urgent email he'd been writing when I arrived. While waiting, I notice a wall-mounted framed citation under a photograph of a guy called Vince Lombardi, the legendary American Football Coach. The text, according to Vince, is the gospel of 'how to achieve greatness' – not his, but releasing greatness in others. All of it is good, but Ed's email dexterity is such that there's only enough time to note the first paragraph: 'Winning is not a sometime thing; it's an all time thing. You don't win once in a while, you don't do things right once in a while – you do things right all the time. Winning is a habit. Unfortunately, so is losing.'

Coffee arrives and we get down to business. Ed introduces himself. 'So, at last I get to meet Mr Walsh! Jon, you're very welcome.'

Ed hopes the flight went well and that the hotel is OK. Like me he has a wife and three kids, and we spend a few moments on introductory stuff. I comment on Lombardi's philosophy, which I guess Ed shares: every person has inherent dignity and potential. The leader's job is to respect the former and realise the latter. Ed wholeheartedly agrees and I remark that one big bonus of transforming procurement is that company culture changes as well.

'Which is exactly what we need here,' he says, and I make a mental note to discuss this more, but later.

Time is money and Ed decides we should move on. 'First off, here's the company structure. Gullmech is part of AeroCorp Division within the Penserin Group. AeroCorp is an international operation with a head office in London and member companies in Europe and the USA. We're all precision-engineering companies in the aerospace business. Gullmech's the largest.'

'How many companies in the group?'

'Eleven. All dynamic businesses, they were private companies until AeroCorp acquired them. We want to get cohesion between them around standards and priorities. Getting better at procurement is one of them. But we need to keep each firm's entrepreneurial spirit without creating a lot of bureaucracy.'

Ed explains the business background. Margins are under pressure and suppliers are forcing price increases. At the other end of the business, customers demand price reductions varying from five to twenty-five per cent. Some purchasing savings have been made, amounting to two per cent of total expenditure, but these are mostly one-off non-repeatable achievements. A more powerful and sustainable way to increase profit has to be found. The opportunity is huge, as a significant proportion of sales revenue is spent on purchases.

'So what's Gullmech's role in this?'

'Well, we're a profitable operation but AeroCorp thinks we're receptive to change and keen to test new ideas. That's why we've been asked to try some. But I'm not a procurement person and I'm uncomfortably aware of how high our supply costs are. They're much higher than internal costs and, boy, we so need to make cost savings, given the economic downturn. How can we do it?'

We talk about procurement's general image in the business world and how many people see it as solely to do with making contracts and placing purchase orders.

'So is that how you define procurement?' Ed asks.

'No, that's more a definition of purchasing. Purchasing's about taking ownership of something in exchange for money, and it's often confined to buying 'things' as distinct from service contracts. Procurement is about acquiring, through one of several legal means, a resource required by the business. It's a broader concept, covering tangible materials as well as less-tangible requirements like services and expertise.'

'Not sure I agree,' Ed interjects. 'That's just a different name, not a different concept.'

'You could say that. But calling it procurement recognises that you don't always have to pay money for something, especially when you find out how much a supplier values doing business with you. Call it "purchasing" and everyone assumes that payment goes along with it.'

'Right, call it procurement for now so we can move on!'

'OK. But here's one last example of what it's all about. There's a successful Scandinavian company that says this about procurement's *raison d'être*: "The purpose of our procurement activity is to ensure that we have access to, and can acquire things from, the supply markets we need to succeed as a business both now and in future."

Ed doesn't play around with words but he gets the significance of this. It's all about managing external resources in order to survive and thrive as a company. I tell him that just before this meeting I'd had a phone call from a CPO in Europe …

'Hold on, what's CPO?'

'Stands for Chief Procurement Officer, an increasingly used term. But this CPO's title is Vice-President, Sourcing. They chose that because it strikes a more strategic note. More sourcing folk report to her, and they in turn manage procurement teams. What's important is not the actual word used but what it means to the rest of the company.'

Ed agrees. He understands all about the importance of image and perceptions.

Back to me. 'Procurement's the word increasingly used now, but only a few firms see it as a vital business process to be managed with the same attention and strategic ambition as they give to generating sales revenue and operating company assets. CEOs have to decide what priority and resources should be devoted to procurement but, too often, the starting point is, "If we invest more in procurement, what will be the payback?" This mentality forever shackles procurement to the cost-savings treadmill.'

Ed fidgets with a mini-Hummer on his desk. 'So what's wrong with that?'

'Nothing,' I respond, 'so long as you don't mind leaving a lot of your profit in your suppliers' pockets. OK, cutting costs is a big attraction. The prize is huge and procurement can deliver. But if that's all you go for it perpetuates procurement's image as an isolated functional activity, dealing with the supply market consequences of a business decision someone else has made. It assumes that a supply market exists and only muscle power is needed to get what you want.'

Ed fidgets some more with the Hummer and isn't overly convinced. 'I'm hearing what you say, Jon, but surely my buyers are here to do what the budget holders ask and to place orders where they can get the best prices and delivery.'

'Right,' I say, 'but you have to ask, "Is that all of the job, or only a part of the job?

'C'mon Jon, that's splitting hairs.'

'No. If it's the former, then you'll continue having users specifying gold plate when less will do, they'll be victims of subtle sales tactics, they'll stay in the comfort zone of using familiar suppliers, they'll be easy meat for monopolies and cartels, poor supplier performance will go unchallenged, they'll feel helpless in the face of aggressive price rises…'

'OK, OK,' interrupts Ed. 'I'm getting the picture and I don't like it. A lot of unnecessary costs are being incurred. But surely it's not the buyers' job to tell other colleagues how their budgets should be spent?'

'No. Budget holders decide what the money should be spent on, or – better – they should specify the need that they want a supplier to satisfy. But then they often spoil things by instructing how the money should be spent and with whom.'

'But if they're held responsible for their budgets, surely they've got to behave like this?'

'They will unless two things are made clear. First, it's not their money they're spending but the company's. Second, they are, often without realising it, part of a procurement process that spans right across the business. Without realising this, budget holders guard money like it's their own but spend it like it's someone else's. The worst behave like prima donnas.'

Ed smiles wryly. 'I guess I can paraphrase our friend Lombardi on the wall there. "Procurement is not a one-person sometime thing; it's an all person, all time thing. You don't buy things right once in a while – you buy things right all the time. Winning great supply deals is a habit. Unfortunately, so is losing them.'

It's time for more coffee. This coincides with Ed needing to leave to preside over the daily business-review meeting. I stay in his office and, under Mr Lombardi's gaze, ponder why procurement's 'image problem' is so widespread.

Ed's executive assistant, Angie, interrupts my reverie with the news that Ed's going to be locked in meetings for the rest of the afternoon. He's allocated more time with me tomorrow but right now it makes sense to return to the hotel. Angie will arrange a car to take me there.

Ground transportation awaits at Gullmech's entrance. I sink into the town car's vast rear seat as the driver, Ray, launches us west into the setting sun and towards the hotel. This offers 'suites' rather than just rooms, accessed from balconies on different levels, all built round a central atrium. Down below is like a holiday resort. A palm-fringed river runs into sandy-coloured pools where goldfish languidly feed off discarded bagels and potato chips floating in the 'sea'. A little bridge leads to a thatched hut whose purpose is unclear. Tables and chairs cluster under more palm trees, served by a bar and restaurant outlet off to one side. Beer is a good idea and is served promptly with a paper chit which I pocket. Scowling, the barman tells me to 'tottleitup'.

'Cheers,' seems an appropriate response, given that I don't speak his language.

'No, tottleitup,' he repeats, the scowl now becoming impatient.

Oh, I get it … he wants a tip added to the bill. Why didn't he say?

One side of the atrium is devoted to retail therapy: a souvenir shop, ladies' fashion, a cigar emporium and a jeweller. There's also a chemist from which I need supplies. They sell melatonin in this country so maybe this'll deal with impending jet lag and sleep loss. I wait for them to find it and read a product-recall notice posted nearby. It's not been a good week. A breast pump recall is required because it's making a dodgy contact, the 'Energy Bounce' nutrient bars have lost their mojo, and the 'Good Mood' anxiety pills have stopped working.

Just as well it's happy hour at the bar.

Chapter 2

NEXT DAY I'M back at Gullmech. Angie has set me up with freshly brewed coffee in Ed's office. It's on the 'management corridor' so the offices have windows, presumably to be able to check on who comes and goes. Walking along the corridor from the reception area is like climbing the organisation chart. The further along you go the higher up you get – status-wise that is. The President has the corner suite right at the end, accessed only through Angie's office where she runs a sort of checkpoint operation.

Ed is still running his daily meeting so there's time to think back to yesterday's discussion about the role of procurement. This is not generally seen as a core 'must get it right' business activity which attracts constant CEO interest and best talent. The problem is that impressive words about what procurement can deliver come cap in the hand of a service provider. Too often the business press refers to procurement being a service or support function, while others claim that a service mentality is key to maintaining effective cross-functional engagement. Unsurprisingly, people identify more easily with these simple ideas than with the more cerebral concepts of value and supply vulnerability. Mainstream business thinking marginalises procurement as a 'supporting service', and this is precisely what is holding it back.

Where has the service mentality come from? Maybe Adam Smith is to blame. His 1776 magnum opus 'The Wealth of Nations' advocated the division of labour whereby huge productivity gains came from breaking down a manufacturing process into separate steps, and then getting people to focus only on one step. Is this how functional silos originated? To do him justice, Smith recognised that taking this concept too far would be detrimental because it would not encourage any sort of mental engagement with the task in hand.

Established in the early 1900s, today's financial accounting conventions don't help either. These reflect what business has been done rather than how it is performed. The biggest sin was to bury external supply costs in total costs of sales. This hides the magnitude of supply-side spend and also taints it with the notion that sales are good and costs are bad. Other ingredients in the 'service' cocktail are the dogmatic pursuit of functional excellence and deferring to the customer as 'king'.

Recent research into artificial intelligence provides further evidence of procurement's lowly status. Three hundred and sixty-six jobs were ranked according to how likely they were to be taken over by a robot. If you are a shelf filler or a bus driver, then … relax. The survey predicts the buyer's job will be axed before yours, while the safest job is being a manager of a pub. What's missing in this research is any understanding of those aspects of procurement's work where human interactions are essential and cannot be replaced by algorithms. This covers internal and external relationships and behaviours, now and in future.

But it's not all bad news. Not long ago a Google search for 'CPOs' came up with 'Community Post Offices' as the top result. Nowadays Chief Procurement Officers do indeed get a deserved mention on page one, and yet, of 278 CPOs recently polled, ninety-nine per cent said their 'function did not have a high enough profile within the organisation'. Better education of top managers was offered as one solution, but it could be said that CPOs should get better at explaining themselves in the first place. Banning the 'F' word would be a start. Describing procurement as a 'service function' perpetuates its image as a mechanistic by-product of someone else's activity.

In recent years, smart CPOs-to-be have been quick to survey what for many companies has been virgin cost-saving territory, and then telling a compelling story of how supply cost savings can increase profit. One CPO said, 'We have to dazzle the board with what we can do.' This successfully won him a new licence to exert influence in the company and paved the way to making dazzling cost savings. However, a savings honeymoon only lasts about eighteen to twenty-four months. CPOs can unwittingly be the architects of their own problems if, at the same time as delivering cost savings, they do not create a very different landscape in which procurement can operate once the easy wins have disappeared. Justifying one's existence solely by cranking out cost reductions loses all credibility when the savings gravy train runs out of steam.

At that moment Ed returns with a breezy 'Good morning, Jon' welcome.

'Jon, I've been thinking about our discussion yesterday. It sounded good but only dealt with some of the causes of procurement's image problem. I'm interested in what can be done to improve it. You're right that business today poses tough questions, and you're saying procurement can provide many of the answers but is often not positioned to do so effectively, if at all. So what can we do?'

I summarise. 'With supply expenditures hidden in total cost of sales, customers as kings, the main value-adding players within the company behaving like functionally excellent prima donnas, and procurement's vision impaired by cost-saving myopia, it's not surprising that procurement's light is hidden under the bushel. The danger is that without a compelling message, told at the right time and constantly retold, it may be extinguished.'

Ed looks like he wished he hadn't asked the question. 'So what can be done to tell procurement's story in a different way and make it stick?'

'Getting back to basics is the main thing. Successful company founders share at least two characteristics. First, they look at both ends of the business at the same time. With little in the way of costly in-house assets or resources, profit margin largely depends on sales revenue minus supply costs. The second trait is to regard suppliers as sources of value, new ideas and goodwill. A firm often loses sight of these characteristics as it grows.

'But not always. Once upon a time a guy called Lord Weinstock built GEC into a company which, under his leadership, survived profitably by prudent, hard-headed financial management. He said, "The secret is to see what the market will pay for a product. You then see if you can manufacture at that price. You then work out what you can get off the costs by squeezing a discount out of the suppliers, producing in bulk and reducing your manpower – and that is your profit." This brutal logic implies that procurement's job is to make cost savings. However Weinstock's message was a different one. Procurement was there to achieve a price target, not a savings one, and the price target was hard-wired into the company's financial plan.'

I continue by telling Ed a story. 'It starts in Kananaskis country, eighty-five kilometres west of Calgary, its jagged peaks and U-shaped valleys a reminder of the last ice age when kilometre-thick, million-year-old glaciers melted to mere remnants just 12,000 years ago. A Canadian petrochem company has chosen this location for a weekend retreat for its top team. The venue, a mountain lodge smelling of pine wood and log fires, enjoys fabulous views. At our feet, a crystal-blue river ripples over multicoloured pebbles. Then, further back, are stands of pine trees and further still a horizon of snow-capped mountains: the Rockies. Huge windows in the conference room make it feel like we're outside although we're not. The company boss opens the proceedings with a few words. Always an anxious time, this, as you never know what they're going to say.

'He is brief and to the point. "Welcome to you all. Now, listen. Business is simple: we buy things, we transform them and we sell things. And we have to excel at all of that to succeed as a business. That's what this meeting is all about: to look hard at the 'buy' side of the equation to find out how we can get even better at it. Not if, but how."

'Now there's a quote that makes impact and is memorable because things aren't often put that way. What a welcome change from the normal overly sales-oriented approach to life: "We sell something, then hope we can make it, and grudgingly place a few purchase orders because we're forced to … but let's at least go for the cheapest price to ease the pain." Sure, this is cynical, but it's exactly the toxic mindset nurtured by the conventions of financial accounting and MBA training overly oriented towards the top line and the way the beans are counted.

'While it may seem that joined-up buy/transform/sell thinking only applies to manufacturing companies, it equally works in service industries and the public sector. An appropriate paraphrase then is, "We acquire value, we organise it and we deliver value."'

Ed's been listening hard. 'OK, I'm detecting some persistent messages here. Jon, I think you ought to meet some of the folks I'd like you to work with. I've asked Scott to show you round and make introductions.'

He buzzes for Scott who eventually appears and we start the round of meeting people. This takes most of the day, at the end of which I report back to Ed. He wants me to meet some of those guys again to start working out how to do things better.

My return to the hotel coincides again with happy hour. I'm beginning to think this is a 24/7 operation. I'm not that hungry but there's a table laid out with cuts of fresh vegetables and a variety of dips. The dips have clearly been well visited as several have bits of carrot and broccoli floating about in them. Not pretty but, for the moment, nourishing. Later in the evening, when a few more fingers have dipped in seeking submerged food, the bacterial brew will probably be life-threatening.

I don't stay around for long and, back in my room, I enter that jet-lagged limbo of feeling tired but not having enough energy to do anything about it. TV proves to be massively un-entertaining so bed really is the only escape.

Chapter 3

Friday

IWAKE AFTER a short melatonin-induced sleep, but refreshed enough to enjoy a spectacular view from the hotel window. Thick, early-morning fog lies low nearby while in the middle distance a higher structure has come up for air and early sunshine. It turns out to be Mount Everest. But this is California, and Everest is a scaled-down version in a theme park near the hotel. The horizon comprises rugged outlines of hills bathed in morning-glory gold and which, for all I know, are alive with the Sound of Music. The image lingers as the TV news reports on a famous male actor caught using a hotel's ladies room. Image and incident merge to create the startling possibility of surprising Maria-the-nun in the 'jahn'.

Scott again shuttles me from the hotel and we dock alongside Ed's SUV.
'Why, hello again, Mr Walsh,' greets Donna at reception. 'Let me take you straight to the conference room. Oh, and have a nice day.'
Procurement people are gathered in the room, an airless place with no windows. But it's bright and business-like and there's plenty of space. Scott ushers me in and faces look our way, some expectant while others have the corralled look that says they've been told to be there.
Shirley is front and centre, this being a fair description of her character and not just where she's sitting. I guess she's in her forties and, I'm later told, does a good job as an experienced senior buyer. She knows how to make suppliers jump and doesn't take hostages. Next to her is Antony, a thin, English, bespectacled guy who's over on assignment from Gullmech's sister company in the UK. He's in charge of a big capital investment project here and its supply implications mean he's interested in what this meeting's about. The project is about automating some production processes. Antony has a mild manner which disguises a high IQ. He could become a good ally in telling procurement's new story. Next is tall, lean Scott, whom I already know. He's fairly new to Gullmech, having been brought in to replace a guy who wasn't up to Ed's expectations. Scott looks like he has a safe pair of supply management hands, but I wonder if he's got what it takes to

thrive in procurement's new dawn, if there is one. Ed is there and talking to a woman with spectacular brown hair which cascades at least to waist height. This is Elaine and she deals with purchase-order operations. Her lively and assertive welcome suggests that she's capable of much more than clerical work. Maybe that's why Ed invited her to this session. Finally there's John, also from the UK and deputed by AeroCorp's CEO to stay tuned to the procurement story in case any of it can be used in the other sister companies. He's an accountant, so could be an asset if we can get him to forget everything he's learned about procurement being a 'cost'.

I sense two moods in the room. Elaine wears the expression of a 'so what's this all about then?' newcomer while Shirley's body language belongs to the 'OK, so here we go again' folks who've seen it all before. She may well resist change, or at least need a lot of convincing. But Elaine and her like would love it as a change from being mired in day-to-day tasks that make anything more than treading water virtually impossible. Ed makes the introductions, emphasising that things have got to change procurement-wise. Not exactly a comforting message to those in the room who represent the pre-change *modus operandi*.

I thought the intro might go on for longer, but suddenly I have the ball and am wondering how to start. A flashback to the view from the hotel finds me mentioning the hills and the fog and, rather embarrassingly, I'm asking folks if they'd prefer to be 'in the fog or up in the hills'. Ed looks puzzled.

'The hills,' they unison.

I guess this is not because they want a holiday but instead hope that their working life can be devoted to a purpose higher than playing King Canute to an incoming tide of trivia. A few words about the 'inevitability of change' might be appropriate. But first we have to deal with 'resistance'.

'Some people like it in the fog and don't want to change,' I observe. 'Fog is comfortable because it hides the nasty stuff that might happen in the future. It also means other folk can't see what we're doing.'

Heads nod through, I hope, engagement rather than hypnosis.

'And then there are those who say, "But Gullmech's already profitable. Why mend what isn't broken?"' Upsetting apple carts and rocking boats come to mind, possibly because boats stop rocking when they sink or somebody drains the pond.

We move on to the need for continual improvement and I give them a shot of Mr Lombardi. Then there's my previous boss who said, 'The day we stop trying to be better is the day we start getting worse. There's always someone who comes up behind and overtakes."

Heads nod some more as we recall prescient words from one of America's best-known change-management gurus: 'In future, job security will not come from employment,' she said. 'It will come from being employable.' That means you need to embrace change and develop new abilities.

'Sounds good,' says Ed, 'but how does this translate to the bottom line?'

I'm granted some thinking time by Angie, who comes in with menus. How come we've got so far without mentioning food? Office life in the USA depends extensively on the life forces emanating from doughnuts and drink machines. Earlier this morning the procurement people were passing round peanuts and I caught myself hoping that this didn't reflect their lowly status in the company's pecking order.

Now Angie hands me a flier from Davina's Deli and asks what sandwich I'd like delivered at lunchtime. I go for a healthy option.

'With fries, Jon?' but I decline on the basis that the one would cancel out the other. Other folks make their choices and Angie exits with a flourish, job done.

With food supply chains now secure, we move to the next topic: how do traditional purchasing mindsets compare with those of strategic procurement?

'Let's look first at the dollars. How much is Gullmech's annual sales revenue?'

I'm intrigued that, apart from Ed, only two folks actually know, and even then there's some negotiation as to whether its seventy-three million dollars or sixty. Ed confirms seventy-three, of which about thirty is spent in the supply market.

'Right. The first point is that "thirty" is a finite number; it's not zero. So just by being in business means you're in procurement. It's not discretionary. Smart companies ask themselves, "How can we do procurement as well as possible?" rather than viewing supply costs as a pain that has to be eradicated.'

'Yeah, but costs eat into our profit margin,' observes Ed. 'I hate costs.'

'I met an airline CEO who said the same thing but, when pressed, changed his position to only hating wasted costs!'

Ed considers. 'That makes sense. Let's accept that costs are a good thing if incurred wisely and we hunt down wasted costs instead.'

I agree. 'So, the old way defines procurement's job as dealing with the "thirty" of costs.'

'And thirty, being a lot less that seventy-three, means that it gets proportionally less attention?' Ed is catching on fast.

'Very often, yes. And that's assuming that thirty is clearly visible and not concealed in the cost of sales number. So better questions would be, "Are we managing our supply markets to enable seventy-three million dollars worth of business to be done in the first place? And have we got those markets poised to help drive our growth in sales revenues and profit margins in future?"'

'So what are people doing differently if they're focusing on the "seventy-three" rather than the "thirty"?' asks Antony. 'Surely the same activities are involved.'

'Yes, but only to some extent, and that's limited to what happens when contracts or orders are actually placed. Traditional procurement kicks in when a requisition arrives from the budget holder and is turned into a purchase order, which gets the supplier moving...'

'Yeah, and usually by yesterday,' mutters Elaine.

'That's looking at the "thirty"', I continue. '"Seventy-three" stimulates a different involvement from procurement, often much earlier in decision-making processes when specific needs are discussed and alternatives considered. Schedules and possible changes in future volumes can also be highlighted, all of which helps the buyer's negotiating position prior to contract placement.'

'How can procurement's contribution be measured then?' asks Scott, perhaps mindful of savings targets that he's got to meet.

'There's a huge difference. If procurement's focus is on the "thirty" of cost, then success will only be measured by how much it can be reduced...'

'Assuming day-to-day deliveries and qualities are on schedule and we're not constantly being jerked around by the scheduling system.' Elaine clearly feels sore about this aspect of her work.

'True. And getting day-to-day stuff right is a must-have before we'll ever get the chance to make a more strategic contribution.'

'Such as?' Ed looks tense, since making big savings is very much on his to-do list. He's thinking that strategic talk sounds good but won't deliver.

'The main thing is to meet challenging price and cost targets built into the company's financial plan. Setting these targets embeds procurement's views about the state of supply markets and trending prices. This is one way of connecting procurement's role directly to the "seventy-three".'

I remind them about the joined-up thinking evident in the Weinstock approach, and continue, 'Simply doing isolated deals that cost less than budgets suggests that the budgets were wrong in the first place. And over-emphasising cost savings perpetuates the idea that making them is the whole reason for procurement's existence.'

'Jon, you seem to be reluctant to talk about cost savings at all,' observes Ed. 'Are we ever going to deal with them?'

'OK. Although meeting cost targets is the main objective, measuring cost savings versus budgets or previous prices shows what can be achieved by doing things differently.'

'Differently like how?' Shirley probes.

'Well, here are some general benchmarks. Many purchases for similar items are done separately as and when they're required. This incurs repeated effort and fails to exploit purchasing power. But aggregating fragmented deals earns volume discounts of around thirteen per cent.'

Antony has an idea. 'I guess even more aggregation is possible if budget holders standardise some of their specifications rather than wanting basically the same stuff but with cosmetic differences which result in different specs.'

'I like that,' says Ed, beginning to look happier at last. 'And the other benchmarks?'

'Collaborating with suppliers can yield fifteen-plus per cent cost savings. For example, customers usually tell suppliers precisely what they want to buy, but it's better to specify the need they wish to satisfy rather than dictate how to do it.'

'I have a great example from my previous job with the food company.' Scott leans forward in his chair, becoming more animated. 'The user wanted sugar to put in the fruit drinks but the cost was way beyond budget…'

'And sugar wasn't what they really wanted, was it?' chimes Elaine, catching on fast.

'Exactly. We got them to realise that sugar isn't the only way to sweeten things and there might be alternatives that give the same result.'

'What happened next?' Shirley's taking more interest.

'We worked with the user and the food-tech folk and found a sweetening product that was as acceptable as sugar, but much cheaper. So we bought that instead.'

People turn to me for a reaction.

'Scott, that's a great example of internal collaboration, and you probably also had to get new suppliers on board with your new needs. Opening up such debates with suppliers allows them to offer alternatives. They can also suggest different delivery schedules or contracting arrangements which fit in better with their own plans and remove wasted costs.'

John's been quietly taking notes, but his antennae twitch at the mention of wasted costs. 'I reckon that's win-win,' he surmises. 'Unnecessary costs on the supplier's side can be saved while leaving their margin intact. So the overall price comes down and the buyer pays less. Neat.'

'That sounds like a great line we can use,' Shirley observes, 'asking a supplier what they can do to remove wasted costs from the current supply arrangements. That'll save me from beating them up to save money my way!'

Ed has been keeping score. 'OK, we've got thirteen and fifteen per cent on the table. Jon, what's next?'

'Outmanoeuvring hostile supply markets.'

'Meaning what?' says Shirley. 'If I have a hostile supplier I terminate them!' People chuckle, knowing that Shirley is capable of doing just that.

'Here's the thing,' says Scott. 'You can ditch some suppliers, but only if you've got alternatives ready to take over. Sometimes you don't have that option and you have to take a different approach. I read somewhere about a four-box grid that clarifies things. It goes like this…'

Ed interrupts. 'Let's not go there at the moment, Scott. I want to hear more about the hostiles.' He looks at me to carry on.

'Think monopolies and cartels. There's a jungle for you. But innocent buyers go in and get ripped off. Cartel prices can be at least twenty-five per cent higher than competitive ones, often higher, even up to a hundred per cent.'

'Surely not?' Antony queries.

'I'm afraid "surely" is the word. Monopoly situations are more obvious, but trying to get lower prices from them is a waste of effort. It's better to get other goodies included for the price paid. But cartels are clever and good at disguising their existence. The sure way to trigger them is for a buyer to go out there asking for several competitive quotes.'

'And I need to hear that we don't do that.' Ed scans the table looking for reassurance, but gets an uneasy silence instead.

John comes to the rescue. 'It's true that seeking three or more quotes is common practice but it makes the big assumption that "three" is some magic number and the lowest quote represents the best deal going.'

Elaine joins in. 'It also assumes the competing sources are actually competing and not conspiring to rig prices.'

'Which brings us back to the four-box thing …'

'Yeah, but not yet, Scott,' Ed interrupts, amused. 'I can tell you're keen to share it and we'll give you the floor later. But perhaps now's a good time to summarise before we take a break. Jon, what you're saying is that getting procurement to focus on the needs of the whole business, and its strategy, opens up many possibilities which aren't there if all we do is cut sharp deals once the budget holder has said, "Buy."'

'OK so far.'

'And then you've said that if we give procurement the time and space to find ways of optimising current arrangements and to really understand markets then we can make some big cost breakthroughs.'

Shirley cuts in on Ed. 'Yeah, but only if we're intelligent and not forced to be stupid.' This earns her a sharp look from Ed, but I don't think it's career-threatening.

Ed looks at his score sheet. 'OK, I've got thirteen, fifteen and twenty-five per cents written here. I want to get my hands on that stuff.'

'But not before we've worked out, from Gullmech's total supply-side spend, where to apply the different tactics. The supply market is complex, and a "one approach fits all" just won't work. Also, these numbers are not sacrosanct but are good guidelines. More may be realised in practice.'

John reflects on something else we discussed. 'I also got the message that we should focus on business needs and cost targets rather than going hell-for-leather for cost savings. Savings have their place but they're not the end game.'

Yes, John is going to be useful. Maybe we can chat sometime to work out how.

For the time being another sort of quote is appropriate. This came from a Norwegian CPO in a company where the buy–transform–sell mindset was alive and well. I'd asked her to contribute to a conference on procurement measurement.

'How do you do it, anyway?' I asked her.

'Well, among other things we measure cost savings.'

I was disappointed to hear this and she sensed it. 'It's not what you think, Jon. In our company we don't feel the need to prove by calculation or example why "procurement" should exist. We already know it's important. The reason we measure things is because we want to do it as well as possible.'

Now that's better.

As if to emphasise this high point in the morning, the delivery from Davina's Deli arrives. We fall on her offerings once people remember what they ordered. Fortunately Angie kept records so there's no hijacking someone else's lunch if it looks more appetising. We have enough to sit out a siege: sandwiches, bagels, crisps, fruit, juices and jugs of coffee. But some of these folk have been at work since six this morning so I understand why they're peckish.

Chapter 4

WE CONSUME DAVINA'S Deli's delicious but diet-hostile offerings and decide to take a break outside. The way out is through the factory where they make the aerospace components. It's a mixture of good ol' lathe-turning and high-tech computerised machinery. Antony's automated pride and joy is getting a test run. It's a machine the size of a shipping container shoehorned in behind protective mesh fencing. Robot arms dart about, picking stuff up at one end, putting it through various engineering procedures before finally depositing finished articles in a bin. This, I learn, is the latest in a string of investments being made by AeroCorp's newish owner, Penserin Group, which is basically a venture-capital operation. But this is a VC company with a difference. It cares about the businesses it buys and does positive things to improve them rather than just stripping out and selling the juicy bits. Penserin is a turnaround specialist.

We continue outside to the parking lot. Although it's late summer we enjoy hot sun, blue sky and ice-cream vended from a machine almost the size of Antony's new toy.

Back in the cool air of the conference room Angie removes lunch debris, leaving us to consider how to make cost savings. I do a quick recap that this isn't procurement's primary objective. However, getting savings is necessary to catch the eye of the CEO and the rest of the company for them to see procurement in a new light.

'Let's just get out there and strong-arm savings out of our suppliers,' suggests Scott.

'Not a smart idea if they're the only one you've got for something critical,' says another.

Scott grins in agreement, suggesting he's got the answer he was looking for. He warms to the theme. 'Right, this morning I mentioned this analytical tool I read about…' He breaks off, half expecting Ed to put the item on hold yet again. But it doesn't happen.

'Do you mean the Kraljic Portfolio Analysis?' Clearly Ed has been on Google. Scott looks disappointed.

'I read that article when I was studying,' adds Elaine. 'It was in the *Harvard Business Review*. Kraljic's approach sorts the things you buy into different categories and assigns them to appropriate quadrants on a four-box grid. The idea is to treat each quadrant differently.'

'So do we do that here?' enquires Ed.

'You must be joking,' mutters Elaine into her bucket-size coffee cup shipped by Davina from the Deli. 'Our entire lives here are jerked about by the scheduling system so we're always playing catch-up, never mind doing things in a strategic way.'

It's always sad to see someone committing career suicide, but my fears are groundless as Ed smiles and doesn't take it personally. 'OK, OK,' he says, 'let's put that on the back burner for the moment. Tell me more about this Portfolio thing.'

'Right,' offers Scott. 'The article was by a guy called Peter Kraljic who developed a four-box grid, calling the x axis "Complexity of Supply Market" and the y axis "Importance of Purchasing".'

'And these labels mean...?'

'Complexity includes things like the competitiveness of the supply market and whether there are monopolies or cartels, pace of technology change, entry barriers, logistics complexity and so on. Complexity is low on the left side of the axis and high on the right.'

'And Importance of Purchasing?'

Elaine comes in. 'It's interesting that Kraljic actually used the Purchasing word because, in the article, he states that "there must be nothing less than a total change of perspective: from purchasing (an operational function) to supply management (a strategic one)". Anyway, sticking with his term, Importance of Purchasing includes things like total costs of materials bought, value added by them, the impact of their costs on profitability and so on. Importance is low at the bottom of the y axis and high at the top.'

This is a new side to Elaine. Interesting, isn't it, how a change from the daily grind allows people to shine in a new way.

Ed has drawn the two axes. 'OK, what's next?'

Back to Scott. 'Starting from bottom left and going clockwise he gave labels to the four boxes.' He looks unsure. 'I guess I can't remember the exact terms but I think bottom left was called "Miscellaneous".'

'Not quite,' corrects Elaine, who obviously has total recall of her study notes. 'It was "Non-critical Items". Top left was called "Leverage Items", top right was "Strategic Items" and bottom right was "Bottleneck".'

I reflect that Peter Kraljic, way back when his ideas were published in 1983, might well have been the first person to use the 'leverage' word which is so widely used now. One grudging reviewer referred to the Kraljic matrix thus: 'In a landscape bereft of any useful techniques which might dispel the idea that purchasing requires anything more than the back of an envelope to work on, Kraljic's Portfolio Analysis has to be welcomed as a step in the right direction.'

These miserable sentiments appeared shortly after Kraljic's idea came into view as an oasis of cool thinking in purchasing's intellectual desert. Its genius is that it held up a simple mirror to real life and revealed what was there, and what had to be done, with stark clarity. Testimony that Kraljic's approach was received as manna from heaven is that it has featured prominently in many presentations over the years made by CPO-hopefuls to their company boards. Typically it opened eyes to the magnitude of supply-side expenditure and the fact that supply markets must be treated in different ways. The result was to give new prominence to procurement's contribution to the firm, exactly as Kraljic intended. What he would not have liked was that 'making cost savings' was embraced as the main driver of change. Kraljic acknowledged that cost savings would be one result of doing procurement properly but its greater purpose was to evaluate supply risk, and then to develop supply strategies to manage it.

While Kraljic's paper provided the key that opened closed doors, it also described the strategic procurement world that lay beyond. The paper is a feast of common sense and gets you thinking about what you're doing when spending someone else's money. The abiding challenge is to advocate that we have to do more than just save it.

But back to Scott who, having been put right by Elaine, continues the master class undeterred. 'You then decide into which boxes you put the things you buy. Items in the bottom left are neither expensive nor mission critical so you don't put much, if any, effort into buying them. In fact it's better to get others to do it for you – perhaps even the budget holders! Bottom right, the Bottleneck Items, represent vital supplies but, since expenditure on them is not great, you don't waste effort searching for the lowest prices. What you concentrate on is supply security, ensuring that supplies are uninterrupted and, in the event that they are interrupted, that there are emergency supplies to call on.'

Ed studies his writing pad and I hope he's not putting the finishing touches to a doodle. But no, he's sketched the four-box grid and his pencil hovers top left. 'So I guess this is the opposite of what you've just said, Scott. There's a lot of money spent on these things and many of them might be vital for us, but our supply chains are not at risk because we have alternative sources and there's spare supply capacity in the market.'

'Exactly,' agrees Shirley, who's catching on fast, 'and that's where we can put the pressure on to get cost savings by negotiating harder.'

'If only we had the time,' growls Elaine, who is now bottom-dredging the coffee bucket.

This is not lost on Ed. 'Look, Elaine, part of my job is to change things to give you that time, and with Jon's help I'm determined to do it. But let's get one thing straight: we can't afford to hire new people and I'm not going to ask you to work 24/7. So we have to find ways to liberate time that's currently consumed by unnecessary tasks. However, like I said, that topic's on the back burner for the moment.'

Far from being on the back burner, Ed's pencil is now probing the hot spot which is the top right box on Kraljic's matrix. 'Surely we can push hard here as well since there's a lot of money tied up in these things?'

Elaine picks up the ball. 'That's right, but they're not called Strategic for nothing. They're highly important to us but we're also vulnerable to supply risks. We don't have the choices that we have for leverage items. So, since we're in a weaker position as a customer, we have to sweet-talk a cost saving from these suppliers rather than beat it out of them.'

'What do you mean, "weaker position"?' asks Shirley. 'Suppliers should be glad to have our business. If they know what's good for them they'll bend over backwards to help.'

'Only if they want to,' Scott explains. 'Look, some of the things we buy that are in the top-right quadrant come from monopoly suppliers. In other cases we know that supply capacity is very tight, so suppliers can choose who they want to sell to. And it might not always be us, especially given the hard time we've given some of them recently by withholding payments.'

'Yeah, why do we do that?' complains Elaine, now fired up on caffeine. 'I just don't understand why our accounts-payable people play these games just to massage cash flow. Don't they realise the damage it does?'

'Most likely not,' I agree. 'This is an example of what Ed and I were discussing earlier, where other people in the company don't realise they're part of the company's procurement process and that their actions, albeit well meant, do more harm than good when they don't look at the bigger picture.'

Elaine looks pleased that she's found an ally. I think she has a lot to offer the company but the current arrangements frustratingly limit any impact she can make. 'So let's get the accounts people sorted out, 'she says, 'before we go rocking the boat and upsetting vital suppliers further by forcing cost savings from them.'

The back burner's getting crowded now as Ed wants to park this topic there as well. 'We will deal with that,' he promises, 'but we've got to get the cost savings ball rolling now ourselves. Jon, what can do right away?'

'In general, focus on some specific targets but remain alert to other possibilities that crop up. They may not be exactly what you're targeting but the opportunities will be lost if you don't act on them now. For example, let's select four or five big-spend items from top left – that's the leverage items – and sweat some savings out of them. That's the main target area initially. But if a strategic supplier comes along with a price-increase request, or causes a quality problem, then seize these as opportunities to examine with them how the commercial and supply arrangements might be changed in order to remove wasted costs and improve supplier performance. The term "examine with them" implies more collaboration than is necessary with the suppliers of leverage items.'

A pause in the discussion alerts us to the fact that other things have to be acted on right now, so we take a short break.

Chapter 5

E D LIKES THE idea of sweating cost savings out of the system.
'So how do we do it?' His pencil hovers over a fresh page on his legal pad. We decide to chart up ideas as people think of them. Angie is summoned to activate the food chain again.

Even Shirley thaws out as the discussion gathers pace. In fact, she starts it. 'We had a good year last year,' she observes, 'and I'm realising that the volumes we bought from some suppliers were higher than expected. I'm going to ask for rebates.'

'Meaning what,' asks Angie, who, having reappeared with food and drink, stays on with growing interest in the discussion.

John supports Shirley. 'It's quite usual for supply agreements to have volume-related formulae where unit prices reduce as we buy bigger volumes. Suppliers use these so-called price breaks as incentives to get customers to buy more. This is because their fixed costs per unit are lower the greater the number of units made, plus there may be other economies of scale. So unit prices, and total costs, reduce.'

'I guess you have to be careful not to be seduced into buying more than needed just to get the lower price,' Angie observes. Hey, here again is someone whose talents may well not be fully realised in their current job.

'You're right, Angie,' adds John. 'And the opposite is also true. When volumes are down, some suppliers use the reverse logic and try to negotiate prices back up.'

'You bet they will,' says Scott, 'so we need to show them the big picture of what our total purchases have been worth, and also extol the virtues of our company as a customer to stay with.'

'They should be glad to have our business,' asserts Shirley. 'But I'm always interested in how I can put more pressure on them. Just tell me how.'

Scott obliges. 'For example, what's the total value of their sales to us over the past, say, two or three years. If we've spent more with them than anticipated, has this meant extra profit for them which we haven't tried to negotiate back? Conversely, if volumes are down, show them that our cash position is strong and we're better able to survive a recession when an increasing number of companies are not doing so. And if they try to weaken our position by using the "but you're only a small customer" tactic, reply that, if this is so, then the money they'll forgo by not increasing prices won't matter very much to them!'

Scott says this with a smile but we know the tactic works. The vital thing in these discussions is to have information available beforehand about the past business done with them and also the potential that lies ahead. And what about their performance? Are they giving us quality or delivery problems that make it costly and painful to do business with them? Or maybe they've not fully honoured some of the commitments they made. If so, seek compensation. There's no single magic bullet available so the trick is to have a number of possible tactics to deploy and then play your hand as dictated by the circumstances. Just getting the information together often reveals what cards you can play. Scott's suggestions are all practical, and there are others as well. They open up the field of play. If the supplier just narrows in on the new price they want then paint the bigger picture along with their place in it.

Ed hasn't said much for a while, perhaps wondering why we're talking about price increases when he started out looking for cost savings.

It's time to summarise. 'Everything we've talked about so far comes under the heading of "Pushing Harder on Existing Deals". This includes going for cost concessions and rebates you think you've earned but haven't claimed. Also, hold suppliers more accountable to do what they promise to do. Resist upward price pressures they try to force on you. And even if you have to accept one or two, then make sure you get something extra in return which is of value. Try also to get increases deferred. All these make cost savings.'

'OK,' says Ed, 'so far so good. Now, are there other things that we haven't looked at yet?'

'Indeed there are. For example, with strategic items where you don't have alternative suppliers, get closer to them and collaborate on cost reduction. Just demanding savings will fall on deaf ears, whereas asking them, "Is there anything you can suggest we jointly do to reduce costs?" taps into their knowledge of how the supply chain to you works. You can follow up by saying you don't want to attack their profitability but instead want to reduce the cost base upon which their profit margin sits.'

'Sounds a bit soft to me,' observes Shirley. 'I think we should be tough with them.'

'You need to be tough with all your suppliers,' I agree. 'It's just that "tough" takes on different guises depending on where you are in the Kraljic matrix. For the suppliers we've just been talking about, "tough" means upping the game with them. Just because you need them doesn't mean that you have to go on bended knee. They also need you, but do you know why? Find out why and draw strength from that knowledge. Maybe they need a bit of help to understand this, so be prepared to "sell" your company to them as being an attractive business partner and differentiated positively from "the others". Do your best to find out how their internal costs build up and ask how good their own procurement activity is. If it's not as good as yours, then you're effectively paying for their poor buying. Knowledge is power, so the more knowledge you have the more powerful you'll come across. That's being "tough" in another guise.

Scott has been quiet for a while. 'Surely there are other things we can do over and above optimising existing deals. What about creating new deals and relationships with new suppliers, for example?'

'Scott, you're ahead of the game,' I reply. 'We're still only starting the journey towards improving procurement in this company. But we'll fail if we attempt everything at once. The secret is to take it step by step and deliver tangible benefits as we go. These successes will contribute to financial results today while also fuelling the change process and silencing the cynics.'

'I still think we need more people to do all this work,' persists Elaine, perhaps now caffeine light and consequently edgy. 'There's no way I can get that close to all my suppliers.'

'No one's asking you to,' says Ed, 'because if I understand Jon correctly we can keep other suppliers at arm's length, especially those who are hungry for business. Obviously we want them to be interested in selling to us, that's the point – keep them working hard to win our orders and let market competition be the driving force. In this context, "tough" doesn't mean being aggressive and bullying them into submission. It means us having high expectations and standards which they'll find tough to satisfy. But we have to behave like the sort of company they want to impress.'

Shirley picks up on this. 'I guess we've also stuck too long with some suppliers without checking who else is out there who can do the job better. For bottom right items there may be alternatives but we haven't looked for them. If we find some, then our current suppliers will be faced with tougher competition than they've been used to.'

Ed decides we've done enough for now. 'What I want you guys to do is select two or three target suppliers on whom you're going to try this stuff and let me know what your plan is. With timings. That's important, since an event may be coming up, such as a pre-planned supplier visit or a contract review, which we can take advantage of. Also don't take your eye off the day-to-day ball because, if you drop one, your cost saving efforts will evaporate. I know it'll be tough, but the first successes, however small, will lead to bigger ones.'

I can hear Vince Lombardi saying this. But it's Elaine who has the last word. 'Hey, Ed, don't forget that stuff on the back burner!'

Outside it's hot and well into a Californian Friday afternoon. It's too late to travel back to the UK so this means another night in the hotel. The manager is offering free drinks again along with more bowls of raw vegetables and dips. The simulated beach on the ground floor is just the place to be.

Happy hour extends to three hours, so there's plenty of time to eat more vegetables than is good for the system and catch up on the newspapers. I can't believe what I'm reading.

UK civil servants have been warned that bringing cake into work for birthdays and celebrations is a public health hazard. A 'well-being' official told colleagues to be 'mindful' of others who have 'difficulty resisting' these treats. A spokesperson said, 'We simply want to remind people of the health implications of eating too much sugar – it's the yeast we can do.' And it did say yeast! I fancy Shirley would make a great 'well-being' officer.

Reading on: a record-holding half-marathon runner is being forced to relinquish his title after race organisers discovered the route was almost 500 feet too short. On race day the fact that ninety-two of the top one hundred finishers recorded personal bests should've been something of a giveaway. A spokesperson said that approximately fifty metres of the shortfall was because the prescribed route was not followed correctly. 'The remainder of the shortfall resulted from the difference between measuring on closed roads compared to measuring on unclosed roads – which was the methodology used in August as a result of notification of essential utilities works affecting the course.' Unravel that if you can.

Then on to a leading barrister claiming he was so good that 'he could get Stevie Wonder a driving licence'. He's now up before the beak himself who criticised him for making a speech that was 'ill-judged, patronising and contained inappropriate attempts at humour'.

Finally a team of scientists reckons humanity can trace its roots back to a microscopic animal that lived on the seabed millions of years ago. Researchers said that one of the most intriguing features of the ancient creature was an 'apparent lack of an anus'. Perhaps just as well... at only one millimetre long the creature would probably have disappeared up it.

What a world.

Chapter 6

NEXT DAY I'M greeted at the front desk with a 'G'day sir, how ya doin'?' It's curly haired Ray, whom I met on day one. He's here to drive the ground transportation to LAX, Los Angeles' international airport with its iconic bowl-shaped building.

Later in the journey I'll learn that, when he was younger, Ray sometimes caught his siblings looking at him with a 'so where did you come from?' expression on their swarthier faces.

'If I shaved off my beard and put a hat on people would think I was white,' he offers, and I am heartened by this cheerful acknowledgement that we are all equal in our diversity. The ground transportation starts rolling and, despite heavily tinted windows, eyeball-searing sunshine fills its interior.

It's a scintillating blue-skied Saturday. I remark on the fine weather although I've heard they've had a lot of rain.

'Well,' says Ray, 'we've had a lot of rain but it's no more than the forecasts predicted. Thing is, these Californians can't handle it. Where I'm from on the East Coast, I'm used to variety.'

Ray's earlier life involved bumming around between New York and Washington DC. 'But I've been in California for thirteen years now and, well, they're different people. Here's the point: I'll see someone in the street and bid them, "Good mornin'." Now this is meant as a courteous salutation to start the day but the expression on their face tells me they think I'm a child of Satan. "OK, OK," I say, "all I wanted was to be friendly but I see your day's already screwed up so we'll pass on shall we?" Now, mid-west, for example, they're friendly folk. They'll invite you into their home for dinner and Grandma will even knit you a sweater if she has the time. Thing is, there's nothin' else to do there. But here? ... make the effort to be friendly and you're toast!'

December, London

The next time I see Ed it's early December in London as he's over to meet his European colleagues. I drive up from West Wales, stopping only for coffee. At one of the motorway services I fetch up at the franchise coffee outlet to be greeted by a jolly, flushed-face girl, basking in the heat radiating from her cappuccino machine. She beams sunnily at me and says she can smell burning. So can I.

'It's me,' she says.

'Shall I retire to a safe distance?' I enquire.

'No, it's OK. I'll stay close and put the flames out.'

'What are you going to use, then? Dry powder or foam?'

'No question, it's got to be foam.'

So… she's into foam.

Interesting.

This evening Ed will travel to Italy. I'll be in the north of England to meet the General Manager of a company just acquired by AeroCorp. But that comes later. For now, we're meeting in a hotel lobby around a coffee table.

'Jon, I want to run over the basics again. What we discussed back at our team meeting makes a lot of sense. When you next visit you'll see we've made good progress. But you said it's not just doing better deals that counts, but getting people throughout the company to realise they must be team players in the procurement process. What I'd like is a precise statement about procurement's role. If we can get that clear then people will find it easier to relate to it.'

'First let's emphasise that we're not creating a functional fortress here, but defining the purpose of procurement activity which involves a lot of people, including, as you say, non-buyers. The best definition I know is one created by a Norwegian manufacturing company which has been in business for a long time and is very successful.'

'And the definition is …?'

'To ensure that the company has access to, and acquires value from, the supply markets it needs for it to succeed both now and in future.'

Each of these words needs fleshing out. For example, 'access' implies two things: the existence of suitable sources and their willingness to do business with you. Neither can be taken for granted, and both can be created. The 'acquires value' bit is better than saying 'buys' since it isn't always necessary to pay money to get what you need. 'Value' can also come in the form of preferential treatment or innovation from suppliers.

The ideas of preferential treatment and innovation, I tell Ed, were evident to the CEO of an American cookie company who was introducing a procurement briefing of his senior management team. 'I have a few questions which I hope will be addressed today,' he announced. 'Here's one: if one of our main suppliers comes up with a great new idea, can we be sure we would be the first, maybe the only, customer with whom he shares it?'

What a star! Here's a guy who sees supply markets as sources of value rather than as a sink for reluctant expenditures.

Back with the definition from Norway, the 'it needs' phrase refers not just to the tangible things like materials and services, but also to the profit margins, cost targets and cash-flow goals built into the company's financial plan.

'What about the "now and in future" bit?' asks Ed.

'This company is one of the few I've come across that lives in the future as much as in the present. It includes procurement perspectives in its strategic plan.'

'Meaning what?' Ed probes.

'It incorporates views on trends in supply costs, supplier activity, ability of the market to supply (both in terms of capacity and geography), keeping up with new product development and innovation, emerging supply risks and so on. All this with the aim of giving the company a competitive advantage. That's a lot different from coping with the "now" of placing orders, general fire-fighting and dealing with price rises and delivery problems.'

Ed ponders. 'I can see the difference, and I guess we're a long way from that at Gullmech.'

'Maybe, but the journey you're starting on will make all the difference. The Scandinavian company has a neat way of putting things, and its President told me, "We make our business out of selling and our profit out of buying."'

'That sounds brutal,' says Ed, 'but it seems they're an intelligent company which uses brain power rather than muscle power to get what it wants from suppliers.'

'Exactly, and the phrase is another example of top management having the joined-up buy/transform/sell view of business.'

'Jon, you seem to carry a lot of interesting quotations in your head. Any more?'

I tell Ed a short story involving the Asia–Pacific operations of a global chemicals company. Its CPO launched a week-long training programme in Hong Kong called 'The Procurement Academy', with which I was involved. As usual, the head honcho, the Pacific Area President, called by to make introductory comments. He turned up again on the Thursday for dinner and made a few more apt remarks. The week went well, so it was repeated, repeated and repeated yet again. The President appeared at all these events, which in itself was unusual, as head honchos have short attention spans and usually delegate someone else to do the public speaking. I asked him why he was so personally committed to the programme.

'Jon,' he said, 'the procurement process is a microcosm of the whole business, and a significant improvement in it not only achieves direct cost reductions but also more powerfully benefits the culture and performance of the business overall. That's why I want this Academy to get us there.'

Pure gold.

Ed gets all this down while making an interesting observation. 'Your first two quotations relate to the actual business done by the company, whereas the Hong Kong one is more about the power of procurement to change things in a deeper way. Am I right?'

'You are indeed. In due course we need to look at the characteristics of high-performing teams, but they do run deep into management style and culture. The thing is, if people try to change these things directly they often fail because the concepts are too vague. But if you make tangible and measurable improvements in the procurement process, the culture stuff tends to happen naturally as a consequence. This is like "culture change by stealth", and it's great because it's paid for by the cost savings coming from doing procurement differently.'

'So,' says Ed, 'I now have two questions: are we doing our procurement intelligently, and are we doing it as well as possible?'

This puts me on the spot. I first heard questions like this from the CEO of an Australian airline and I'm trying desperately to remember how I replied. I buy some time by activating Plan B: 'Ed, how about more coffee and a freshen-up first, and then we'll get back to your questions?'

'Good idea.' Ed stands and reaches for his phone as he realises the folk back at Gullmech will be starting work now and he wants to gee them up.

To stretch my legs I take a turn round the vast reception area. It's a prestigious, modern hotel with lots of space, greenery, glass and a reception desk the size of an airport check-in area. Elevator doors open and close with a Star Trek swish. One departed just a minute ago but has returned to the ground floor with the same occupants on board. The expectant look on their faces suggests that they've arrived, but they haven't. The hollow centre of the building offers a view all the way up to the roof. Flat TV screens adorn most of the walls. One of them shows a vigorously crackling log fire, while over by the grand stairway another lists what functions are happening today. Apparently Mr and Mrs Lee will be celebrating their golden wedding anniversary.

Chapter 7

E D RETURNS, PRESUMABLY satisfied that all is well back at the ranch and that supply chains other than Davina's Deli are up to speed. 'My questions then. Are we doing procurement intelligently?'

Privately, I think, 'Probably not, but they have the potential to.' 'Intelligent' implies possessing knowledge and using the brain. Unfortunately, the busy-busy climate at Gullmech doesn't help. It has smart people and sells good products but the question remains as to whether human talent and motivation is hitting its full potential. I list what it takes to tick the 'intelligent procurement' box.

First is to have good data about supply expenditure: how much is spent, with whom and on what. Next is to understand how the company's business model depends on suppliers. This means clearly knowing what needs the supply market must satisfy, and then determining which suppliers are mission critical. Third, thorough market knowledge is vital: capacity, key players, cost drivers and trends, innovation, new entrants and exiting suppliers, competitiveness, risk soft spots, regulations and so on.

All this covers sources of intelligence. But how well is this knowledge used? Consistency depends on mandatory procurement principles which represent the DNA of procurement behaviour and decision-making. These apply across the company since many folk are part of the procurement process. There should be a clear framework of authority, delegation and management control and all expenditure should happen under the influence of the procurement process, including measuring what's happened. Buyers don't directly need to spend every dollar, as other folk can be authorised to commit company expenditures, but this must be done in a controlled way and recorded.

Summarising so far, knowledge feeds the brain while the control frameworks ensure that purchasing power is used in an enlightened way. Finally, knowledge and power must come together to deliver useful output. This requires a proven process for developing and implementing risk-managed acquisition strategies, with the right resources in place to execute them and sustain impact.

Or – looking at the negatives – no facts and you're flying blind, no strategy means less ambition and lost opportunities, no control framework equates to writing blank cheques, and no risk management invites nasty surprises. That's not intelligent!

I glance over to the row of elevators. The hapless folk who previously arrived but did not arrive have successfully got off somewhere. Perhaps it was Mr and Mrs Lee searching for their golden wedding party.

Ed brings me back to earth. 'So how good is our procurement? Remember my second question: are we doing it as well as possible?'

'This is where measurement comes in. Some companies only measure outputs from the procurement process. For example: prices paid versus budget, delivery accuracy and promptness, supplier performance and so on. In fact, I think all companies measure these metrics, but it's what the smart ones measure in addition that makes the difference. They focus on the process that produces good outputs rather than the outputs themselves. But even that can bring problems.'

'Such as what?'

'Well, measuring how long it takes to turn a requisition into a purchase order, or how much expenditure is handled by each buyer …these are very crude measures of efficiency. It's wrong to ignore them but they perpetuate the mechanistic functional image. It encourages box-ticking and slavish adherence to procedures. Another important thing is to be clear why measurement is happening at all: is it to compare how well our procurement compares with "best in class" elsewhere? Or is it to check whether we're hitting our business targets? And those targets should flow directly from the company's business plan.'

'Like sales volumes, margins, cash flow, developing new markets?'

'Exactly.'

'Hmm, I can see how that hardwires procurement activity directly to the needs of the business.'

'Correct. The ideal is where the company has board-approved procurement strategies covering the acquisition of key things the company needs, and then the CPO tracks how successfully the procurement team is implementing them. If that's the main focus of management attention then it's a lot different from just reporting cost savings to justify the existence of the buyer community.'

'Although we're not going to ignore cost savings, are we?!'

Boy, this guy's tenacious! I like Ed more and more, the more I see of him. He's highly skilled and experienced and has excellent leadership disciplines, but is still hungry to learn. That doesn't automatically make me a Lombardi-calibre coach, but it's refreshingly stimulating to operate in this environment without the ritual head-banging that usually goes with trying to convince the cynics.

'Certainly not, because delivering cost savings versus price targets built into the financial plan contribute directly to profit. But, as we've discussed, there's a higher purpose for procurement activity over and above making deals. Ready for another story?'

Ed looks at his watch, then at me with an 'OK if you must' look on his face.

'Martin was Procurement Director in a public-sector organisation. Every month he appeared before the so-called Tender Board to gain approval for high-cost contracts which exceeded his expenditure authority. This box-ticking frustrated him, and few of the board members had useful knowledge of contracting. The only good news was that they could all say that they'd followed the rules by quizzing Martin before signing off.

'At the following board meeting he did the usual stuff and then, for the last five minutes, he gave them a heads-up about a contract he wished to review next time. Future meetings went the same way, with more and more time being given to previewing upcoming contracts and the strategies that went with them. Board members showed they had much more to contribute to strategy formulation than checking contracts.

'Breakthrough came when the board's chairperson said, "Martin, don't bring any more contracts for us to sign. We're more useful contributing to strategy development." Martin felt the same. "So in future, once we've all agreed on the strategy you have our authority to execute it in its entirety, so long as everything stays within the framework of what we've agreed. If you have to change things then come and discuss them, but otherwise you're free to act without further reference to us."'

Ed was listening intently, possibly wondering why some organisations got themselves so bound up in formalities in the first place.

'That's win-win for all concerned,' I say. 'Martin gets to use his time more effectively, both at the meetings and afterwards, and the board members make a genuinely helpful contribution, which he values. The story illustrates the difference between following procedures without giving too much thought to the subject matter versus really engaging people's brains and experience and focusing on the actual business being done.'

'Good story. I guess that's another example of intelligent procurement. It also shows the benefit of making changes to the way we do things. Which brings us back to, are we doing procurement as well as possible, and what changes can we make if not?'

'Taking the first part, Gullmech certainly can do better. That's not saying it's rubbish now. The way things are done has served the company well, but the world is changing and it's time to take procurement to the next level. While I remember it, there's also the question of how Gullmech procurement compares with other companies. That's about benchmarking, but we'll deal with it later. For now it's better to focus on how Gullmech's procurement process can be improved.'

'Sounds pretty straightforward to me,' says Ed.' We just keep motoring along doing better deals and getting a bigger bang for our buck. We'll then get more recognition.'

'Well, actually, no. You'll only succeed if more and more people in the company get involved in what you're doing. If you were driving your SUV towards a low-cost utopia with only buyers on board then it'd stop when cost savings dry up. So alongside the journey to get cost savings there has to be a parallel journey. I call it Route 42.'

'And where does that take us?'

'To a new level where you exhibit the characteristics of high-performance procurement.'

'So do you have an improvement template to measure how good we are and how to improve? And why forty-two?'

'Yes, the template looks at seven aspects of procurement activity and scores it on a scale of one to six, one being poor and six being excellent. Forty-two represents high performance. Seven times six is forty-two.'

'I can do the math,' grins Ed, 'but what are the seven aspects?'

Boy, this guy's appetite is insatiable, and I'm wishing that Davina's Deli was here to deal with it.

'Er, we'll do that later, if it's OK with you. But we must do it, because the two parallel journeys respectively deliver financial benefits at the same time as increasing procurement's profile and impact. In this way, cost-management innovations kick in and break through the barrier that's encountered when simple cost savings dry up.'

'OK so far, but I'm still not getting this parallel journey thing.'

'Right, let's say that one journey is about procurement practice and the other is about procurement process. The "practice" bit starts with doing the simple things better.'

'Like aggregating orders and pushing for deeper discounts, like we discussed back at Gullmech?'

'Exactly, and then becoming more strategic, like dealing with monopolies and cartels and developing new sources and relationships. But the further you go on that journey the more you need internal support for the changes you want to make, and the authority to make them. The parallel journey, called "process", equips you to do that.'

It's getting too late in the day to explore much more, but Ed still has a moment or two before he heads for Italy. We have time to summarise the three stages of the procurement practice journey.

'The first is "Cost Reduction". This is essentially a leverage game played by procurement teams with little involvement from others in the company. It covers the things we talked about at the Gullmech team meeting, like increasing leverage by combining similar deals. It's also worth looking at the total amount of business being done with a supplier, for example when buying different things from the same company but they can't be standardised. Expanding this, sister companies in a group may be using the same suppliers or buying similar things. Looking at the whole accumulates more purchasing power.'

'What's next?' says Ed.

'"Cost Management". This phase sustains the initial cost savings but goes on to use other approaches to gain further benefits. Continuing to leverage cost reductions is futile, and strong suppliers will not be interested in this game anyway.'

'Yes, I recall Shirley's comments back at the team meeting. We sure have some suppliers who would turn off the taps if we got aggressive with them. In some cases we're our own worst enemy because we've kept them at arm's length and treated them as if we had other options and lots of suppliers knocking on our door to get orders.'

Kraljic's message lives!

Ed continues. 'Give me examples of what you do here then.'

'With those important suppliers, open up dialogue with them along the lines of wanting to collaborate with them to hunt down wasted costs. Or invite their ideas about what new products or new specifications could be interesting to you, again with the aim of reducing the cost base or increasing competitive advantage. Another tack, especially if you're experiencing quality problems with their product, is to help them improve that quality. They may not have the disciplines or resources needed, but you do. It's another way of removing wasted costs.'

'And the other suppliers where we can be business-like but don't have to get close?'

'Play the market and switch to cheaper suppliers when price dips justify it. Also, get tougher with contract management and insist that suppliers honour the commercial and performance commitments that they've signed up for.'

I haven't the heart to tell Ed what one of his Gullmech colleagues told me: that they have a supplier who often delivers sub-standard stuff. Gullmech rejects it but also pays to return the goods to the supplier. Why would it do such a thing? But it does.

'Finally, don't get caught out by last-minute price increases. Anticipate them, head them off, don't be seduced by their logical justifications, and negotiate more into the deal if a price rise is inevitable. It's also worth looking at total lifetime costs and making buying decisions on that basis rather than on the initial price.'

'Lifetime costs?'

'If you buy engineering equipment, say, during its life maintenance costs will be incurred, it'll consume utilities and ultimately be disposed of. Calculating the lifetime cost of ownership and factoring in the time value of money might show that it makes more sense to pay a higher initial price for more efficient and reliable equipment and then to benefit from lower subsequent costs.'

'We can do a lot of these things,' observes Ed, 'but it means more effort and also management's commitment for buyers to spend time on such activities.'

'Correct, but it doesn't necessarily mean hiring more people. It's about the same people spending the same time but doing different things. This in turn needs the boss to clear the decks for the new action. That's what I mean when I say the cost reduction stage can be done by buyers alone, but cost management needs collaboration with others: suppliers, users and management.'

It's getting dark outside and we need to wrap things up. The elevators are now buzzing as some of the Lees' party guests emerge, high on happy memories and too much bubbly.

Ed puts away his papers. 'Jon, we haven't time right now for the third stage, so just tell me what it's called.'

'"Sustained Value Acquisition".'

'That's a grand title, but I guess it's just common sense that you charge good money for!'

'I'm very happy to charge money to tell you, but it'll be worth it!'

He smiles and proffers his hand for one of those all-American bone-crushing handshakes that brings tears to the eyes.

'I'd like you to come over to the States in a couple of months' time, and I'll confirm exactly where. Meanwhile, give my best to the folks up north and tell them their procurement needs sorting out too! I don't actually know that but I bet it does!'

Chapter 8

North-West England

LATER THAT EVENING the train ride to England's north-west is uneventful, but the weather deteriorates en route. An early cold snap forecast by the pundits has arrived and the stifling warmth of the train plummets to near-freezing conditions on the station forecourt. A keen wind provides extra chill. I wait to summon the ground transportation. If only! Ray and his cavernous Californian cab are a distant memory. Anyway, a taxi arrives and takes me to the smallish town near the industrial area I'll be visiting tomorrow. The hotel on the main street is a faithful rendering of a 1970s hostelry brought up to date with aggressively patterned carpets, non-matching sofas and lots of white gloss paint, the smell of which hangs in the air just strongly enough to mask the cooking odours that accompanied the dinner I've just missed. A pleasant girl dressed in the usual uniform of white blouse and black skirt welcomes me and assigns me a room.

It's… interesting. The curtains, carpet, furnishings and bed covers are possibly leftovers from upgrades in other rooms, as nothing seems to match. The bed sits on a small plinth but it's not clear whether this is for aesthetic or medical reasons. I think it's the former, as there's a row of LED lights as well. Moreover, there are different light settings to change the mood: from lights chasing round the bed through gently pulsating warm effects to a night-time setting. Sadly, it's only the lights that are warm, as the room's freezing and the heating doesn't work.

Oh, for a palm-treed atrium and happy hour.

In search of warmth I head downstairs to the bar.

It's an opportunity to finish writing a short piece for a business magazine wanting a quarterly Q&A column on procurement. It's due tomorrow. There's nothing like a deadline to stimulate creative writing. But that doesn't mean it's fiction. All the questions are real, and the one I'm dealing with now is about procurement's role in a legal services firm. At first sight it's the high-rolling lawyers who are the prima donnas in the company, with everyone else deployed in support. That's how *prima donnas* stay that way. But there's a huge difference between 'doing the business' and 'running the business'. The high-charging lawyers do the former. They won't like this but, from a business viewpoint, they are simply the agents of revenue generation.

But what is the business strategy for the future? Should it carry on soliciting in its individual locations around the world, or is there a grander scheme? It was the latter. The company wanted to become a truly globally connected entity. A relatively easily specified IT infrastructure was identified as a key requirement, but here the firm faced a new challenge: its IT spend was small compared with Goliath customers in other business sectors. The law firm believed this diminished its purchasing power with the major IT supplier who already had its foot in the door of routine operations. The CPO felt differently and developed a story that persuaded the supplier to see the company as an attractive customer. A great global networking deal was struck, helping the firm to achieve its strategic objective. Without that strategy – and it was not just procurement that brought it into being – the firm would have stayed as a network of provincial solicitors.

I don't know if the CPO had helped to create the company strategy in the first place, but let's hope so. There's no divine law that says it's only the CEO, CFO, COO and Head of Strategy who are gifted with foresight and business acumen. If a CPO is involved, then his or her role is to contribute to the creation of company strategy, distil out its supply implications and then manage teams who'll make those parts of the strategy happen.

This story shows how procurement can help a company achieve its strategic objectives rather than just supporting the status quo, although both are vital. It doesn't matter if it's one person or a hundred-plus people in the procurement team; the significance of procurement's role depends how much the CEO sees it as a core activity.

Time passes quickly when writing. I look up and find I'm now alone. The girl behind the bar busily polishes glasses, looks at the clock, then at me, then back to the glasses, then at me again. I get the message and retire to the mood-lit executive suite.

Next day I visit the factory. Lenwall Engineering is another company in the AeroCorp Division to which Gullmech also belongs. I'm here because Procurement Director Mike wants to run through things he should be doing because the growing recession could spring some nasty surprises. He's an approachable guy of medium height and much experience of Lenwall's operations.

'Jon, I don't want *War and Peace*,' he cautions, 'just a few pointers to check we're doing the right things short term. I also want to share some of this with our smaller suppliers to make sure they're going to survive the storm.'

'OK, let's start by making a few assumptions. First, I hope you have good data showing how much you're spending, on what and with whom. Also that you've analysed supply expenditures and supply markets, knowing who the critical sources are and why.'

'Yes to all that so far,' confirms Mike.

Peter the CFO looks in to say hello, so I pose him a couple of questions. 'Do you have a good debt-collection process in place and are you stopping customers from playing delayed-payment games?'

Peter, a tall, bespectacled, analytical type, says 'yes' to both. These are pertinent questions as they refer to Lenwall's own performance as a supplier. They also affect Lenwall's margin just as supply costs do.

Mike has also been thinking about some internal angles. 'We're maximising usage of internal stocks before buying new. This includes reusing old materials where possible and adapting stuff we already have rather than buying new. We're also checking our other company sites in the UK and overseas to see if they have spare supplies we can use before buying new.'

Peter approves. 'This means we're reducing the debt finance part of our overheads by saving money using the unused or little-used assets we already have.'

Mike joins in. 'And our new planning system means we now have reasonably smooth forecasts of what we need to buy. We can give sensible planning forecasts to key suppliers which don't fluctuate wildly every day. That said, we're also looking for suppliers' special deals and picking them up as needed.'

Clearly, here's a company well equipped to survive economic turmoil.

'But were not complacent,' Peter warns, 'so what else can we do?' This guy's as hungry as Ed.

'Well, in no particular order, there are four priorities. First, ensure your cash flow is tightly managed and keep payment systems under control. This means you don't pay suppliers twice!'

'It has been known,' Mike ruefully agrees.

'Then ensure that supplies keep coming, and have contingency plans ready if deliveries of critical items or services are disrupted. And lastly, protect your company where you've spent money – down payments, for example – but haven't yet taken delivery.'

'Anything else?' Peter enquires.

'Yes, don't leave cash on the supplier's table and identify quick cost savings and go for them. You'll know that Ed over at Gullmech is already hot on the trail of these, so I'm assuming that you're also busy in that area.'

Peter agrees, and reminds himself to organise his travel for the next meeting in the USA, where Ed will be checking the scores.

It's time for a break, and refreshments arrive. The sandwiches are smaller than their Californian cousins, a sure sign that Davina's Deli doesn't yet feed Europe. Neither, unfortunately, does the Californian weather. It's cold and wet outside and I hope the mood lighting and aircon back at the hotel room have a fireside setting. That's if they've mended it.

But first there's more work to do. AeroCorp's CEO Carol joins us, possibly lured out of her office by the food that Mike is paying for. She's up from her London HQ for a day's meeting. I hope she's got a better hotel room than I have.

'We've seen huge price increases for commodity raw materials over the past year,' Carol observes, 'and my hunch is we'll see some big falls now because suppliers' sales are dwindling. Should we negotiate some long-term agreements to lock in these better prices? Jon, what's your view?'

Unfortunately the question comes while I'm biting into a wholemeal sandwich that lives up to its name by taking ages to deal with. An opportunity, though, to think of an answer. People wait patiently. 'No, not as an automatic reaction.'

'Why not?'

'Partly because you want to stay free to play the market and partly because long-term agreements create a false sense of security. But there are advantages. They do save buyers' time, as it's easier to call off from a term agreement than to keep setting up new purchase orders from scratch. Also you can include a price review mechanism to lock in a good price for a time but then control how that price changes in future.'

'What about the security thing you mentioned?' quizzes Peter.

'Suppliers aren't obliged to keep their promises in these agreements. In legal jargon they're "standing offers". They don't guarantee deliveries because suppliers can cancel them. Trade under their terms only becomes "legal" by placing purchase orders.'

'OK, so we must be careful,' observes Peter. 'Are there any more benefits?'

'Well, they do remove some uncertainty about the future and provide a better basis for planning ahead: you have price schedules to work on and suppliers have an idea what volumes are coming along. Suppliers also gain confidence to book future raw material supplies although, again, this doesn't guarantee supply security. So it's dangerous to set up long-term agreements and then forget about them.'

'I didn't say we were going to forget about them,' retorts Carol. She's like Ed and will keep her finger on the pulse.

Mike has been quiet because he's worried about another aspect of economic hard times. 'We've got some suppliers who are slashing prices in order to attract business, but there are others who are really trying it on.'

'Meaning?' enquires Carol, who's still with us.

'I've got two or three suppliers who've become very aggressive. I don't know if it's born of desperation or because they think they have us over a barrel, but they want big price increases and don't really want to discuss them. It's "take-it-or-leave-it".'

'I know what I'd do,' offers Carol. 'If I had alternatives I'd just say no. But if you don't, then I suppose more subtlety is needed.'

Peter explains that the majority of these demands will be justified by 'prices-based-on-costs' mathematics, especially if volumes have decreased. However, such 'reasonable' explanations often conceal a supplier's true motives.

Mike agrees. 'We must have faith in our own information, logic and opinions, and not be fooled by the "facts" peddled by suppliers. Information and planning makes for more powerful negotiations.'

'And don't lose sight of our own targets,' adds Carol.

Chapter 9

S O FAR IT'S been a good discussion. Interestingly, it's dealt with procurement matters as they affect the business rather than focusing on narrow functional issues.

It turns out that Carol has called the Managing Directors from Lenwall's different factories together for a pep talk as well as to look over the factory here. They're meeting for a routine review of company results and have asked me to join them for a short while to consider procurement issues as well.

We gather in the conference room, which is almost totally filled by a long wooden table, a sideboard with refreshments laid out, an electronic whiteboard and windows looking out over the factory. Carol, Peter and Mike are there along with five others. These are the men and women who run Lenwall's factories in the UK, including Nick, the MD of the plant where we are right now.

Carol introduces me and wants me to say a few things about what other companies are doing to improve procurement's impact. There's some general chit-chat around the table, which provides an insight into how the company operates. Apparently, the London-based Penserin HQ where Carol is based runs things with a light touch, allowing the heads of each of the businesses a lot of freedom to run things their own way. In other similar setups I've seen it often means the individual companies behave like fiefdoms run by turf-protecting barons.

Mike gives a quick summary of the UK operations from the procurement viewpoint. They buy several raw materials, one major component coming from a big supplier who is now virtually a monopoly. Its take-it-or-leave it attitude has led Lenwall to conclude that there's nothing more it can do to squeeze lower prices.

I think this is an assumption, as Lenwall hasn't probed into that supplier's situation to search out weak spots or to understand how Lenwall fits into its overall sales strategy.

Anyway, back to Mike. 'About forty-five per cent of our expenditure is outside the main raw material category, so we think it's worth looking there for cost savings.'

It may well be, but the chances of success seem slim when they tell me how procurement works. It's not all good news.

One MD observes that front-line folk don't think strategically and senior people haven't the time to. Another says, 'We don't have buyers; we have clerical administrators.' Across the board, procurement is not considered to be as important as sales, therefore the question of doing it better is a shall we/shan't we decision. Carol's listening intently but stays quiet most of the time, sensing the discussion's flow.

There's one guy, Graham, who says a lot of good things and is happy to be candid. 'We've spent a lot of money getting people to sell more consistently, but nothing to get people buying more consistently!'

'There's no procurement training at all?'

'No.'

'Right,' I say, 'so who are your sales folk selling to?'

'Our customers' buyers of course, as well as their users and technical folk.'

'And are your suppliers training their sales people as well?'

'We know they are, just like we are.'

'So the situation is that your suppliers' highly trained sales people are selling to your untrained buyers. You know that, but you're not doing anything about it.'

An uneasy silence falls in the room, with only Graham looking like he's happy with the way the discussion has gone. I think this is the point when they don't want me there any more. That's the price you pay when you tell it the way you see it.

I also sense that Carol wanted this paradox to be exposed. However, the problem with her light touch approach is that she isn't ready to put her foot down, and the other head honchos there won't be told. Anyway, they don't like me very much now.

'Jon,' says one of the MDs, 'I don't think you understand how difficult it is to sell to customers, especially when there's hot competition.'

'Look, I'm not for one moment underestimating the importance of skilled salespeople. But to portray sales as difficult and buying as easy just doesn't reflect real life.'

Privately, I recall a time when I negotiated with a salesman from a US company on whom we were totally dependent for supplies of a critical raw material. We spent millions of dollars on the stuff and the supplier wanted a hefty price increase. Negotiation? No way. It was take it or leave it. OK, we hadn't been very smart in allowing ourselves to get trapped in this corner, but that proves the point. If we'd correctly identified the criticality of the raw material, established a different relationship with the supplier, given high priority to managing that relationship and the supply chain, and had a contingency plan up our sleeve, then that would have been a lot more intelligent. And strategic. In fact we would have exhibited all the commercial skills that a key sales account manager would exert on a critical customer.

The hard-headed MDs remain silent so I continue. 'Companies aren't in business to sell stuff; they're in business to make a profit. While selling might affect only one end of the company, profit depends on what happens at both ends of the enterprise. An extra dollar earned on sales is in principle worth just as much as an extra dollar saved on supplies, although there is some fancy maths proving that a cost saving has a bigger impact on margin than making an equivalent sales increase.'

The folks round the table look as though they'd like to debate this as a timely red herring, diverting attention away from the seller–buyer training inconsistency.

Again I need to continue, and quickly. 'This puts a new light on procurement's role, and we haven't even started talking about managing supply risks and strategies for attracting other sorts of value from key suppliers.'

'What "sorts of value"?' asks Peter.

'Like preferential treatment and innovation.' But I feel I'm flogging dead horses here. If these guys are fixated on procurement being so simple that they don't need to train their buyers, then they're not going to buy into a more strategic approach.

Another, longer, silence ensues. But we're not quite finished.

'OK,' says one of them, 'just supposing we were to agree to do our buying differently, what should be our action plan?'

I summarise the 'procurement practice' part of the two parallel journeys, or at least the cost reduction and cost management stages that I aired with Ed. I decide not to mention the 'procurement process' bit because these hard-headed operational types wouldn't see much mileage in it. People are polite enough but I sense they'll resist making changes to the status quo. Oh, the problem with egos! I think they want to assert that 'they're in charge', and diktats from head office to change their ways are not welcome.

Talking of which, it seems that my own welcome has now expired. Carol thanks me and the robber barons politely concur. She follows me out of the room and ushers me into the spare office she's using for the day.

'Jon, thanks for that, and I'm sorry you didn't get an easier ride. But we can definitely improve things. Personally I'm absolutely committed to doing so, but it'll be a while before those guys are won round. What we must be clear about is precisely what procurement's business role is. If I can persuade the MDs it might get the ball rolling.'

'Yes. A lot of today's discussion has been about both ends of the business and the in-house activities in between, which is good. It's better than focusing on procurement in isolation. But it's clear that procurement doesn't get the same management scrutiny as you give to sales and internal operations. When things are more balanced, suppliers get as much attention as customers. Both live in the real world, both are subject to competitive forces or otherwise, both can be hurt by trading partners with their own agendas and both are vulnerable to risk.'

'And money changes hands between both communities and us!' observes Carol, always with an eye on the money.

'So, in the more even-handed approach to managing the business ...' and I tell her about the 'buy/transform/sell' equation, ' ... procurement is positioned at the top table, and the role of the person heading it up is "to contribute to creating company strategy, then distil out its supply implications, then manage those activities which make that part of the strategy happen".'

'Right,' says Carol, 'here's my plan.' She breaks off as Julia, Nick's PA, comes in and asks if we'd like more coffee. Why not? She's taking more to the main room anyway.

Carol continues. 'It was me who asked Ed to get cracking with improving procurement at Gullmech. That's why he wanted to meet you. They're a good bunch and doing good work. They're receptive to change and not afraid to do things differently. They also don't hang around. So they'll make fast and significant progress – to the extent that the other folk like those you met today don't have an excuse for sticking with the status quo.'

Carol's engineering background is evident in the logical way she's planning things, but she's obviously well up in management psychology too. She knows that 'telling' the MDs to change will be taken as a challenge to their autonomy. But having them realise that they are laggards as Gullmech powers away from them will make life uncomfortable until they, too, do things to catch up. The 'no hiding place' tactic.

We need to wrap this up as the others are waiting for Carol to return. She shares one final thought: 'Although Ed doesn't know it yet, he'll be asked to be the change agent for procurement right across the AeroCorp Division. He'll carry on with his Gullmech VP job but he's got plenty of energy to take on the Division thing as well. But we need to get some results in the bag at Gullmech first, so I'm hoping you can help make them happen.'

And with that, she's gone.

Nice one, Carol: a bit of carrot to attract me to help AeroCorp overall, and some stick to make sure we beat savings out of supply costs at Gullmech first. No pressure, then.

I leave Carol's temporary office to find Mike hovering outside. He's not needed at the other meeting now and, as it's approaching late afternoon, he offers to take me back to the hotel. We drive through heavy rain which has the semi-solid consistency of water uncertain as to whether or not to freeze. Mike declines the offer to stay for a meal at the hotel, and departs.

The same girl at the reception desk recognises me and hands over a key. I've been given another room because they couldn't fix the broken heating in the first one. The new room is also styled 'Executive'. The mood lighting and everything else conscientiously follows the design concept of the original room, with the addition of a black and white photo occupying the entire wall opposite the end of the bed. In the far distance I can see the sea with, nearer, a bikini-clad lady making for it. The foreground features two hairy legs stretched out in front of, and presumably belonging to, the bloke on the sunbed who took the picture in the first place. Not great art.

Chapter 10

February – Kansas

TWO MONTHS ON and I'm at Chicago's O'Hare airport. This is *en route* to the heart of cereal-rich Kansas, the breadbasket of the world. I remember how flat it is around where I'm headed, the state's largest city. The highest piece of land within a hundred miles of the city is its waste tip. There must be an equal and opposite hole somewhere, from which they got the raw materials in the first place. Although it's winter outside, O'Hare is hot. Over there is an ad for cool beer. 'To Ensure Responsible Alcohol Service we ID 100%', proclaims a notice. 'Please Prepare to be Carded' says another. I show my passport for the fourth time since landing.

Broderick at the immigration desk was the first to see it and in my mind I relive our encounter. Over his shoulder I saw the 'Homeland Security' sign and I pondered what subversive and draconian political agendas are pursued in this folksy way by countries of all colours in the name of 'The War on Terror'. Broderick lets me into his country.

Moving towards the domestic terminal, I'm stopped by a lady called Rita who also scans my ID. Perhaps I should put a few family snaps in there to make it more informative for the folks who are so interested in me. Rita looks up from the passport and, having glimpsed something of the future in its well-stamped pages, announces, 'Jon, you're going to have a wunnerful day.' I volunteer that she's already given it a great start, despite it now being past lunchtime. I'm instructed to remove coins from my pocket and realise this is not for the purpose of crossing her palm but a small gesture in the interests of Homeland Security.

Next up is the X-ray machine. Sophie, bandana-bedecked and baggy-trousered, asks for the laptop to be out of its case for screening. I negotiate the X-ray force field and the laptop joins me on the other side. The guy behind me has taken his shoes off and comes through barefoot.

After I've made it through the security assault course, a sign for cool beer stops me and I buy one. Duly carded to prove I'm older than eighteen, I adjourn to a table nearby. A hearty-looking lady camped alongside pushes a mangled baguette to one side and opens up on her mobile phone. She has a voice that deafens the PA system into second place. 'Hey, I've been away on a training course for four days so I'll keep this short as I have no voice left.'

Could have fooled me. A number of fellow travellers are also startled by this non-flight announcement. A few of us exchange glances and silently disagree with her on the subject of her vocal capability. As to content, I'm bemused.

'Listen, when I'm back I'll write you a diet programme and also a schedule for using the bathroom.' Beer glasses stop in mid-drink as we tune into this freely broadcast lifestyle advice.

'You see, he's probably stressed by his new surroundings.' Uh-oh, so there's a man involved here as well.

I go for another beer, assuring the sales lady that I am now a little older since last being carded so she doesn't need to ID me again. She agrees. Silence falls as the lady on the phone shuts up. The conversation was about a dog. How easy it is to get these things wrong.

An adjacent triangular plinth supports a full-size World War Two fighter plane. It's an F4F-3 Wildcat, looking a little portly as if its belly contains kittens. Flying it might induce them, though. It's a mean machine, capable of exceeding 300 miles per hour. Two hundred and eighty-five of these aircraft were built, and saw combat action between December 1941 and August 1942. This plane's undoubtedly heroic pilot was Lt Edward Henry 'Butch' O'Hare, and a comprehensive history of his exploits occupies some twenty feet of one side of the plinth. I notice that Butch had been promoted to Lt Commander by the time the sign-painter reached the next side of the plinth to continue the story, so Mr O'Hare was either as swift up the career development ladder as his name implies, or the scribe was a slow writer. Either way, Chicago's fine airport is right to honour the pilot who went on to become the US Navy's first 'Top Gun'. He died on 26 November 1943. Silently, I thank him and his kind for what they did, and for what they have therefore enabled us to be and to do.

But now it's time to board the aircraft. Another Sophie, this one a stewardess, starts her welcome spiel. 'If you don't want to go to Kansas then you probably shouldn't be aboard this plane.' But I do, and I am.

I'm visiting another of AeroCorp's companies for a couple of days at its factory. With Carol's cost-savings challenge still ringing in my ears, it's fortunate that this session will be all about them.

Since I last saw Ed it's been announced that AeroCorp wants him to look at procurement in all the Division's companies as well as make changes in his own. That's why Ed and the CPOs from the other businesses, including Bryn from this one, are gathered here in the boardroom. John from the UK and Scott are also there. We're welcomed with presents from the locals. Mine is an outsize insulated mug sporting the company logo. We thank Dora, our VP host.

The boardroom is long and narrow with windows down one side offering views of the flat, snow-dusted Kansas skyline. The waste tip isn't in that direction, then. Eight by four sheets of faux wood panelling adorn the walls, providing the backdrop for pictures of the company's founder and the products it makes. The US of A does things on a grand scale, and the conference table is no exception. It fills the room while leaving just enough space around the edges to accommodate deep leather chairs sized to accommodate generously proportioned backsides. They're very comfy, but are so low that the table edge is around chin height – for me, anyway. I guess a diet of Kansas cereals propels its sons and daughters to be taller than me because everyone else in the room looks to be sitting normally.

Ed clears his throat to signal the commencement of business.

'Right,' opens Ed, 'what success have we had pushing harder on the deals? Let's go round the table.'

'Hold on,' says Mike from the UK. He looks tired after what must have been a jet-lagged night. 'I've got things to report but I'd like Jon to explain again why pushing harder works anyway.'

'Yeah, sorry, Mike. I forgot. You weren't with us in LA when we went through this before. Jon?'

I look round at expectant faces. 'It starts by being tougher with suppliers with whom we've been too lenient in the past. Maybe they've delivered too much or too little or been late. Maybe they've conveniently forgotten to charge a lower unit price when our volumes went above an agreed threshold. Maybe we got too involved in solving problems for them that they should have sorted out themselves. All this amounts to below-par performance and, directly or indirectly, it costs us. I know one company that paid the transportation costs to send defective materials back to the supplier for reworking.'

'That's crazy,' mutters Ed.

'But it happens,' Scott chimes in.

'Not on my watch, it doesn't.' If he only knew!

I continue, 'OK, guys, we won't argue about this. In the world at large, a lot of this stuff happens simply because buyers are working in sub-optimal conditions. They're stuck with fire-fighting and never get to see through the smoke for long enough to know what's really going on, let alone have time to deal with it. When this happens it's not because buyers don't care; it's simply that they're doing their best in seriously unhelpful circumstances.'

Ed scribbles a few notes. Perhaps he's remembered feisty Elaine back at the ranch and the items he's put on the back burner for her.

'Hmm,' murmurs Ed, 'we do have some issues here. Jon, I'm thinking of travelling back to Chicago with you after we finish up here. En route I'd like to discuss what we can do about "sub-optimal conditions", as you put it.'

'Perhaps we'd all like to have that discussion,' observes Diane from Seattle. Others agree, but we need more time. People consult travel plans. I'm happy to trade extra time here for a quiet return journey without Ed, so we agree to extend our meeting into a third day. We return to 'pushing harder' and I carry on.

'We started with being tougher with complacent suppliers, insisting on what we believe is due to us, and tidying up sloppy systems if we have them. We can then go on to make larger deals by adding together what would otherwise be fragmented purchases. Sometimes we issue too many small purchase orders instead of fewer bigger ones, or it may be that other parts of the company are buying the same stuff we buy but we don't get our act together. None of this makes full use of our purchasing power.

'All this seems pretty easy to rectify,' observes Mike.

'Yeah,' says Dora, 'but only if other parts of the company are happy to standardise things in order to make bigger deals. Is this often a problem, Jon?'

'Fraid so, but we'll come to that in a minute. It's another ball game because it involves changing the minds of other people over whom you have no direct authority. This is more difficult than doing things differently ourselves. Also, we often don't probe enough into what exactly is going on. Poor information can mean we don't fully use our purchasing power.'

'OK,' says Ed, 'if I get you correctly, you're saying that producing cost savings is initially a leverage game which can be played by procurement teams without involving others in the company. The initial object is to add together and streamline current supply arrangements, then push harder for better deals. Typically there's little market analysis, and activity stays within the procurement team, whose main job is to find the best sources and then use contract negotiation skills on them.'

'And, as in our case where the Division is made up of independent businesses, to make sure that different locations covered by a "group deal" stay loyal to it,' Diane adds. She's come down from Seattle for this meeting.

Ed sits back thoughtfully. 'We're getting ahead of ourselves,' he observes. 'Let's deal with company structures later. For the moment I want to concentrate on the deals. Where do the savings actually come from?'

The spotlight is back on me, so I heave myself out of the depths of the settee-sized chair into which I've been gradually sinking. Ed and I discussed this issue back in London, but I guess he's asking the question again so the other folk can catch up.

'If we improve poor supplier performance then we obviously save the costs of poor quality and of running around rectifying things that have gone wrong. Once this is sorted out, then more savings come from economies of scale if you give suppliers bigger orders. You also save the internal costs that build up from placing lots of small orders. More benefits come from tighter and more consistent contract management. Further, suppliers can be willing to offer part of their profit margin in return for larger orders which give them continuity of business.'

'Alternatively, they might include additional benefits in the deal without increasing prices.' Diane is coming across as someone who's done this before.

'Absolutely. They might also push their own suppliers harder. All this forces us to examine overall costs in more detail to search out and eliminate unnecessary ones.'

'I'm hearing two things here,' observes Diane. 'There are benefits from pushing harder, and then other benefits if we make larger orders. Can we deal with these separately?'

'Right on,' agrees Ed. 'But first let's hear from Scott how Gullmech's been getting on from just pushing harder.'

Over a protracted lunch eaten in the conference room we do just that and hear about cost savings being made in several of the businesses, not just at Gullmech. They've obviously realised the heat is on at Gullmech and want to get ahead of the game.

Some examples of cost savings are around ten per cent, with others considerably higher. How have these been achieved? Some locations justified retrospective volume rebates or negotiated a lower volume threshold above which cheaper prices kicked in. Elsewhere, delivery or quality mistakes have been rectified. Some suppliers purchased back obsolete parts and have also been encouraged to reuse materials that still have some life left in them. With suppliers' help, internal stock movements have been reduced, consignment stocks have been agreed without increasing prices, and a national freight agreement has been set up to replace lots of local deals.

This was picking the so-called low-hanging fruits. What has to be done often becomes obvious after time is devoted to getting more information about the current situation and probing 'why'.

In one case a buyer decided to reopen dialogue with a supplier they hadn't used for a long time, having been very much wedded to an existing incumbent.

'We thought you were married to them,' said the "new" supplier, 'but since you aren't we'd very much like to see if we can do business together.'

It turned out they had some new technology and other productivity improvements which put them on a much more competitive footing than the current source.

Sometimes the grass over the fence is greener, but we don't see it.

We take a quick comfort break and return to the fray, spending more time discussing how folks have done things differently so that lessons can be learned to apply elsewhere. Excitement has been mounting, but Ed brings us back to earth with a reality check. 'Guys, this is good but it's not transformational. Jon, I hope you're not going to disappoint me.'

I hope so too. 'Transformation will come, believe me, but we must put results on the table first so that your management colleagues stay convinced that doing things differently is worthwhile. They need to see some payback from having invested in meetings like this, for example!'

It's early dusk outside and the reflected lights of passing traffic show that the slushy snow of midday has morphed into the malevolent ice of night-time. Ed sees this, stands up and stretches.

'Let's call it a day,' he declares, 'and we'll reconvene in the morning to see what else we can do over and above simply pushing harder. 'Night, everyone.'

Outside, the temperature has fallen like business confidence in a recession. Bryn offers to convey me back to the hotel in his classically gargantuan, brilliantly chromed, tail-finned auto. He eases into his seat, the size and rake of which suggest that he's settling down to watch TV rather than drive me home. Up front, under the hood, a deep-throated power plant heaves this Detroit dinosaur into life, while rearwards a surprisingly small-bore exhaust pipe steams languidly into the chilly night. We arrive, I disembark, and Bryn and his mobile sitting room ease away from the hotel just as languidly, leaving me to contemplate the evening ahead.

The hotel isn't busy so it looks like it's going to be a quiet evening and an early night. After a day in a conference room, though, fresh air is needed, so I decide to take a quick stroll. This turns out to be a careful stagger as the pavements have iced up. Then come the sprints across the no man's land that is the highway, empty only while cars are held at the lights and raring to go. Wide, very wide, roads keep shopping malls apart, like firebreaks designed to prevent runaway retail therapy. Crossing these roads requires patience first, and then the launch speed of a NASA rocket when the red light turns green. Halfway across, the green hand that distantly beckoned now abruptly starts flashing red again. To falter would be fatal, and I wonder what level of Olympian fitness is required to make it all the way on green.

Chapter 11

IT'S THURSDAY AND we reconvene for daily start-up routines. If this was Hong Kong everyone would be outside for Tai Chi. But not here. Early-morning rituals involve checking emails, replenishing doughnut stocks, scaling Everest-sized muffins and laying in supplies of non-alcoholic liquor. Are we here to work or withstand a siege? I try root beer and privately make a deal that if it doesn't repeat on me then I won't repeat on it. Strange flavour.

Ed wants to see how buying power can actually be increased as opposed to flexing muscles more vigorously.

'Adding similar deals together is one way of getting a bigger bang for the buck, I suppose,' observes Mike, 'but I guess there's a limit to how much of the same stuff you can combine and give to one vendor?' An overnight stay in mid-Kansas has noticeably improved his American vocabulary.

'That's true,' I agree, 'but piling the same stuff higher and buying it cheaper isn't the only option. For example, think of the total value of business you give to a supplier. I met a CPO with a pharmaceutical company. Doug had a global remit and added up what all his company's purchases were really worth to a key supplier, also a global company. He found that his pharma colleagues in country A were buying product X, those in country B were buying product Y, and colleagues in country C were buying service Z. They were using what seemed to be independent suppliers, but they were actually all owned by the same group parent. Doug went to the supplier's Global Sales VP and successfully negotiated significant cost savings which more realistically reflected the total value of the pharma company's custom to the global supplier. The VP's comment still rings in Doug's ears: "Gee, Doug, I just hate it when customers get their act together."

'There was another case where collaboration was between two unrelated companies with no "group" connections at all. One made paint and bought a pigment that was a vital ingredient in its formulations. As a relatively small customer it felt weak dealing with a major chemical supplier. So it found a company in the paper business that used the same chemical for surface coating and allied with them to set up a joint purchasing agreement with the chemical supplier. Bigger bang, fewer bucks. Bingo.'

'I have a variation on the fragmentation theme,' offers Diane. 'I was at a conference the other day and met a CPO from a company that makes food products. His complaint? He said, "We buy thirty-seven types of chicken flavouring! Surely just one or two would do?"'

'Sounds a bit like the spice cupboard at home,' muses Mike, 'but Jon and I talked about something like that back in the UK.'

I can't remember talking chicken with Mike, and look puzzled.

'C'mon, Jon, it's the situation where we had several engineering shops making stuff for us from similar raw materials. We reckoned that, based on the total volume of business that we spread over those subcontractors, we could negotiate lower raw material prices than they could. So we did that, got a much better deal with the raw materials supplier and let the contractors buy that raw material under the terms we'd negotiated.'

'Why spread the business out in the first place?' enquires Diane.

'Because we're dealing with small shops, none of whom have the total capacity we need.'

'By the way, what happened to the chicken flavours?' John asks Diane.

'They settled on three different varieties, bulking up the volumes of each variety and saving a load of money in the process.'

'Makes a lot of sense,' says Ed, 'and I want to stay with the fragmentation problem a bit longer. Jon, we need more examples where this was successfully overcome.'

Sometimes, building bigger deals enables a supplier to offer cost savings larger than might be expected from simple volume discounts. One division in an oil company wished to purchase four motor-driven centrifugal pumps and had already received offers from three suppliers to provide them. However, a search for similar requirements in other divisions revealed that forty-eight were required throughout the company. The suppliers were notified of this. Two of them offered five to ten per cent price reductions in light of the larger volume. Generous on the surface, but maybe that's all the buyer deserved if his negotiating tactic was to go straight from four to forty-eight. However, the third supplier quoted fifty per cent below its first offer. Two factors contributed to this. First, the new volume was sufficient for the supplier to dedicate a whole production line to this customer's work, giving twelve months of continuity. Second, it formed an alliance with the motor manufacturer, who adopted a similar strategy. Cost savings? They exceeded one million dollars. A nice example of how savings can be made by understanding underlying costs rather than chipping away at surface prices.

I resume. 'That's just one specific case. Remember, cost savings produced by combining fragmented deals can generally be thirteen per cent plus.'

'Very, very interesting,' says Ed. 'We must have many opportunities like this that will show up when we look for them. All of you, let's search! However, I can already hear some of our budget holders saying no to some of this.'

'Why?' asks Mike.

'Because they're comfortable with their current suppliers, and they also believe that their precise specifications are sacrosanct. Thirty-seven flavours for thirty-seven users!'

'True,' adds Diane. 'And there could be thirty-seven reasons why this happens. Part of the problem might concern the composition, quality or performance spec of the item or material that's actually being bought. But these may simply reflect user preferences rather than make a tangible difference to performance. Users also tend to specify suppliers by name, which restricts the buyer's choice.'

'Surely it's the buyer's job to select a supplier?' Dora is still with us, and aims the question at me.

'Yes, it is in principle. But nominating the supplier occurs because the user has confidence in them and is nervous about untried alternatives. When this happens, the buyer must probe exactly what operational needs the user insists on and then be creative in suggesting other ways in which these needs can be met.'

'Such as?'

'Testing a new supplier for a trial period and involving the user in monitoring them. Or putting the user in touch with a colleague in a similar role elsewhere in the company who has already tried the new source and can pass on positive comments. These tactics do work and demonstrate that buyers must influence things earlier in the procurement process rather than waiting for a final requisition to turn up when it's too late to do anything about it.'

I look at Ed and sense that he too is thinking of what Elaine would say at this juncture. 'Dreaming on' might be involved.

Bryn comes in from another angle. 'What about when budget holders – you called them users, Jon, but we can all think of other names for them – just don't want to change the spec or supplier at all, and in any case think that buyers are exceeding their authority when they suggest it?'

Diane, who seems to spend a lot of time at conferences, remembers another one she went to and someone she met there. 'That can be tricky,' she recalls, 'but elementary psychology works here. This lady I met is the procurement boss for a hotel chain and wanted to get the Head Chef, the equivalent of our Engineering VP here, to change meat suppliers. But he exhibits all the volatility and self-belief that goes with being a celebrity chef. It's not the best idea to go to him and say, "I've got a new meat supplier for you." Not if you value your life. Chefs have knives. So she says to him, "Chef, every day meat suppliers call me wanting our business. But I'm not qualified to say if they're any good, so I need your help. If I organise a tasting session would you be prepared to try their products?"

"'Mais oui," he says, being French, "just let me know when you need me." So she organises a blind tasting which includes offerings from the existing source. The chef comes along, tries the stuff, doesn't like the meat provided by the current supplier although he doesn't know it's theirs, and pronounces another meat to be magnificent. It actually comes from a different source.

"'Ah yes," says our chef, "it is very good. I have been thinking we should change suppliers sometime, and now, now is the moment. Go do it, s'il vous plaît.'"

Job done, clever psychology and a thirty per cent cost saving in the bag.

We're mesmerised by Diane's total recall as well as her French impression. A muffin moment seems appropriate so that we can savour the psychology some more. Diane has a point. If you can convince a chef to change his spots then leopards would be easy meat. I decide to give the root beer another chance. The flavour hasn't improved so I check the side of the can for the ingredients. They include spikenard, pipsissewa, guaiacum chips, sarsaparilla, spicewood, tree barks and roots from burdock and dandelion. Oh, and vanilla beans, liquorice, dog grass and molasses. There's also a bit of history on the tin. We owe root beer, it seems, to Charles Hires. He was a Philadelphia pharmacist and apparently discovered, while on his honeymoon, a recipe for a delicious herbal tea. Presumably he discarded this and made root beer instead, because it still tastes weird.

Since we've stopped, someone suggests that this would be a good moment to look round the factory. It turns out to be fairly old and nowhere near as modern as Gullmech's, and that's even before Antony's new machine is up and running. It's a welcome break, though, after which we return to the boardroom, joined again by Dora.

Ed attacks a last muffin, flushes it down with another swig of root beer and gets things going again (probably in more ways than one) with a quick summary. 'Right, we've looked at getting better deals by being tougher about them, increasing leverage by combining otherwise piecemeal purchases, and heard one great example of how a tough user can be persuaded to do things differently. I guess it's about making it possible for them to say "yes".'

Diane nods in agreement with this insightful comment, but suddenly looks thoughtful.

Ed notices. 'Perhaps there's one thing we need to be careful about, though. Diane, if you're thinking what I'm thinking, it's how far can we go wielding purchasing power like this. How do we know when to stop? Jon, what's the secret?'

'One quick answer is, when the supplier to whom you're awarding all this business is unable to cope with any more, or finds it so painful that they want to pull out. I know one big company that had put virtually all its eggs into one supplier's basket. Then all of a sudden the supplier said, "Thank you, but no thank you. This business is now unattractive and we want out from it. We'll honour our existing commitments and then we're out of here."'

'Big problem if it's a key supplier and you don't see it coming,' Dora observes. 'So what happened?'

'The customer won a stay of execution and then initiated a whole new programme of closer supplier relationships which were very different from the arm's length albeit cordial relationships currently in place.'

'So why did this make the supplier feel better about the situation?'

'Because the customer stopped banging away at price and instead worked more closely with the supplier to see where and how underlying avoidable costs could be removed. For example, reducing waste, improving communications about forecasting and scheduling, eliminating unnecessary packaging and adopting the supplier's advice about changing some of the specifications to be more cost friendly. This enabled costs to be reduced without diminishing the supplier's margin. Beforehand, all the customer was doing was pressing down on the margin to reduce prices.'

Mike's been taking all this in. 'I guess this customer was lucky to come out of it OK, but it's dangerous to let things get so bad before they're put right.'

'But it's what a lot of companies do. Leaving it late is human nature.'

'So what's the advice?' probes Diane.

'Stay close to the supplier, because the more business you give them the more important they are to you. Establish a rapport that allows the seller to be honest about whether or not the relationship is working. But be realistic. They may not be totally open with you, so watch out for signs suggesting they're cooling off if their interest in you wains.'

Bryn is spurred into action. 'And how do we detect that, for heaven's sake?'

'You can sense this when things start backsliding. For example, they put a junior sales rep on your case where previously you dealt with senior account managers. Previously there were few, if any, problems, and if there were, they were on top of things from the word go. Now they're slow to put things right, and that's assuming you can find someone to talk to about the problems in the first place. They adopt "take-it-or-leave it" tactics when imposing price increases. And so on. This is how you get the feeling you don't matter so much to them any more.'

Dora is now hooked and has postponed another meeting to which she was going. 'Who said the customer is always king? You're giving me a whole new perspective on what our procurement folk should be doing. But what do we have them doing in practice? We have them chasing ever-changing schedules and solving "urgent" problems for users. We're not being smart, are we?'

Elaine would concur. Ed gives Dora a quick nod but wants to explore another aspect of dealing with disaffected suppliers.

'We've talked about how to build bigger deals with suppliers, the dangers of being too aggressive, the benefits of closer relationships and the tell-tale signs that indicate a supplier's lessening interest. But how do we increase interest if it's on the wane and we actually do need the supplier because we don't have alternatives?'

'Recognise that "piling high and buying cheaper" is not the only way to obtain maximum value from the supplier. Look for other reasons why doing business with you is valuable to them.'

'Examples?'

'Think of good behaviours that your company exhibits that might differentiate you from others. I hope there are some. Having a reputation for paying on time is a good start. Be demonstrably fair and ethical. You might also be more willing than others to help suppliers improve performance, or involve them in R&D or field-testing programmes. Are you the sort of company that tells suppliers what they must do for you – which is not a good stance – or do you listen to the supplier's suggestions about how things might be done differently? Encourage suppliers to question your specifications if they are different from what other customers find suitable…'

'Hold on a moment,' urges Mike. 'I'm having difficulty getting this down… OK, carry on.'

'If you're recognised widely as a high-class company, then a supplier would be glad to say they have you as a customer. They could use this as a reference when talking to other potential customers. Your order book might be growing when others aren't, or you might be operating or wanting to expand in parts of the world where the supplier also has ambitions for sales growth. Do you give your suppliers decent forecasts of upcoming needs or are you always hustling them into urgent deliveries and then changing your mind?'

'OK,' says Ed, 'I think we get the picture, and it's quite possible that we don't tick many of these boxes.'

Dora is now really with the programme. 'What about other situations where the supplier does want our business and we've given him a lot, but there's the worry that they may go bankrupt? Is there a maximum volume that one should give to one supplier while giving the rest to another?'

John, with his finance background, has something to offer. 'There aren't any general rules about the maximum amount of business that can "safely" be given to any one supplier, although some companies say they will not let contracts exceed x per cent of the supplier's turnover. It's a risk-management issue. However there are tell-tale signs that indicate an impending supplier crisis. So you have to look for them! This needs an ongoing relationship-management plan, or at least a watching brief that shows up early warning signs.'

'Signs? What signs?'

'Maybe they start factoring their invoices ...' I begin.

'Hold on, what's factoring?' asks Scott.

'It's when the supplier gets a bank or other finance business to remove the burden of chasing unpaid bills. The bank pays the supplier for all the invoices owing after taking off a management fee. It justifies the fee by collecting the money owed. So the supplier gets its money now – or at least most of it – and doesn't have the cash flow problem or the hassle of chasing unpaid debts. Other signs of problems include deteriorating quality and delivery, maybe even production stoppages because their own suppliers aren't supplying as a result of stopped payments. One leading insolvency practitioner reckoned a company was really in trouble when its board's main interest was redecorating its headquarters, fitting deep pile carpets and putting bigger goldfish in the lobby fish tank!'

Silence falls as people remember there are emails to be dealt with before the end of play and the afternoon is almost done. But Ed isn't. 'Yesterday, I think it was, you mentioned that procurement teams often labour under seriously unhelpful conditions which reduce their impact. Can you explain?'

General body language in the room says 'no'. In any case, people remember this to be the reason for going into a third day.

It's not lost on Ed. 'OK, OK, I get the message. That's the agenda for tomorrow morning, and you've all made plans to stay over. Tonight there's a ball game we need to see, and the drinks are on me.'

Thanks, Ed, and I hope it won't be root beer.

Chapter 12

IT'S THE END of the week and day three of the muffin-fuelled marathon. Bryn's mobile sitting room has brought me from the hotel, packed and ready to leave when we're finished. The limo slipped and slid on hard-packed snow, but when you're seatbelted into something like a sofa you feel you can hit anything and only spill coffee. I'm alarmed to see more snow falling, though.

We're inside the offices again, and the boardroom is full of luggage as everyone wants to make a quick getaway when we're done.

Ed opens with a recap on progress and reminds us what he said yesterday about the successes so far not being transformational. 'Guys, I think I was a bit hard on you. The Division's latest results have come through and I'm delighted to say that our procurement initiatives are making an impact. And that's AeroCorp's CFO saying so. It's certainly grabbed a lot of attention. Well done to you all.'

'So what about the lack of transformation?' probes Dora.

'I mean that what we've achieved has been basically through our own efforts. But we can't sustain this impact by ourselves. So we have to create fundamental change in the company about how people view procurement and the part they play in it.'

Dora understands. 'And I guess our leadership teams have to stimulate those changes. But I'm not sure what the problems are.'

Ed looks at me. 'Jon, you said procurement's impact is often limited in some way – you called them "sub-optimal circumstances". What are these?'

'Problems include too much time spent on handling non-strategic purchases, and being involved too late after specifications have been fixed by users who, to worsen matters, have often hinted to suppliers that they'll get an order. And then management push for short-term savings, not knowing or caring that these might damage longer-term relationships. All these lock procurement into a functional box and isolate its activities from mainstream decision-making.'

'Sounds like home,' says Scott, earning a dark look from Ed.

But, to continue. 'There's more. Many procurement folk don't talk about their work in the language of the boardroom. They often don't know

65

where the business is going and so can't relate their work to the company's objectives. And if they can't explain procurement's contribution, no one else in the company is going to do it for them.'

'Why's that?' says Dora, who's now taking a full-time interest in the proceedings.

'Because folk are trapped by their own perceptions and prejudices about what the buyer's job is.'

'Still sounds like home,' persists Scott, but Ed grins this time. He recruited Scott to fix these problems. 'Surely the possibility of capturing big savings will get people working together in the right direction?'

'Scott, this certainly gets people's attention. Many consultants advocate the need to cut costs, and procurement is the go-to place to do it. The prize is a big one. But if that's all you're going after, then it perpetuates the image of procurement as an isolated functional activity dealing with the supply market consequences of a business decision someone else has made. It assumes a supply market exists and all you have to do is exert muscle power to get what you want.'

'I think I've heard you say that before,' remembers Ed, 'but it's good for us to hear it again. Now, I want you to explain the difference between tactical buying and a more strategic approach.'

'Right. Tactical Leverage is what buyers do, frequently acting in isolation from colleagues elsewhere in the company. It's a functional thing and involves optimising current transactions to prise cost savings from bigger deals. Some costs can be eliminated through economies of scale. Suppliers can also be persuaded to yield some of their profit margin back to the buyer to recognise the buyer's larger commitment. But the fact that cost savings are made this way means there's a cap on the total savings available. These can be big, but if they've only come about by optimising a current situation rather than changing it for the better, then it isn't strategic. Doing big deals isn't necessarily strategic.'

'How do you define "strategic procurement" then?'

'Strategic Procurement is what a company team does before, during and after making a contract. It influences and links supply market behaviour directly to the current and future needs of the business overall. It also changes things rather than makes the best out of the way things are.'

'Changes what?' asks Dora.

'It could be developing a new supplier ...'

'But we do that already when we approve a new source,' argues Bryn. 'That's hardly strategic.'

'Yeah, but that source already exists. The example I'm thinking of is where an organisation used a haulage contractor to deliver its liquid products in bulk. But the service was rubbish: product contamination, vehicle breakdowns, missed deliveries and so on. As a result, the company was losing customers.'

'So why not ditch the contractor and use someone else?' probes Scott.

'Because it was the only game in town, believe it or not. Then one day the procurement supervisor was gridlocked in traffic – in Bangkok, actually, so nothing new there – and was stuck behind a really smart road tanker carrying dry powder. She thought, "I wonder if they can help?"'

'So what happened?' Dora is intrigued.

'The supervisor called the truck company, who said they didn't do liquids.'

'So back to square one, then?'

'Not at all. She persisted. "Look," she said to them, "we're in the liquids business and we know all about handling them. And your lorry is like one of our tanks on wheels. But you know all about the wheels bit. So why don't we help you convert one of your trucks to handle liquids and we'll take it from there?"'

'We wouldn't have the time for this,' complains Scott.

Ed counters. 'That's the sort of thing we've got to fix if we're going to get strategic. Jon, how did it end?'

'They did the conversion, jointly ironed out teething troubles, found the result really worked and switched contracts to the new haulage company. Not a huge saving in cost but a vast improvement in quality, and hence more customers retained and less wasted costs. The new contractor was delighted because it not only gained a new customer – the one that helped them – but many more as well through diversifying in this way.'

Folk are becoming too comfortable in the giant chairs, and those who have jet lag are also battling with the effects of watching late-night baseball. We decide to move about a bit, and I take the opportunity to tell another story from the real world as we do so.

'An oil company regularly needed to upgrade its petrol stations for new technology, rebranding, new customer facilities, etc. These projects were called KDRB: Knock Down Re-Builds. In one particular city, it took nearly 200 days to complete such projects and each one cost, let's say, "one hundred". Several contractors could do this work and each project was treated as a one-off, each time seeking bids and awarding to whoever came in with the best offer. But they never changed much from costing "one hundred". Then the procurement folk decided on a new approach which involved, after testing the market, engaging just one contractor for the next year to do several concurrent KDRBs, not just one. The first one was completed according to the costs and duration of previous projects, but then things started to change. The contractor was on the learning curve, helped along because he knew he had several projects to do. He started to pre-fab stuff off site, not just for one project but for several, and was also able to order larger volumes of the materials needed. This wasn't speculation as he knew they'd be used. The construction teams settled into a rhythm and got faster and faster. The result? After one year they were completing projects for a cost of "seventy-eight" and, astonishingly, in thirty days. This meant that stations were back in business far quicker than previously and way ahead of their competitors who were doing similar projects but on the "old" schedules.'

Ed thinks Vince Lombardi would approve. 'That's a great example,' he observes, 'of a different procurement approach not only saving costs but also creating huge competitive advantage for the company by getting it back in business so quickly.'

'It's also a superb example of how creative procurement contributes directly to achieving part of the company's strategy, in this case to increase sales versus competitors. The road tanker case and the KDRB projects both created responses from the supply market the company needed to achieve its objectives. They demonstrate that procurement's role is to create, sustain and ensure access to the supply markets the company needs for it to succeed now and in future.'

Surprisingly, Scott wants something more generic. 'OK so far, but can you give examples of the different things that strategic activity involves? What are the principles distinguishing it from tactical purchasing?'

'Here are three for starters. First, it looks below price and attacks the supply cost base upon which price sits. Second, it looks beyond the transaction and into relationships, engaging supplier expertise and innovation where appropriate. And third, it detects and outmanoeuvres hostile supply market behaviour like monopolies and cartels.'

Ed is in his calculator again. 'And what sort of savings can we get by doing this?'

'Previously we talked about the leverage route, which generally gets thirteen per cent cost reductions, and often much more. Engaging with suppliers in a collaborative way can yield fifteen per cent up-front savings plus much bigger benefits when the supplier gives you preferential treatment. Examples are not being rationed when supplies are short, or it might mean you're the first to benefit, maybe exclusively, from supplier-led innovations. Then there's the competitive advantage, as just mentioned.'

'What about monopolies and cartels?'

'Beating these produces at least twenty-five per cent savings, often much more, while it also eliminates the risk of being the victim of suppliers' price-fixing games.'

Ed's on the case now. 'OK Jon, now let's see some examples of how we might get these savings.'

'Sure, but in a moment, Ed, as Mike is looking thoughtful.'

'Yes,' says Mike. 'I hear the numbers, Jon, but I'm still not clear why procurement can't deliver them on their own. Why is it necessary for other people to be involved?'

'Remember the chef and the meat, or the thirty-seven chicken flavours in the food company? Buyers can't unilaterally standardise on just one or two flavours because it's the technical specialists who are the arbiters of what's acceptable. And if they think buyers are telling them how to do their job, then you can forget getting their support for change. Likewise, an IT Operations Manager, for example, will be confident dealing with a long-time service provider and will resist changing to a newcomer who might be more competitive. This is partly because it's outside their comfort zone, but also because they think the "new" supplier has offered a cheap price just to get the job.'

'You haven't mentioned budget holders,' observes Diane, probably recalling some run-ins she's had with them as well.

'I'd rather not mention some of them too!' adds Bryn.

'OK, we all know they can behave like prima donnas. That's because they have the money and believe it empowers them to dictate precisely how it should be spent, when and with whom. But in a company with effective management controls, budget holders have the authority to decide what they should spend money on, but they don't have the authority to choose suppliers or commit to legal contracts with them. The checks and balances provided by the controls should ensure that things like over-specifications, untimely commitments, perhaps even fraud, don't happen. But even the best systems don't prevent budget holders having commercially naïve moments in which they reveal budget amounts or company decision processes to supplier personnel who are out fishing for this useful market intelligence.'

Mike is now on board. 'I guess it's difficult when buyers need others to cooperate but they can't demand it. Surely these problems are easily fixed by issuing an edict or two. People will then take notice, especially if it comes from the top of the company.'

'Edicts don't work,' says Diane. 'I've tried it. What we must do is change the whole environment within which people operate, and that includes non-buyers as well as buyers. What do you think, Jon?'

'Diane, I totally agree. Everyone from top to bottom in the company and right across it must realise they are part of the procurement process.'

I recall a meeting with a global pharma company having just this ambition for the entire business. The company's inspirational boss put it very neatly and I know I wrote it down somewhere. I search for the reference, finding it just in time to stop the others from taking an impromptu toilet break.

'Here it is, guys, listen to what their boss said,' and I quote: '"We plan sweeping changes to enable us to achieve the pre-eminent organisational effectiveness that's so crucial to our future. We must develop an organisational structure that reinforces shared accountability through multiple reporting relationships. In fact, all employees have multidimensional roles. We aren't simply experts in one functional area; we also have key roles to play in the business decisions. To create the 'new company' we must embrace each of our own roles in achieving the goal.'"

Privately I wonder how long it would have taken Shirley to dismiss this as horse-shit, but Scott clearly feels it's worth digging a little deeper.

'How on earth do we achieve that?' he says, poised for intensive note-taking and hoping to get answers to a lot of problems.

I say, 'We need a pincer movement,' but Ed calls for a comfort break before we carry on.

Over coffee, people want to know who the pharma company is, but it's not fair to tell. However, it does provide an interestingly different slant on the subject of cost-reduction. The company wanted me to visit them overseas and called beforehand about travel arrangements.

'Jon, we've looked at your ticket cost and have another suggestion which will save money. Would you agree to come over on our executive jet which leaves Heathrow on the same day?'

'OK, OK, just this once!'

It's easy to relive the experience. A private part of London's airport was set aside for these executive functions and a gleaming Gulfstream with beaming hostess welcomed our party of seven: three folk who would be at the procurement meeting, some corporate suits and me. We settled into leather seats big enough to make Bryn's sofa look like economy class. Large drinks dispensed, the aircraft scorched off the runway and headed skywards in a near-vertical trajectory. It only stopped doing this when the curvature of the earth came up in the window. We flew high, fast and northwards, noting icebergs far below looking like polystyrene balls spilled from a beanbag.

Landing was equally brisk, and wheels had no sooner kissed the tarmac when the pilot hung a sharp right and headed, still seemingly at launch speed, for a silver hangar on the airfield's perimeter. We hurtled towards what appeared to be the solid wall of a building, but well-concealed doors opened automatically just wide enough to let us through before gliding silently shut without pausing for breath. The plane's engines wound down, a small staircase was attached to the fuselage and we disembarked our spacecraft for swift and courteous immigration formalities. James Bond never had it better.

Chapter 13

THE KANSAS SKY looks pregnant with snow and I wonder if I'll be able to leave at all when we're finished.

Ed is thinking the same and calls us back to the table. 'Right, Jon, a pincer movement?' He refers to his notes. 'You said that "pretty well everyone in the company is part of the procurement process, from top to bottom of the company and right across it". Where does the pincer come in?'

'It's a rather inadequate analogy, but it takes a pincer movement to squeeze high performance out of the procurement process. Pincers need two arms to work, and one of them concerns procurement practice. This is the work involved in making contracts, running supply chains and managing costs. For maximum impact, non-buyers must realise they're part of the process and collaborate. The other arm involves the CEO giving a new licence to procurement to operate in a strategic way.'

'Why do you need both?'

Diane's insight comes into play. 'I think you need both to make lasting change. If all you do is make a few savings which impress budget holders then individuals may be won over, but that leaves others still thinking that buyers are there just to take orders. Likewise, if it's just the CEO demanding that things be done differently, then most users will give lip service to this without really being convinced of the reasons why. Like I said before, edicts don't work.'

John's analytical mind is at work, observing. 'Let's start with the first arm of the pincer. Two questions arise. One is, how specifically are non-buyers part of the procurement process?'

Scott joins in, 'And how do you get them to realise it and do things differently?'

'OK, first things first. If procurement is thought only to be about placing and expediting orders, then no one apart from the buyers will feel involved. On the other hand, if you define the procurement process as one that includes all interactions with suppliers, then everyone is swept into the net.'

'We need examples of these interactions,' says Dora. 'Let's go round the table and see what we come up with.'

Here's what we produce:

Technical folk talking to their counterparts in supply companies;

Budget holders and users asking suppliers for indicative prices and availability;

Operations people discussing problems with suppliers' after-sales teams;

Maintenance supervisors receiving visits from suppliers' sales people;

Quality teams auditing suppliers' production processes;

Our CFO meeting a supplier counterpart at a conference;

Our law people discussing a claim with a supplier;

Accounts clerks dealing with invoice queries;

A sales director paying a courtesy call on our CEO or President or inviting him or her out for a meal;

Our CEO meeting a supplier equivalent at an industry conference;

… oh yes, and a buyer negotiating and placing a contract.

It's a good start and, while not exhaustive, the list covers people across the company and up and down it. But it's very 'functional'. People in task boxes. This seems a good time to bring up the so-called 'separation of duties': a fundamental and valuable aspect of management control. This principle defines three separate authorities: the authority to 'requisition', the authority to commit the company to a legal contract and the authority to pay money out of the company. The requisition authority is exercised when a budget holder makes a decision to use company money to satisfy a business need. This might mean allocating part of a budget to create a service contract, but does not authorise the user to go ahead and let it. Moving along, a buyer is formally acting as a legal agent of the company when he or she signs a purchase order. Again, in principle, only the buyer possesses this authority, delegated from a CEO or CPO. The buyer's job is not just about setting up watertight contracts but also about establishing suitable sources and evaluating which of several quotes received represents superior value. Finally, on completion of the contract, an accounts payable person will settle the supplier's invoice once certain verifications give the green light to do so.

That's the basics of management control. Within this framework there can be some sideways delegation – for example, a user being given the authority to make purchases below a designated expenditure level. That helps efficiency but it needs someone, such as the CPO, ultimately to be accountable for the delegation structure and how it is used.

Essential as it is, the separation principle unfortunately perpetuates the concept of the procurement process being a sequence of isolated activities, the first being an operational stage leading to a requisition, then a commercial stage culminating in contract award. In real life it's more like a continuum. Early on, although the emphasis is on technical or operations matters, there is a commercial element. If this isn't recognised then commercial exposure exists. Then, approaching the point of commitment, commercial issues come to the forefront, although there will be residual technical considerations.

People seem overwhelmed by this deluge of management principles and it's Dora again who suggests a circuit round the table to give examples of commercial exposure. We decide not to point the finger at guilty parties but simply to identify misdemeanours and explain why they are identified as such. So we come up with:

Budget or urgency is unwittingly revealed. The salesperson will adjust their quote to be what the buyer can afford rather than reflect actual costs.

We reveal why other suppliers are not acceptable to us. The supplier concludes there is little or no competition for their wares and will price accordingly.

We divulge who has the authority to sign the order. Supplier will prefer only to discuss and negotiate with that person.

We say, 'You're the only source we're looking at.' The supplier puts on a 'monopoly hat' and prices accordingly.

We give the names of other suppliers we're talking to. This can trigger a cartel.

We hint to a supplier they will get the contract before we actually award it. Bang go any further concessions they might have made had they still been in 'selling' mode.

Commercial exposures unwittingly give away information that undermines the buyer's purchasing or negotiating power and hands the advantage to the seller. People look glum, so I decide they need cheering up.

'However, there is a brighter side. There's the CEO who looked in on the procurement team and said, "The Sales VP of our main raw materials supplier is visiting me this afternoon. Is there anything you want me to do, or ask, while he's here?"

'On another occasion a quality assurance expert was about to visit a supplier. The buyer got to hear about this and asked her QA colleague to investigate, during the visit, the supplier's cost base and the state of their order book. She also wanted to know who they saw as their main competitors. That's a great way of identifying other sources we may not know about. These are examples of commercial opportunities. They work because the other party, for example the supplier's technical guru, sees the QA visit as a technical matter and information is revealed without realising its commercial value. It certainly wouldn't be given directly to the buyer.'

Folk want some tips on how we can make our non-buyer colleagues more commercially aware.

'A half-day briefing, perhaps led by the company's own salespeople, would stimulate awareness and encourage street-wise behaviours. Demonstrate that suppliers' prices are usually "made up" but are made to look as though they've been "worked out". The former reflects what the seller "thinks they can get", whereas the latter implies a cost-plus logic which, being logical, cannot be disputed.

'Show that there are many different pricing policies, each intended by the supplier to achieve a specific objective. For example, low pricing to get rid of old stocks or to encourage buyers to try a new offering; high pricing if a new product has been launched with limited supplies to make it initially exclusive; cost-plus pricing to ensure a profit margin over and above manufacturing cost; high pricing if proprietary spare parts not available from other suppliers are becoming obsolete but buyers still need them to keep machinery going, and so on.

'Emphasise the difference between what budget holders and specifiers would "like" to buy as opposed to what really should be bought to meet the true business need. Then describe the tactics used by successful salespeople and how "strategic selling" can so effectively penetrate behind the company's lines of authority, thereby influencing "buying" decisions in a covert, and thus highly effective, way. And teach your colleagues the politician's skill of not answering questions!'

Ed summarises where we've got to. 'Jon, so far we've seen how non-buyers are part of the procurement process. Their behaviours can affect the quality of a deal done and how suppliers react. Equally, their help can be enlisted to find market intelligence not easily available to buyers, and we can do things to make them more commercially aware.'

'All true. An internal survey in one company found that two-thirds of the people spent fifty per cent or more of their time on activities linked to the procurement process. You can see how the figure arises when it's realised that anyone's contacts with suppliers are as much a part of the process as are tangible activities such as inviting quotations, placing contracts and so on.'

'Right,' says Scott, 'now please explain why, in addition to all you've said, we need more involvement with users in our quest for cost savings.'

'We've touched on that already, Scott, but that was some time ago so it's worth mentioning again.'

'Talking of time,' says John, 'I need to take a break. Back in five?'

We reconvene and I kick things off again. 'Scott, you were asking why user involvement is eventually essential. I say "eventually" because in the early stages of the cost savings journey buyers can do things without reference to others.'

'Like aggregating volumes, pushing harder on deals?' recalls Bryn.

'Exactly. But when it comes to changing specifications, standardising things or adopting a different contract strategy, then the user has to be involved because it is, after all, their business need you're addressing. It's only when they're on board that you can push forward and really get your teeth into cost management and reach for seriously challenging targets.'

'I've tried this at our company and it really works,' says Diane. 'Users can be very creative and supportive once they realise that, far from making savings by doing purchasing on the cheap, you're trying to make their budget go further.'

Another example from a pharmaceutical company, already well along the cost-savings road, is relevant. Its CPO was discussing possibilities with the head of Research and Development. Big savings are forecast. 'Hey,' said the R&D colleague, 'if we can get those savings then they free up funds in my R&D budget to pay for research into a whole new treatment area.'

We've reached an important point in the discussion. It's natural to use logic to persuade a user why they should collaborate more, but they may still resist. Psychology is needed.

'Psychology? Please explain as you probably covered this when I wasn't present.' Dora is intrigued.

'You've got to make it easy for the other party, whether they're a technical expert or a budget holder, to say "yes" to what you propose.'

Ed recalls yesterday. 'Hey, Jon, you said something yesterday about a CPO and Chef. Actually, that sounds like the beginning of a joke…'

'Or the name of an English pub,' comments Mike, perhaps wondering if the deepening snow will ever let him through to visit one again.

Ed waits patiently. 'Is that the sort of thing you have in mind?'

'It certainly is.'

'And,' observed Diane, 'I expect that chef is now procurement's ally.'

'Indeed so, and right now they're collaborating on a big project to upgrade hotel kitchens as part of their global refurbishment programme. Funds are tight but the chef and the tech experts are convinced that procurement holds the key to maintaining the programme's scope, despite capital cutbacks. They'll be searching suppliers for the latest ideas.'

Scott looks up from his legal notepad like a courtroom stenographer ready to take down the next bit of evidence. 'Surely results like that speak for themselves and any other budget holders will fall into line automatically and want the same treatment?'

'Not quite. Our hotel CPO did win over some hearts and minds, but only of those who were willing to listen. Other folk, even those without prejudices, have what to them are legitimate reasons for keeping her at arm's length so they don't join the party. So already we only have partial impact. Further, although that particular CPO's style wins respect and cooperation, the same won't automatically happen with her successor when she moves on. So if a company relies only on a CPO's courage and charisma to produce results, they're likely only to be temporary ones. Backsliding can be expected when the successful CPO gets promoted to run another part of the business, as indeed she was.'

But backsliding didn't happen. Why? Read on.

Chapter 14

A FTER A SHORT break, Ed summarises. 'We've looked at the procurement practice part of the pincer you mentioned. What does the other part do again?'

'This is the lever exerted from the top of the company. The message has to be, "Ladies and gentlemen of the company, given that excellent procurement process is a must, how can we all play our part in it and when will we do it?" The "we endorse what procurement is doing so please feel free to be involved" invitation is the road to nowhere.'

'But Diane says edicts don't work,' Mike reminds us.

'They certainly don't if they come across as instructions without any explanation, and also if people think the company's leaders are aloof from the action. Also, edicts can often signal a prevailing boardroom fad. So people keep their heads down, don't do anything, wait for the first fad to be replaced by a second, and then don't do anything about that either.'

'I didn't think you could be so cynical!' observes Ed.

'Not really, but it's how people cope with uninspiring leaders, especially when they've seen it all before.'

There's a powerful phrase, attributed to Joel Barker, about the management of change: 'Vision without action is just a dream. Action without vision just passes the time. Action with vision can change the world.' I privately apply this to procurement's pincer scenario: 'Edicts without buy-in create the illusion that things will change. Cooperation without leadership is only a temporary fix. Inspiring leadership plus motivated people will move mountains.' Hmm. I'll keep quiet about this for now... it's definitely a work in progress.

Diane speaks. 'Just supposing the CEO really buys in to what procurement can do, how would things be different?'

'First, there'd be a powerful statement about procurement's purpose. Why it exists. This *raison d'être* links the process to the fundamental goals of the business, and gives procurement the licence to operate. It's amazing that this isn't properly articulated in many companies. As a consequence, people make up their own minds about what buyers are there to do. And it's also "them and us", with no feeling of procurement being a shared process.'

'Got that,' says Scott. 'What next?'

'Procurement will stay on the leadership team's radar. If it's on theirs it'll be on everyone else's. So every time a major business proposal is reviewed at the top of the company, you'll hear them ask, "What procurement considerations have you built into this proposal, and who did you involve?" or, "We have a major challenge or opportunity for our company; how can procurement help us address it successfully?"'

John joins in. 'And at budget time, "What's the basis for the materials costs in your budget, and what sourcing strategies will you employ to make these promises come good in practice?"'

Scott still has space in his notepad. 'Any more?'

'Yes, agreeing important sourcing strategies at leadership level should be the norm, just as it is with the other strategies that are more commonly reviewed there.'

Dora observes that this seems to involve the leaders in a lot of the action. 'What's left for the buyer to do other than to follow the plan as agreed by the boss?'

'That's where delegation comes in. The other thing that can only come from the top of the company is the framework of management control, delegation of authorities and so on. Most companies say something about this and set operating procedures in stone, but in many cases procurement is woefully served by them.'

'Woefully? Do you have examples?'

'Buyers' authority levels are often too low, so management spend time rubber-stamping stuff. The distinction between the three key authorities – requisition, commit, pay – is usually blurred and open to misinterpretation. This triggers turf wars. Heavily audited procedures are internally focused and fail to reflect the reality of the supply markets with which they're supposed to deal. For example, decreeing that three bids must be obtained before awarding a contract is absolutely wrong some of the time – when cartels are active, for example. If you want to throw money away big time then this is how you do it, but many rule books still require this approach to be followed.'

Just like the snow outside, silence falls again as folk ponder this gloomy diagnosis. Ed brightens. 'What about some good news – if there is any?!'

'There is indeed. Imagine a two-day gathering in Thailand of senior folk drawn from the various companies in a group operating around Asia–Pacific. The company, and its HQ, is also present in the northern hemisphere but they'd already had a separate session in the snow-clad mountains of Norway. The company President closes with these words to his colleagues: "My friends, I want you to remember two things about procurement…"'

'Hold on,' says Scott, 'I want to get these down.'

'"One is that when you take action today, make sure it's also part of a longer-term plan. In this way, meeting today's needs also moves you a step further along your strategy."'

Scott scribbles. 'And the second?'

'"Remember you are part of a family, and any decision or action of yours will have an impact on someone else. Consider this before you do anything."' This wisdom neatly summarises what we all have to do as stakeholders in the procurement process.

'Surely that's a one-off?' says Mike. I don't hear people round here talking like that.'

'Not yet you don't, 'chides Ed, 'but it will happen.'

The 'two things' story stands out in my memory. It's no surprise that it concerned the Scandinavian company succeeding today by living in the future. I'd been invited to a two-day gathering of the leaders of their businesses in the southern hemisphere. It was in Thailand, up north at Kanchanaburi. During one of the breaks we'd visited the POW camps where so many brave soldiers had been incarcerated and allowed to wither away to shadows of their former selves while working on the so-called Death Railway. We were all very thoughtful, and in the company of their ghosts, on that visit.

In the evening we gathered in the hotel lobby. Buses awaited and, after a short journey, we were on the banks of the River Kwai. We boarded a flat, barge-like structure which turned out to be a floating restaurant. There was no one else on the river and the only soundtrack was from the cicadas. And so we drifted downstream under the famous bridge, an iconic structure silhouetted against a full moon. The atmosphere was not celebratory, and it was not intended to be. Rather, it was a shared moment among a family of business friends acutely conscious of what had gone before in this theatre of war, and appreciating that they worked for a company that cared about people.

Ed's increasingly frequent consultation of his watch suggests that we're nearing exit time. He starts tidying up his papers. 'How about we stop now and Jon and I will continue the dialogue over the internet. By the way, I also want to hear more about what strategies actually look like, especially the monopoly and cartel ones. You promised me this a couple of hours ago!'

Nothing get past this guy, apart from those folk now making for the door.

'Safe journey home everyone – and better take those left-over doughnuts in case you get snowed in.'

I wonder if that last can of root beer could act as a de-icer, and whether or not Charles Hires thought of that application on his honeymoon.

Lunchtime, and it's time to leave Kansas country and say goodbye to one of that state's cities that styles itself as the 'air capital of the world'. I'd thought this to be, well, fanciful until I'd learned just how many aerospace companies are based here.

At the airport I check in and approach Security, manoeuvring uphill through a zigzag of police tapes before reaching the Guardians of the Gates.

'It's like slalom in reverse,' I observe. 'What was my time?'

'Nine seconds,' comes the uniformed reply. I appreciate these folks' sense of humour.

'Not bad, but hardly Olympic standard. Making "go to departures" like a workout explains why you guys win so many gold medals.'

'You've cracked our secret,' says Wayne the security chap. 'Our Olympic teams have never been as good as they were when they trained here.'

I move on to security screening and find ten people eager to welcome me. There are no other travellers, so perhaps I'm the only reason why they're here so late on a snowy Saturday afternoon, plus possibly the overtime package. This crack security crew is composed entirely of veterans. The impression is that otherwise slack weekend afternoons are scheduled for refresher training.

Jacket removed, bags opened, shoes off, pat-down search. A small tube of toothpaste is found on my person but deemed not to be a weapon of mass destruction. It's right that they do this, though.

'Where are you from?' continues the by now friendly interrogation.

'Wales,' I say, and they all assert they want to go there one day.

Only a handful of people occupy the departure lounge, watching basketball. Outside there's thick snow and a fast-greying sky pregnant with imminent precipitation. The warning lights on a dayglo yellow snow plough wink through the window. Off-white, low, flat buildings squat across the other side of the runway, but no planes. One rolls into view and I realise, gratefully, that planes push themselves across the snow rather than rely on traction between tyre and tarmac. It looks as though I might actually get out of here and make Chicago on schedule.

Chapter 15

Chicago

I MADE IT out of Kansas and am at Butch O'Hare's Chicago airport again in bright sunshine waiting for the between-terminal transport. A notice catches my eye: 'Ironic, isn't it? The city you never want to leave has the airport that can take you anywhere.'

Some posters really stick in the memory. One in Melbourne showed an Aussie airline taking a pop at British Airways: 'We don't want to be the world's favourite airline... just yours.' Other notices are resigned to things being beyond their control, as in, 'You are in a No Entry area'.

But it is possible to be more proactive. There's a stout oak door to the bell tower in St Patrick's Cathedral, Dublin. A notice proclaims, 'No entry to unauthorised persons. If you don't know whether you're authorised, then you're not.'

And there's one about recycling. It pictures a large toilet roll with the caption, 'In a previous life I was a political manifesto.'

Now that's ironic.

The last time I heard the word 'ironic' was during local elections in West Wales. The nearby chapel had been commandeered to count votes rather than souls. Dilys from the village post office and her daughter Megan provided a glamorous reception committee. As I arrived, Dilys' husband Tomos was lurking outside enjoying a holy smoke, as it were. We greeted one another.

Tomos pointed to the small gate to the chapel and then to the larger entrance for the burial ground. 'I was just thinking about the time that big gateway was made,' he said. 'Dai Morgan was here and a JCB was working in the road outside. Dai persuaded it to dig a hole in the roadside bank so we could have a wide gate to drive into the graveyard. He died shortly afterwards and is buried here so he was the first person to use it! Ironic, isn't it?'

Sure is. See JCB and Dai, as it were.

Ed also made it to Chicago on a different plane and is somewhere in O'Hare's domestic terminal catching up on our discussions while waiting for onward transport, in his case to LA. My phone bleeps, announcing the arrival of his first question.

'Jon, I hope your journey's going just fine so far. I was behind you leaving and only just got away myself. Some snow, that! Anyway, how do we get the board interested in what procurement can do for them?'

'Ed, you've put your finger on the answer,' I respond. 'One way is to judge what the CEO's current priorities are and then show what procurement can do to address them. For example, many companies are challenged by the current economic tough times. So procurement's message is, "We can cut costs," at a time when company leaders are hungry to do so.

'A CEO recently asserted he was "anti-costs", then admitted he really meant wasted costs. That's a big difference. Incurring costs with suppliers is part of a positive trade to obtain the resources needed to be in business in the first place. These costs are the precursors of revenue generation. Any waste at any place in the cost-incurring process damages profit or busts the budget. By all means go for immediate cost cuts, so long as they are enlightened ones.'

I zap the 'send' button and relax, but Ed comes right back. 'But what's wrong with saving costs? Surely doing this will automatically get people interested?'

'OK. It will, and procurement will shine brightly on your CEO or CFO's radar while the tough economic times persist. But after eighteen months or so the cost savings made by procurement folk "by themselves" dry up. You'll have nowhere to go if you've not by this time established procurement as an activity in which the behaviour of everyone in the company is "on side". Remember Route 42 and the parallel journeys?'

Zap.

Oh joy, the sound of radio silence. I guess Ed is busy digesting this lot or, like me, is moving towards getting airborne.

I'm on the terminal transport, arriving at International. Yet again I go through the laptop out, jacket off, grin-and-bear it routine, and then head for the lounge. It's a KLM flight but, as a result of its merger with Air France, the lounge promises a taste of gay Paree. I rattle the locked door but to no effect. Customer friendly or what? I recall another occasion when a trip around Oz and Asia involved five different airlines. The last was Air France, departing Tokyo. A Japanese chap in the next seat inscrutably asked what I'd been doing and which place I felt was 'most foreign'. 'Right here on this plane,' I said. 'Everything is in French and it feels that I'm tolerated as a lesser mortal while also being a useful bit of fare-paying cargo.'

Don't get me wrong, I love the French people I know and many of their customs. I ponder on the gulf between the impression we form about a country based on the highly spun self-serving behaviour of its leaders and the reality we enjoy in the company of its people.

I rattle the lounge door again and decide a phone call might be more productive. A lady called Rose at Al Italia reception gamely calls my airline who insists the lounge is open. I return, searching nooks, crannies, toilets and garbage disposal areas for a secret door that I might have missed previously. Eventually I arrive at the first door again. It is now open, though the lounge is empty of both passengers and sustenance – apart from wine (French), but then you'd expect that. I try some, a delicious red, 1998 Cotes de Castillon (12.5%). I have four hours to wait until departure so decide to give the lounge staff a sporting chance as it's still early.

Ed has been busy while I've been foraging.

'Still here, Jon. My flight's been delayed, so we can talk.'

No hiding place, then. Ed is a great guy and I like him, but he doesn't rest.

The message continues, 'Understand what you say about cutting costs. Is there another angle here that relates procurement's role to costs, but not necessarily to cost reduction?'

This doesn't seem fair. Ed asks the short questions while I'm lumbered with the long answers. I wonder if it might be better to converse by phone, but decide to reply longhand.

'OK. Try this. Take a look at your company P&L report. You have top-line sales and then, underneath, the costs of sales. One minus the other leaves profit before accounting for taxes and lots of other stuff. The point is that all the costs – internal costs and supply costs – are all hidden in the one number. One manufacturing company's cost of sales was eighty-seven per cent of top-line revenue. Its procurement chief reworked the figures to show that, if sales revenue was put at "one hundred", the corresponding supply expenditure was "sixty-five". The difference was a gross margin. She then subtracted the internal company costs – twenty-two – from this to give the original net margin before taxes, etc. Sixty-five plus twenty-two being eighty-seven. Not exactly high finance but, astonishingly, this was the first time the CEO realised the significance of the supply costs. This doesn't necessarily mean the company was paying high prices. It could just as easily reflect considerable outsourcing and so on. But they realised procurement involved much more than just placing orders. It was more an external resource management activity.'

Zap.

Buzz. Guess who? The man is irrepressible. He's either walking home or bedding down for the night at the departure gate.

'Jon, you mentioned changing procurement's licence. What exactly is this and do you have an example?' Another short question lobbed from Domestic to International.

'I'm not the greatest fan of mission statements but that's what the licence is. It's simply a statement of what procurement is there to do for the company. We've already looked at one or two, but here's another one from a major advertising company: "To improve profitability through professional management of the group's external resources."'

The phone falls silent and I surmise that Ed is airborne. Meanwhile, activity in the Air France oasis increases as new staff arrive for duty. There is much laying out of newspapers and opening of more wine. Solid food takes the form of a few peanuts and a biscuit or two; maybe ice as well, but I don't check. Some real-time training is going on as staff members practise inserting a special pourer funnel into the wine bottles, of which nine are now open. I try a little more. The one available wine glass I used earlier has been confiscated, so this next slug is in a tumbler. I suspect the glass I used before was part of a table decoration. But no matter, it worked just fine.

Another message arrives from Ed, presumably using in-flight telecoms.

'Gotcha with the mission statement. But if I propose something like that, won't the company President feel defensive – meaning he should have thought of it first? After all, he is in charge.'

I put down the tumbler and start texting again. 'Good point. It also applies to any procedures you want to change. If you say, "This policy is wrong and we need to change it," then board members will say to themselves, "Hey, wait a minute; I generated that policy. If I agree to change it then it suggests I got it wrong." And so you meet resistance. What works is a bit of psychology. Try this: "The policies (or whatever) have served us well in the past and have contributed to our company's success. This is a good platform upon which you may wish to make further change. What I propose is ..." and on you go. This makes the board members feel they've already decided it's time for change and you've come up with a way to help them achieve it.'

I glance up from writing as a portly 747 Jumbo lands, burning rubber as it reconnects with terra firma. The sound of rustling paper draws my gaze away from the window. It's a serving lady who has sidled up and removed my tumbler and tattered nut packets. I ask if there's any real food coming.

I'm told that the chap's still doing it. I hope it's quick, as the lounge is filling fast. What's not clear is whether 'doing it' refers to pre-flight life support, or the light breakfast which will be served in ten hours' time as we approach journey's end. I begin to fear it's the latter. Boy, I'm hungry.

Bottles clunk and I check what's happening. We're now down to six bottles of wine. I'm curious to see how many biscuits remain and stroll nonchalantly, though weakly, to the counter to check. There are three. But, to be fair, more are being produced from a packet which clearly hasn't travelled too well given the number of broken bits cascading onto the plate. I remind the lady about the food. She smiles delightfully, seems to curtsey, and says something in a foreign tongue which leaves me feeling slightly hopeful, though hungrier. It's only a short time now before take-off, so the chap who's 'doing it' needs to get with the programme. He should have 'done it' by now.

Ed is still online. 'OK, Jon, it's looking good. We're making progress. Any more suggestions?'

'Just two. It's what you might call a stealth strategy. In one case a CPO submitted a monthly report to the board, as requested, but always put in a comment which he knew would trigger a question from one or more board members. He used this question as a hook to catch their attention, and his answer would enlarge their understanding of what it was all about. And then if you remember back to our meeting in London there was the Procurement Director called Martin who got the Tender Board to be more interested in strategy than contractual small print.'

'I like the sound of all these ideas. What I'm going to do now, Jon, is put together a presentation for the AeroCorp leadership team. We're meeting four weeks from now to look at the budgets we've agreed for the year. It'll be a good time to hit them with what procurement can do differently from then on. Any thoughts on how we set our cost targets?'

'Ed, I'll send a note as soon as I'm back at base. OK? I'm out of here very shortly.'

'Roger that.'

A plate of sandwiches has appeared. And cheeses. They look, and are, so good. Despite extreme need I don't grab handfuls but use the tongs provided. The cheese sticks to them immediately and won't be dislodged. I think this is how they do portion control. I hand the tongs to the next guy. He selects a grape, drops it, and I tread on it. I wish I wasn't walking around in my socks.

Outside it's become a beautiful late afternoon. In contrast to Kansas, there's a clear blue sky and a searchlight sun shining on the snowscape. An

Air France Airbus is parked outside the window in the place just recently occupied by a Lufthansa version of the same plane. I never saw it go. Perhaps it had a quick paint job. A 'Flying Food Group' container is poised to disgorge its contents into the open mouth on the side of the aircraft. I hope they're getting more than wine and broken biscuits. That said, I haven't seen any food going into the adjacent aircraft, which I assume is the one for which I'm destined. Better get another sandwich or two, and the grape stuck to my sock might also come in useful. It's time to be gone – especially as the food has.

Chapter 16

THE FLIGHT BACK from Chicago provides the opportunity to think about setting cost targets. Partly this depends on how much business the company thinks it will do in the forthcoming year. The finance people will know standard materials and labour costs and then add overheads and profit margins to them. But that's just for starters, and it assumes continuing with the normal *modus operandi* in each AeroCorp business.

Ed has other ideas and wants to achieve cost reductions by doing procurement differently. But the heads of each business are hedging their bets, claiming it's difficult to forecast what the actual business levels will be. For sure, Ed won't be happy with these guys sitting on their respective fences. The answer is to create a planning basis for each business. Doing this allows me to get on and suggest where cost savings can be made, and how. At least it's a basis for action, and the numbers can be fine-tuned in due course.

OK, that's sorted, then. Time for a film and some sleep.

The film isn't good. Conversation with the guy in the next seat reveals he is in the aerospace business, specifically involved with leasing engines.

'So what qualifications do you need for that?' I enquire.

'OTJT.'

'OTJT ... what?'

'On The Job Training.'

'Oh, right. So what did you study beforehand?' I know I'm interrogating him but I'm understandably interested in how well this guy knows his engines. They are, after all, largely responsible for getting me home. He's a fresh-faced, neatly turned out chap, and probably more articulate than these initial exchanges suggest. I put him down as an engineering graduate, or at least a finance person.

'Sociology and media studies.'

Bloody hell. So here I am, 30,000 feet up and kept there by engines leased from a guy whose study programme involved getting up late, ordering pizza and watching films. But perhaps that's an old-fashioned view. Another G&T comes along just in time for me to adjourn my line of enquiry and return to the planning basis.

For each business I start with the typical annual spend, separated into the various categories of items purchased. This represents reality without being an exact financial forecast. It's usually easier to get a business to agree to a planning basis rather than predicting the future. It also gives a basis from which to pro-rate figures if actual expenditures turn out differently.

From the total AeroCorp annual expenditure I select about two-thirds as holding the most promise of cost savings. This is done simply by inspecting the different categories and ignoring those with little savings potential. The selected category expenditures are listed line by line as the first column of a spreadsheet. I then decide what 'per cent focus' should apply to each line of expenditure and write this in column two. Tooling, for example, gets an eighty per cent focus, meaning that only eighty per cent of that category's spend will be targeted. This is necessary because not all the 'tooling' items can be standardised to become candidates for consolidated-volume discounts.

Multiplying the target expenditures by the 'per cent focus' numbers gives revised target-spend figures in column three.

The fourth column is called 'per cent saving' and shows the figures thirteen, fifteen or twenty-five per cent as discussed before, assigned to each line item. For example, the 'Outside Processing' category would be assigned fifteen per cent, as collaborating with these contractors is a good route to obtain cost savings. Categories governed by monopolies or cartels would be assigned twenty-five per cent, while consolidation targets get thirteen.

Multiplying the third and fourth columns gives the potential cost saving in column five. A sixth column could be added, showing the 'probability' of getting a result. This gauges how easy or difficult it's likely to be to cut those costs, depending on how tough that supply market is and what has already been done to reduce costs.

Multiplying the fifth and sixth columns gives column seven, which is the expected annual saving, line by line.

The stewardess comes by with a drink as I contemplate these figures. Overall, I reckon the planning basis shows how to deliver savings amounting to six per cent of total spend for the forthcoming year. Individual judgements in the planning basis can be debated and adjustments made in light of reasoned argument. All this gives an outlook which is far more credible than just pulling a percentage-saving number out of the air.

Thinking about this stuff works like a sedative and my last thought, before losing consciousness, is that I'll email the analysis to Ed in the morning. Maybe he'll use it in his upcoming presentation to the company Presidents.

October – London

I'm train-bound for London again, having boarded at a different West Wales station for a change. This involves less driving, which is good news. The bad news comes in the form of a train with only two coaches. Fortunately I'll be changing at Cardiff. It is crowded. People are standing everywhere. Bicycles block the way from one carriage to the next and the lady with the refreshments trolley can't get through. She's talkative and addresses all of us within earshot. 'By the way, people, one of the toilets is blocked.'

A lady passenger joins in. 'And the other one's not working either. It's one of those modern ones with electric doors and when I was in there all the lights went out, including the buttons, see? So there I am in the dark. I didn't know which button to use for a flush, so I didn't press any of them because I didn't want the door to open instead.'

We all quietly appreciate the humour of the situation while noticing that the carriage is cold. Our tea lady explains. 'We can't manually control the heating because all the settings have to be adjusted by a supervisor back at base. I think they want to keep the fuel bills down.'

An in-train announcement interrupts her discourse. 'This is the guard speaking. I can't get through the train to sell tickets because of passenger numbers. Please buy them at your destination.'

Fat chance.

'Next stop, Bridgend.'

'We were lucky to get that,' observes trolley lady. 'There are lots of buttons he has to press to make an announcement and sometimes they don't work.'

Despite the unwitting entertainment, we ponder these dire times where the lives of train staff and passengers alike are ruled by invisible men in grey suits back at base, intent only on optimising costs and generally dehumanising things in the interest of generating profit. If they knew we were getting entertainment for free they'd probably charge for that as well.

'What are you going to do about the toilets, then?' comes an anxious voice from halfway down the carriage. Presumably the enquirer is computing the time it'll take to push through to an unflushed but serviceable loo on the train versus the time it'll take to reach Bridgend.

'Don't worry, luv,' says Mrs Trolley, 'what we're going to do is have a longer toilet stop at stations with public lavatories.'

'How are you going to make sure everyone who gets off for a pee also gets back on the train before it leaves, then?'

Mrs Trolley is stuck for an answer, so we all silently hope the men in suits are working on it.

Chapter 17

E D AND I meet over coffee and sandwiches in a quiet corner of the vast lobby in one of London's swankier hotels. Ed has style. He's also in great form and seemingly pleased with himself as he's been asked to lead a Division-wide review of procurement as well as continue with his VP role at Gullmech. This is what AeroCorp's CEO advised me back in the UK's north-west,

'Jon, the Presidents' meeting went well. I used your planning basis and built the numbers into a presentation for the guys. They bought it totally and we've got the green light to do Route 42 as well. They also want me to increase authority levels and implement new systems to release buyers from the low-value dross that bogs them down. So what's next?'

'Hang on. Tell me what went into the presentation. You certainly bet the farm on it. What did you say?'

Ed produces his laptop and charts spring to life. 'Someone once told me how to make a powerful presentation. You need to use logic, show pictures and induce fear. So that's what I did.'

I can't wait to see how this turned out and lean forward to see the charts better. Ed shifts to the edge of his seat and scrolls through his thriller movie. 'This first chart states our business model, the buy/transform/sell thing, and then says that over our whole Division between thirty-five and fifty per cent of sales income goes right through the business to be spent with suppliers. It raised a few eyebrows so I challenged them with a couple of questions.'

'And you're going to tell me what they were!'

'Yup. One: what value is acquired from this expenditure? And two: what risks are the businesses exposed to given their high dependence on external resources which are effectively out of their direct control?'

'That sounds like the "managing a large part of our company, which we do not own, cannot see and which is staffed by people we don't employ" way of describing procurement's role.'

'I wondered if you'd spot that!' Ed is enjoying himself. 'I then put forward five arguments for action. The first said that procurement is not mechanistic and that there is science and strategy in it. I showed them the Kraljic grid and where our purchase categories sit within it.'

'A good picture to show them.'

'Exactly. I then hit them with another one: the Supplier Preference Overview. This supported the second argument, namely, "We may need suppliers more than they need us." This worried them.'

'Hang on a moment, which version of the Supplier Preference Overview did you use?'

'You sent me an article about it. It's where a supplier looks critically at its customers and decides how attractive they are, or not. It's another four-box grid where the x axis is "Competitive Position of Supplier", low to high. The y axis is "Attractiveness of the Account", again low to high. If the supplier has a weak competitive position, for example, the customer prefers another source and if the account is not attractive, then the customer is labelled a "nuisance".'

'But obviously not told so!'

'No way. And while the supplier may be selling to them, they don't give any favours. It's take it or leave it territory.'

'And the opposite is where the customer is "core" and treated with great care?'

'Correct. But we're only "core" to some of our suppliers. With others we have varying degrees of attractiveness.'

'You're on a roll here, Ed. What was the follow-up punch?'

'A picture of a huge, mean-looking gorilla under the caption, 'Supply Markets Are Jungles.' These include monopolies and cartels where prices can be twenty-five to one hundred per cent higher than competitive ones. Some of our initial cost-saving projects revealed suppliers' profit margins up as high as fifty per cent, which led to the key question, "Who's profiting from whom?" The Presidents were not happy.'

'Pictures and fear seem to be playing a big part in the story so far, Ed. Did logic ever get a look in?'

'You're forgetting the Kraljic and Preference Overviews. But I also used logic to support the fourth argument for action, namely that company in-fighting and chaotic expenditure cost money.'

'I'm all ears. What was the story?'

'I showed them a chart with "Relative Cost" as the y axis and the key steps of the procurement process along the x axis: Identify Need, Requisition, Contract, Deliver and Pay. A rising cost line showed how doing the wrong things "burned up hard-earned sales revenue". Actually, this was the chart's title.'

'This is becoming an Oscar performance. So what were the "wrong" things?'

'Well, roughly following the procurement sequence, I told them about over-specifying, giving buying signals, approaching supply markets in the wrong way…'

'Meaning?'

'Seeking three bids from cartel suppliers, for example. Then constantly changing specifications, making bad contracts with performance and legal loopholes, accepting poor supplier performance, leaving the door open to fraud, and paying late.'

'Ed, I'm surprised you've kept your job. Why didn't they blame you for allowing this to happen?'

'Fortunately, they didn't ask. I think they were too bowled over by what I was saying. Had they got nasty I would've used the formula you mentioned a while back.'

'Which was?'

'I'd say, "Guys, we're not in the blame game here. Our procurement focus up till now has been to serve the internal customer. It's worked reasonably well and has helped us to get where we are. But we're growing as a company and the world is more challenging, so we must raise our procurement game accordingly if we really mean to be up there with the best."'

'Good work. No one could argue with those facts of life.'

'Fortunately they didn't. But I hadn't quite finished because there was the fifth argument, namely, "User prima donnas can ruin things. Only focused, purposeful teamwork delivers best procurement process."'

'Surely this repeats your fourth argument?'

'No. That was about how specific mistakes increase costs. This fifth point is about culture and people's appreciation of how their role fits into the procurement process overall. They may be a technical expert or a budget holder but they're still part of the process. Realising this, they'll understand the sales tactics used on them and know how to get commercially useful information from the salesperson which can be passed on to their buyer colleagues. They're no longer living in a technical or user bubble. They'll also be familiar with the research highlighting the massive cost-saving benefits of involving procurement early in the development of a requisition or a project. This compares with keeping the buyer out in the cold until the specification has been finalised with too little time left to carry out effective sourcing and contract negotiation.'

'How long did this story take, Ed? Remember, senior people have short attention spans!'

'Too true, but there wasn't a problem. To answer your question, about fifteen minutes. I then signed off, stating, "Procurement is a fact of business life, and the only question is, are we going to be outstanding at it?" And just in case they thought the answer was "no", there was a footnote saying, "The company that says no is automatically building in its own competitive disadvantage.""

'Sounds like a tour de force. Was that it?'

'Basically, yes. I had some back-up charts showing what strategic procurement looks like in practice. Also what Route 42 is about and where I thought we were on the journey at the moment, using the seven times six benchmark.'

I forgot that we discussed this sometime somewhere. Ed was referring to the seven facets of procurement effectiveness, namely: procurement's image and influence, relationships, organisation, operating framework, infrastructure, people, and agility and ability to change. A six score in each area would denote best practice.

'So what did you reckon the overall score for the group was?'

'Twenty-three.' Typical Ed precision. 'So they agreed we had some work to do.'

'And they all bought into it?'

'Yes. Well, most of them. The diehard who runs our other Californian operation dismissed much of what I said as consultant waffle.'

'OK. So long as the majority are with us we can proceed. It's important to get some results as soon as possible. Then it'll be more difficult for the cynics to hide behind the excuse, "It won't work." They'll have no hiding place, and rather than us justifying why they should be "in", they'll find it increasingly difficult to justify staying "out".'

'So, coming back to my question, what next?'

'First is to continue pushing and probing harder, as we discussed with the team back in Kansas.'

Mentioning Kansas activates Ed's muffin button and he calls for more coffee.

I continue. 'Since your presentation has got buy-in from other AeroCorp companies there'll be opportunities to build bigger deals covering two or more businesses that have similar needs. But this needs coordinating. Do you have anyone who can be authorised to knock together heads from different businesses?'

'I've got just the person lined up: Mishal. She's based at AeroCorp's HQ in the UK. She has an MBA and came to us from a leading engineering school. She's a bright cookie and on our fast-track management development programme.'

'Sounds great, especially as she's not a dyed-in-the-wool buyer.'

'What have you got against them?'

'Nothing at all. But Mishal's appointment will send a big message to the company.'

'This being…?'

'That the bosses see procurement as a major priority needing a high-calibre business person to drive it forward. It'll also promote procurement as an essential part of the company's forward strategy, needing excellent change-management skills to make things happen.'

'And Mishal is already well known and highly regarded in the Division. So she's the one. Now let's grab that coffee and finish up here. I have other things to do this evening but we can take it further tomorrow at the Group HQ. I also want you to meet Mishal. You'll be impressed.'

Chapter 18

IT'S A CLEAR, crisp morning the following day and I decide to walk to AeroCorp's London office. It's a smart, marble-lobbied address in Mayfair which is shared with Penserin HQ. The receptionist announces my arrival at the office and ushers me, along with the enticing fragrance of her perfume, into the lift. We head skywards and I step out onto higher-altitude marble. Another lady operates wall-mounted buttons and allows me into the inner sanctum. This is Tasmin, PA to the Penserin CEO. She gives me a big welcome smile, shows me a seat, offers coffee and sashays away across the room to get it.

They say first impressions matter, and we're already into double figures and counting. There's a lot of space in this office. Tasmin and her own assistant have desks in the middle of it, partially screened by tall, green, palm-like plants. These and the sand-coloured carpet convey the impression of an oasis of calm efficiency. Confirmation soon arrives in the form of delicious coffee served in delicate china. It's all a long way from the bucket-size, plastic, logo-embossed mugs deployed in Kansas. I wonder if muffins and root beer are on the menu, but probably not. Not very Mayfair.

Floor-to-ceiling windows along one long wall look out over London landmarks. Another wing accommodates offices. Penserin's conference room occupies the end wall opposite the one that Tasmin allowed me in through. There's lots of glass, steel, leather and... space. Nothing ostentatious here, but just an atmosphere breathing style and purpose into those who work in it. And that, apart from Tasmin and her assistant plus another lady who's just emerged from the oasis, is just eight people: the Penserin CEO, Chief Finance Officer, Chief Operations Officer, two high-powered adviser types and a trio of finance folk. It seems we have a team here who could run an entire country, but no, these are the names that top brass go by in today's business stratosphere. A couple of other offices are there for visiting folks like Ed, and I can see him in one of them. He's on the phone, pacing the room and issuing orders, just as you'd expect from an interplanetary SUV commander. An office door opens. A pin-striped-suited guy comes out, sees me, changes course, proffers a handshake and a nice smile, and says that I must be Jon. Welcome. It turns out he's the Penserin COO. He is clearly on board with what Ed is doing and my part in it, and he knew I was visiting today. He takes a seat alongside mine at the coffee table.

'We're delighted you're helping us, Jon. My name's Alan and I'm looking forward to hearing what you and Ed are cooking up. Carol's away today, I'm afraid, but she sends her regards. We have big plans for the company and I'm hoping the procurement side of our business can help us fulfil them.'

First impressions continue to be positive, with Alan coming across as a genuine guy with no ego problems. But he's referred to the procurement 'side' of the business and also used the 'fulfilment' word. Does this mean he sees procurement as servicing the business by satisfying what the production planning schedules demand? Here's an opportunity to check this out, especially with Ed still glued to the phone.

'Thank you for inviting me to be involved. I've already met some great people in the company. There's considerable excitement about what procurement can do if it gets into a higher gear...' but Alan cuts me off before I can go any further.

'Jon, it's not about a higher gear. This suggests going a bit faster in the same car. I want this company to be transformed into a truly high-performing vehicle of value creation,' at which point he stops, smiles, apologises for the crap metaphor and confirms his view of procurement transformation being the catalyst for change that the company needs.

'So you don't see procurement as a back-office activity, then?' I've got my fingers crossed.

'Far from it, although I know that's what a lot of people think. Procurement's a process that spans right across the business – that means within each company and across the Penserin Group as a whole. Transforming the procurement process is a vital part of our strategy to transform the business overall. How do you feel about helping us on the journey?'

I get the impression that this chap knows a lot more than I do about corporate vitality and the life forces that propel businesses to great achievements. Maybe he's related to Vince Lombardi.

'Funny you mention "journey", as this is what Ed and I have started on. Two parallel journeys in fact: one to deliver cost savings and the other to lift procurement out of its functional box and establish it as a core process in the company.'

'You must mean Route 42.'

So the word has already reached him. I wonder what else he knows.

'The very same. I didn't know you knew about that.'

'Well, Ed does talk to me, and we have pretty short communication lines in this company. In fact, I recruited Ed when I was in one of the businesses – the Seattle one, actually – and he's one of our rising stars. He's damn good at his day job and he's got enough spare energy and ambition to handle this procurement assignment as well. What do you think of him?'

I'm saved from answering by Ed's arrival on the scene. 'Hi, Jon. You and Alan seem to be getting on well.'

Alan stretches long legs in front of him, steeples his figures and smiles benignly at his protégé. 'We are indeed, Ed, but you should've given us another minute or so. I was just asking Jon what he thought of you.'

Our all-American hero raises eyebrows in my direction. It's time to change tack. 'What's impressed me so far is Ed's determination to extract from me everything I know about procurement. Alan, I get no rest from him! Questions and then more questions. But it's great because here is someone who's not interested in superficial change but wants permanent improvements. That said, one guy alone isn't going to do it. We've talked about a pincer movement, and we need the right message to come from the top of the company at the same time as Ed and the procurement teams are serving up the short-term cost savings.'

Brown-eyed Tasmin's been observing us from her oasis and decides that this impromptu meeting needs sustenance. She glides towards us on sky-high-heeled shoes, elegant and cool in a simple, figure-hugging black dress. She'd look great on a catwalk, although admittedly the desert sand does very nicely instead.

'Gentlemen,' she breathes, 'what about some refreshment? Or maybe you'd like to move to an office and I can bring it to you there?'

'Don't worry about me,' Alan replies. 'I need to be elsewhere. What about you, Jon?'

'More coffee would be great, thank you.' Mayfair-style china cups don't have the capacity of their Kansas cousins. Ed is also thirsty and orders water, and says we'll move to an office momentarily. Tasmin smiles demurely, gives all three of us some eye contact and melts back into the oasis.

Alan shifts to the edge of his chair, ready to leave, but has a final question. I hope he's not wanting more impromptu feedback on Ed's undoubted attributes. 'You mentioned a message from the top. Such as?'

Four top-management eyes drill in my direction.

'What we don't want is a simple endorsement of what Ed is doing. This suggests to others that you're supportive but not involved. Instead, say what you've already said about procurement being a cross-business process having the power to transform the company. It enables people to be even more successful in their work. And when you peruse budget plans, R&D programmes, requests for capital investments, operating plans and so on, say you'll be seeking assurance that procurement considerations have been fully explored early on. Tell them your periodic business reviews will place as much emphasis on procurement and supply chain issues as they do on in-house operational performance and sales results.'

Tasmin reappears with the coffee. She catches Ed's eye, raises finely shaped black eyebrows and nods in the direction of the office we're going to use. Ed nods back but doesn't have the classy eyebrows to match Tasmin's performance.

Alan has listened intently. 'OK. I'll obviously put it in my own words but that makes a lot of sense. What's more, it's what I do actually believe.'

'Involving an even-handed approach to procurement, production and sales?'

'Absolutely. Look, our *raison d'être* is to acquire companies in the sort of business we understand but which are underperforming. We then reinvigorate and invest in them, make sure their new performance level is self-sustaining, and then sell them, making a profit in the process.'

'Where does Carol fit in?'

'Carol is CEO of the AeroCorp Division, currently one of the main businesses in our portfolio. She operates from another floor in this building. Here in this office we're basically the holding company, but we do much more than sit back and wait for the companies to turn themselves round.'

'Such as?'

'We look for synergies between companies in the Group. Be very sure, though, we're not asset strippers, nor do we sell companies with only a twenty-four-hour guarantee. We may only own a company for a few years, but we genuinely want to do lasting good for them while they're with us.'

I hadn't realised any of this but am impressed by Alan's candour. It seems to be part of the corporate DNA. He goes on. 'So in the time we've been doing this, we've noticed what differentiates good companies from not-so-good ones. They're very clear about what their core activities are and don't exhaust themselves running things that aren't. They realise trade is done at each end of the business and they have to be equally good at both, as well as running the bit in between.'

Ed, possibly now caffeine-deficient, has been quiet, but now fires up and mentions the buy/transform/sell equation we discussed before.

'Exactly,' says Alan, 'but I've overstayed my welcome. Really good to meet you, Jon, and I hope we'll meet again. Ed will keep me in touch with how you get on. When you need me to do anything over and above what we've discussed, just let me know.'

'Many thanks. We will, because we need to do something about procurement principles as well.'

'I'm sure we do, but not now! I'm off. Ed, call me tomorrow with an update.'

'Yes, sir,' says Ed, but we all know that this is the American way and not the utterance of a subservient employee.

Chapter 19

E D AND I adjourn to the office where he immediately fires another question. 'What do you make of Alan, then?'

What is this obsession with first impressions?

'Seems good news to me, and I think he'll be a real ally. He's instinctively in tune with what needs to be done about procurement's message, priority and principles.'

'Yeah, what was that bit about principles? We don't want to create a bureaucracy here.'

'You won't need to. That's what happens if you have too many procedures. Principles set the basic rules of play. If they're defined, then people can decide how to deal with situations based on what those principles require. They provide central terms of reference around which to work out a course of action rather than trying to force-fit procedures to handle events they're not suited for.'

Ed grabs a last biscuit as Tasmin deftly scoops up cups and crumbs and silently withdraws, but not before doing the eye-contact thing and smiling enigmatically. I wonder what she thinks of all this?

Perhaps the subject of principles seems too theoretical at this juncture. Ed muses for a moment, then snaps back into action. He suggests putting them on the back burner and warming up yesterday's discussion instead. 'We covered a lot of ground then, Jon. The picture I get is that traditional buying deals only with what's in the shop window of the deal, whereas we've been discussing what goes on behind the scenes.'

A useful analogy.

'Correct. People usually only look at the price on the label, maybe haggle a bit, then buy. The procurement we're talking about is more like making an investment. You don't just look at today's price. You also take into account costs paid tomorrow – for example, if there's phased payment – and also any returning cash flows. And all these future money movements are discounted back to present values using the "discounted cash flow" technique.'

'That's not a concept I'm familiar with'

'Try "time value of money" then.'

'Now I'm with you. We discussed that a while back. It's where one hundred dollars today is worth more than the same amount in a year's time because you can invest it now and earn interest. So money in the future has to be brought back to what it's actually worth today. But you mentioned "returning cash flows". What are these?'

'It's what you might get by selling equipment when you've no further use for it. Mind you, you might equally have to pay out money for equipment disposal. Whichever way it is, these lifetime cost issues are more important than they once were, especially as technical advances happen so fast these days. Obsolescence strikes almost as soon as you've bought something.'

'Too true,' agrees Ed.

I continue. 'So when a buyer evaluates one supplier's quotation versus another, we must look at overall lifetime costs and not just up-front purchase price. This total cost approach also allows negotiations to be more creative.'

'Explain?'

'It's like playing cards. Having more cards gives you more options. In buyer–seller deals, each card is a negotiable item. Examples are unit price, payment terms, delivery cost, volume discounts, spare parts, training and so on. All these affect total cost of ownership. So as a skilled negotiator you can "give" on some points, like paying a slightly higher price, but "take" on others by having things like training, software upgrades and extended credit included for free. What you must do is keep score to ensure that the total value of what you win is greater than any extra costs incurred or conceded.'

Ed obviously reads business journals and cites negotiation research showing that it is easier to resolve things when there's deadlock if there are several negotiable items under discussion. This is because you have the flexibility to agree to a 'must have' wanted by the other party so long as you get bigger concessions in other parts of the deal where they can move their position. If you're only negotiating on one or two items, then you've got nowhere to go if you get stuck.

He adds, 'It's important when preparing for negotiations to be creative about identifying these items in the first place.'

'Exactly. These are the negotiation variables which we'll talk about later.'

Lovely Tasmin appears and asks if sandwiches would be desirable. She's obviously got a comprehensive catering operation going on in the oasis. We think this would be great, as Ed has to be elsewhere soon. The slim, gold watch on Tasmin's tanned wrist tells me that, if we finish soon, I can get the early-afternoon train back to base. She catches me looking and asks if I have to catch a train. I'm not sure if she's joking or just anticipating my every need, but I say I do. She will book a taxi. 'When would you like it, Mr Walsh? I know, I'll check the train time and synchronise with that.'

And so she leaves us to it, with me thinking that she probably synchronises perfectly. But we're here to work, not fantasise. I pull the chair up to the table with renewed purpose. It's time to look at the planning basis again, and we quickly review which AeroCorp companies are going to do what.

Tasmin arrives with sustenance and news that the taxi is booked. She asks Ed if she can help with anything else.

'Tasmin, you're a marvel. No thanks. Now, Jon, we need to split when we've finished these sandwiches. You need a train and I need a plane. I've also scheduled an AeroCorp buyers' meeting back in LA. I won't ask you to come over as it's basically a catch-up review. But what do you suggest we cover?'

'First you need an update on what they've achieved with the pushin' and probin', as you put it, both individually and then collectively when Mishal gets going. Then you ought to see how the various things we've discussed over these two days can be built into a supply strategy plan rather than left as isolated things to do. In the meantime we'll stay in email contact, and if any buyers have specific issues they want to sound me out on then they must feel free to do that.'

'Sounds fine to me. Until we meet again, then!'

'Hang on a minute. I thought you were going to introduce me to Mishal.'

'Ah, yes, change of plan. I found out she needs more time to finish her current assignment and then she's all ours. I'll give you her contact details so you can arrange a trip to Ireland in due course.'

'Well, thanks very much! Do you think I need a holiday?'

'No way, not with what we're paying you! No, we've got an operation over there which does pretty well and could be a model of best practice for us to follow. I'd like your views, and it'll be a great opportunity to get Mishal on board. OK?'

'That's fine, and I'll link up with her. Meanwhile, I'm off to the train station.'

'We'll stay in touch. Safe journey.'

I make it to the station in time to board a train that I hope has been sorted out loo-wise. It's much longer than the stricken one I came up on so statistically we should have no problems. The men in grey will have done the calculations. We're delayed leaving, though. When we do, progress is spasmodic and we find ourselves stopped again out in the country. Customers get restless and mobiles are deployed to advise waiting loved ones not only that 'I'm on the train' but also that 'it's going nowhere'.

At least the guard understands the need to keep people informed. An intercom crackle and bonk announce he's going on air. 'Ladies and gentlemen, this is your train manager. We are stopped at the moment so I'm going up to the driver to find out why.' Privately, we wish him well with his mission.

More crackle and he's on the line again. 'Right, I'm with the driver now and I can see a red signal.' So... that's why we're stopped.

More updates follow and the train manager's concern to keep us in the picture succeeds in lessening the strain brought on by the delays. But not to the extent that people will let it pass. They demand customer complaint forms. A harassed employee passes along the train announcing that he's run out of them. Perhaps the men in grey will stop the train for longer at stations that have a writing room.

Chapter 20

Ireland – November

A COUPLE OF weeks later, Mishal and I are in an airport hotel, having met yesterday and flown over to Ireland's west coast. We spent a convivial evening together. Over dinner we learned about each other's background but didn't talk much about the procurement project.

I am struck by her beauty. She is tall, slim, olive skinned and has tightly curled, close-cut, black hair. Her parents were high-flying professionals working as ex-pats on the African continent, having come themselves from some exotic location bordering the Indian Ocean. She was educated in international schools and business academies in the USA, and now has two degrees under her belt: one in engineering and the other in business studies. So she's a citizen of the world, enigmatic and with an air of nobility about her.

We meet in the hotel club lounge and chat before getting down to business.

'So have you met Ed yet?' I ask her.

Mishal confirms that she has. 'Yes. The day after he met you in London he came out to the factory where I was finishing an assignment. He's on the ball, isn't he?'

'Absolutely. So what's the plan for us in Ireland?

'Three things. This afternoon you and I visit the company here and tell them about Route 42. Tara is their CEO and she wants her management team to get up to speed. They're already pretty good at their business and, like Gullmech, are a benchmark for others in the Division to follow. But they're still keen to improve.'

'So what are you going to tell them?'

'I thought I'd use Ed's presentation to the AeroCorp Presidents' meeting. He took me through it and I can see why it works.'

'You mean the one about pictures, fear and logic – including the big gorilla?'

Mishal grins. 'The very one!'

'Sounds good to me. By the way, where's the firm located over here?'

'About an hour's drive away, near the coast. I've organised a hire car. Their place is out in the sticks so I thought it best to stay at the hotel here in town.'

Mishal clearly knows how to make things happen. This bodes well for Route 42 and the transformation we hope it'll lead to. She checks her phone, zaps something, smiles demurely and gives me some Tasmin-style eye contact. She carries on. 'Right. That's this afternoon taken care of. We have this morning to ourselves and I want to focus on two topics.'

'Which are?'

'Your advice on how best to monitor the cost savings reported by the businesses, and then to get a flavour of what "best practice" procurement principles look like.'

'OK. Let's take the principles first.'

'Why?'

'Because they define procurement's DNA in the company, and if you get them right then good things happen.'

Mishal looks like she needs convincing. 'I hope this won't be too theoretical. Ed also mentioned something you said about the difference between principles and procedures. Can you explain?'

'That's a good place to start. Let's get some coffee first.'

We move to a quieter part of the lounge. Refreshments follow us. Mishal takes charge and I appreciate her presence more closely. She's slim, sinuously curvy and wears elegant jewellery, the slim bracelet of a gold watch complementing a fine chain-link gold necklace. All this looks great against dusky skin that, in her early years, was caressed by sun a little hotter than the UK's.

'Are you OK, Jon? You're looking a bit out of it.'

'No, I'm fine. My mind was wandering.'

'OK, but can it wander back to principles and procedures?'

This is a rude awakening but I decide to latch on to this as a small step towards restoring credibility. 'Actually, the wandering idea's a good start point. That's what buyers do if they don't have guidelines or procedures to work with. Of necessity they make things up as they go along, are unsure about where they're going and are probably unable to account for where they've been.'

'Sounds like a recipe for chaos and inaction.'

'Exactly. So companies create procedures to avoid this. The trouble is that these can be prescriptive and restrictive. Often they don't reflect real life, and buyers have to force-fit actual situations into them. They're like a straitjacket.'

'But surely this stops maverick behaviour?'

'Yes, in theory, but not in practice. Buyers will manipulate procedures if they have a mind to. They can even commit fraud.'

I show Mishal a current news report naming procurement as the top type of private and public sector fraud, ahead of accounts receivable fraud and treasury fraud. She looks alarmed but is reassured that I'm talking generally and not about AeroCorp.

We sip coffee and I continue. 'We're talking about controls here. "Management control" is a healthy and necessary aspect of corporate life, but there are good controls and bad ones.'

'What's the difference?'

'Good ones state the fundamental principles the top management folk believe are necessary for the conduct of successful and responsible business dealings. They recognise that people must be accountable for their actions, especially to stakeholders in the business, and also that laws and regulations have to be obeyed. So they emphasise things like codes of conduct, ethics and the importance of separating delegated authorities.'

'Say more about the last bit.'

'Delegated authorities?'

Mishal nods.

'OK. If the company's a one-man band it's not a problem. But when the business grows the boss can't do it all and the people employed have to be allowed to make decisions and approve things. So, for example, a production manager would have a budget and the authority to decide how it is used on production activities.'

'I guess this is the "requisitioning authority"? Mishal's now taking notes. An expensive-looking pen glides across the pages of a burgundy-coloured, leather-bound note book. This lady has style.

'Correct. It's a widely used term but often misunderstood. It's simply the authority to convert one type of company asset – budget money – into another resource needed to do the job. Raw materials, spares or service contracts, for example.'

'Seems clear enough, but how's it misinterpreted?' Mishal's pen is poised.

'The budget holder gets a power complex. They think the budget is "their money" and they should decide how it's spent, and who with. So they often go too far, have discussions with suppliers, give a nod and a wink to a supplier indicating an order is on the way, and then get the buyer to do the clerical stuff.'

'I guess a lot of people would think this is pretty slick and anything different would slow things down. But I agree that such behaviour won't get the best deal going. It may also fall foul of contracting law and, dare I mention it, leave loopholes for fraud by a bent budget holder.' Mishal's business education has clearly been enlightening.

'Right again. Also, many budget holders are not commercially aware and haven't been told the secrets of sellers' sales tactics or how prices and costs are established.'

Mishal shifts in her seat. Non-verbal signals indicate she's ready to move on. 'Jon, let me stop you before this turns into a training course! I'm getting the picture and the part the buyer plays in it. The budget holder defines the needs and allocates the money to satisfy them, but mustn't go the whole way to prescribe exactly how it should be done. The buyer understands what's available in the supply market, how competitive it is or isn't, who the best sources are and how to deal with suppliers to get best results. They then formalise this with a purchase order or contract ...'

'... and in doing so they're using their delegated authority to commit the company legally.' We're on a roll here.

'Just what I was going to say!' says Mishal with a tolerant smile. 'OK, we've sorted out requisitioning and commitment authority. Who's going to pay the supplier when the time comes?'

'Mishal, you know very well. The finance people or accounts payable folk have their own delegated authority which allows them to pay money out of the company.'

'OK. So that's dealt with the three authorities.'

'Correct. The principle of separated responsibility prevents one person from possessing all three. But once it's established it makes sense to allow some, let's call it "gentle", merging of authorities in the interests of efficiency. Perhaps a topic for another day?'

'Indeed it is,' Mishal agrees, 'or we'll run out of time.' A glance at the bracelet timepiece confirms the need to move on.

'Right,' she says, 'we've seen how general principles set standards for business practice. Are there others relating to procurement?'

'Yes, things like the company's terms and conditions of purchase, the ways in which suppliers will be invited to offer prices, and the requirement only to use suppliers who are deemed acceptable to do business with. These and some others define the code of procurement practice within the business overall.'

'So is that it?'

'In many companies, yes. But it doesn't go far enough because it portrays procurement as a separate function within the business. However, if you define "procurement process" to include all activities involved in dealing with suppliers, then other people come within its remit.'

'People in engineering, quality teams and so on?'

'Yup. So their behaviours must be guided by other principles dealing with supplier relationships and what reputation the company wants to have in the supply market. There should also be statements requiring early involvement of procurement folk when requisitions are being developed, and others to prevent people making contractual commitments when they don't have the authority to do so.'

'OK. We've done the principles. Where do procedures come in?'

'In a good company, after the principles. In a bad one all you get are the procedures. The principles are buried somewhere in them but they don't stand out, and the purpose of each procedure is seldom made clear either. It's like telling the buyer, "Look, don't ask, just get on and do it." Hardly a recipe for high performance.'

'So, in a good company...?'

'In a good company the principles are the headline stuff. Then come procedures. But they have an important proviso. This says, "These procedures cover most situations that a buyer will encounter. You can use them knowing they comply with the principles and will save you time by not re-inventing the wheel. However, if you are dealing with a situation not covered by the procedure, then you the buyer have the authority to take alternative actions that are more appropriate, but only on the basis that the principles are adhered to."'

'Jon, you were almost in dictation mode there, but I get the point! It's an important and empowering one. Let me try an analogy to check my understanding. Over-control would be like telling a car driver they must use a prescribed route to get from A to B. But if there's a blockage en route then they're stuck. Better control is to let a driver choose his or her own route while complying with fundamental principles like driving on the correct side of the road, stopping at red lights and observing speed limits. Is that OK?'

'Very OK. How's the time?'

'Marching on. Anyway, I'm happy with the procedures topic now and know what sort of stuff Ed wants me to formulate. Earlier you referred to it as procurement's DNA.'

'I did. It's like a source code.'

'Now that would make a good title for a book!'

Definitely.

Chapter 21

SOMEONE FROM THE hotel reception comes over to say the hire car is ready. Mishal adjourns to deal with the formalities and returns with details of the car. Apparently it's a fast two-seater. So Mishal has style and is in a hurry too. This trip gets ever more intriguing.

'Right, that's done. Now before we go, just a bit more on "measurement".'

'The first thing is to be clear why you're doing it. Is it to justify procurement's existence, or to show how well you're doing it and achieving specific objectives?'

Mishal scents there is more to this and wants to carry on. The burgundy book is open and waiting, and fine eyebrows are raised expectantly. I take the hint.

'In business, "measurement" is another form of management control. What gets measured gets done. But it's more productive to measure inputs.'

'So what's an example of an input?'

'This could be to measure where we are with our plan to develop another cost-effective supplier.'

'And what would be the corresponding output?'

'You'd record the cost saving produced. Measuring steps along the way confirms that strategies are on track. And if they're not it reveals what's needed to get back on course.'

'So are you saying that we shouldn't report cost savings? If not you'll have some explaining to do, as Ed is gunning for them!'

'No, go for them. They're motivating, provide examples for others to try, and convince people that Route 42 is worth the effort. But when you report savings, give equal emphasis to what you're doing strategy-wise and encourage senior folk to be interested in it. This'll widen their perception of what procurement is all about.'

'OK. Sounds sensible. Now, how should we define what is a cost saving?'

'These have to be tangible benefits arising from deliberate actions by the buyer and not simply a result of favourable market movements.'

'Tangible benefits like ...?'

'Shorter lead times which permit lower inventories; price stability when others face rises; faster times to market with new products; innovations you've worked out with a supplier to give you competitive advantage; business continuity when supply chains go wrong and hurt competitors but not you...' I pause while Mishal gets it all down.

'Anything else?'

'OK, try this for something different. One of the AeroCorp businesses did a great job collaborating with a supplier to prepare what turned out to be an order-winning bid when one of their customers asked them to quote. The supplier's cost-saving ideas were incorporated in the bid, but this wouldn't have happened if the old practice had been followed.'

'Old practice?'

'You know, where a potential customer asks for prices. Your sales people work them out by themselves, don't have the benefit of supplier input, quote too high and don't win the business.'

'You make it sound like we never win any at all! Anyway, I see what you're saying. But how do you measure cost savings when collaboration created a successful outcome?'

'I wouldn't even try. The point is that when they did it, they were well into Route 42 and people didn't need convincing it was a good idea to do procurement differently. By then the thinking went more along the lines of "Here's a business challenge – in this case the need to compete for a new order – so how can we use our procurement process to help us win it?"'

'I can hear your Scandinavian friends saying that sort of thing.'

So Ed's obviously told her about them. This company's very connected, communication-wise.

'Exactly. The trick is to know when to stop measuring savings and to focus on more strategic things. If you don't do it that way, measuring savings becomes an industry in its own right and gets you nowhere in terms of changing procurement's image.'

Mishal starts gathering things together, checks her phone, stretches long limbs, uncoils from the chair and makes to go. 'Jon, that's good, but now we must hit the road. Ready?'

Mishal's driving is a master class in road craft, and it turns out she's done some track days. We've selected the Irish voice on the satnav, more for entertainment than enlightenment. It's a great country where the navigation instructions come across more like an invitation to have fun.

We sweep up to the main entrance of the company we're visiting. After a few moments waiting in reception, CEO Tara appears, offers the warmest welcome and takes us to the conference room. En route I catch a noticeboard full of stuff about employee welfare. One advert, though, poses an unintended challenge: 'If you have trouble reading this notice then you need to join our adult literacy class.'

The leadership team welcomes us and we get down to business. Mishal's presentation goes well, and I notice she's added some good front-end material to Ed's story. She makes these points: external costs often exceed internal costs, procurement's impact on profit is greater than that created by sales price increases or staff cuts, customers often need suppliers more than the other way round, and lots of colleagues spend more than half their time on activities related to the procurement process. She's been talking to Ed again.

The folk here are clearly keen for Route 42. There's no question of 'interesting, but it won't work here'. The reaction is definitely along the lines of 'that's just what we're looking for, how do we do it?'

The visit has encouraged us.

With Mishal again at the wheel, the car sweeps away from the office onto the road beckoning seawards along the south bank of a large river. Today's work is complete but it's too early to check in for the return flight to England. Time therefore to savour the space and open-faced beauty of Western Ireland.

I glance at Mishal's elegant features. I think we'll make a good team. AeroCorp is a well-organised network of companies wanting to get even better at what it does without creating a lot of bureaucracy and a burdensome head office. Already it is a highly devolved and slim organisation and keen to transfer good practices from one business to another. Overall the destination is the elusive 'best practice'. Old attitudes and organisations are being dismantled to create space for transformed, empowered processes. But what should the boundaries and controls be within these new frontiers? Hard questions hunt elusive answers. Perhaps the search for best practice will reveal the ideal to copy.

One answer comes sooner, and unexpectedly. A sign painted on a corner in the road ahead says. 'Slower'. I react to that.

'Hey, that's interesting. In England these signs usually just read "Slow".'

The sign only touched Mishal's subconscious but my remark registers its presence and prompts a response.

'Obviously a consultant wrote it: why use one syllable when you can paint two?'

Ensuing laughter shakes free a new thought. Best Practice: an ideal or an illusion? For many companies it is merely the performance exhibited by a good firm they happen to run across, which looks to be worth copying. So they try to get there too but it turns out to be a mirage. Arriving, they find that the faster and fitter company has already moved on. There is no such thing as best practice: the real goal is to do better. 'Best' is a static concept, while 'better' suggests momentum. It's like the sign in the road: 'slower' demands you have to change whatever speed you're doing at the moment. But 'slow' is an absolute concept implying that no change is needed. I voice these thoughts aloud, and Mishal's take on them is typically concise.

'"Good-buy to best practice."' We laugh at the pun. 'That's what you've said. Creating good buying processes is a tangible and certain way to make cerebral management concepts become reality. This causes behavioural change which enables firms constantly to get better. That's neat.'

I'm not sure I said exactly that, but it sounds right so I don't argue.

Mishal slows the car on the cliff road to take in the view where the mouth of the river opens wide but is itself swallowed by sea. A spectrum of colours arc across the grey sky some way offshore where sunshine meets squall.

'That's where many search for the gold of best practice: rainbow's end,' she muses. 'But it's far simpler: just get better each day rather than reach for the mirage of "best".'

A little later and we're at the airport, Mishal to head for the States and me back to the UK. But this is only a short separation. Early next year I'll be stateside as well for a meeting of the clan in LA.

Chapter 22

February

MISHAL'S ENTHUSIASTIC ACCEPTANCE by the team in Ireland suggests we're stepping up a gear on the journey along Route 42. She's quickly made friends with the other AeroCorp businesses in North America, UK and mainland Europe. Encouragingly, the Division, although sizeable, is not mutating into a behemoth. Somehow it is working the trick of becoming a serious player while at the same time maintaining a family atmosphere – a feeling of togetherness focused on the ambition to be world class.

I keep up with progress via Ed's bombardment of emails to me in West Wales. Mishal also calls and says she has tabs on all the businesses and chases them for progress reports on their cost-saving achievements. No hiding place there, then.

Since considerable momentum is taking us in the right direction we've decided that face-to-face meetings aren't needed so much, and internet and video-conferencing are being used instead.

But now it's early in the New Year and time for LA again. It will be another gathering of the buyers drawn from different AeroCorp businesses. It's Thursday and, preparing to leave the office, I notice a waiting voicemail. It's from Scott. 'Jon, I'm telephoning to ask you to cancel this trip as we're not ready for you. I am sorry for this inconvenience.' Click.

This doesn't ring true as, while preparing for the visit, we corresponded about the questions buyers need to ask in order to think strategically. I decide to ignore Scott's message. I need to visit Gullmech anyway and, en route to the airport, I check back to recall exactly what the questions were:

'Buyer's name.' Of course.

'Name of the category which the plan is about (for example, raw material "x").'

'What will be next year's expenditure on this category?'

'Who are the main suppliers (with individual spends) currently used by AeroCorp?'

'What are the problems currently experienced in buying these items, or, if there are no problems, what improvements could be made?'

'Are current purchases covered by long-term agreements or are they spot deals?'

'What, if any, key "relationship events" are coming up within the next three months? (For example, a price review, a contract renewal, a meeting to discuss problems, a trial with a new supplier.)'

'What do you think you can do differently with this category to improve things?'

'Describe in a few words what the supply market for this category would look like and how it would behave if, in your opinion, it was "ideal".'

'The top five most important aspects of supplier performance for this category are arguably volume flexibility, consistent quality, competitive cost, delivery accuracy innovation, and others. Put them in order of importance.'

'What are the top two things about the current arrangements and supplier performance which, in your opinion, put AeroCorp's manufacturing and commercial performance at risk?'

None of this is too taxing for a buying team with its finger on the pulse, even if it's a faint one.

The air ticket for this trip includes chauffeur transport from home base. The long journey gives driver Terry the opportunity to pass opinions on many matters as they occur to him. We're nearly at Heathrow and Terry points out Windsor Castle off to the right.

'I had an American in the car the other day,' he volunteers. 'He was wondering why they built the castle so near Heathrow.'

C'mon, Terry. That's an old one.

With Americans in mind, I plan to call Ed once I've checked in at the airport. The phone call confirms what I already suspect: Scott has gone.

'He had a few issues,' says Ed, 'and he wasn't managing the team in the right way. Pity, he came over well at the interview, but...'

His voice fades out, as, indeed, has Scott. I'm sorry this has happened, but frankly it seems for the best. Good politician and deal-maker that Scott might have been, he couldn't see the wood for the trees, didn't probe for causes of problems and failed to create strategic direction and relentlessly follow up on actions. Ed's energy and optimism seems undimmed by all this, however, and he says he'll get it right next time.

'Jon, I'm interested in your view about what skills we should look for.'

'OK, I have a bit of time before the flight is called so I'll email something about what the priorities are and what skills are needed.'

The message I'm sending Ed goes along the following lines. The new recruit must thrive in a dynamic atmosphere. This is because young and/

or entrepreneurial companies can be 'unruly' as regards management disciplines. Responding to constantly changing priorities consumes effort and distracts buyers from addressing external supply issues such as poor performance or rising costs. So changes are needed for them to rise above just coping with daily issues. Also, for the important items purchased, cost savings must not take place in isolation but should be part of an overall strategy.

So Scott's replacement must do four things to succeed. First, free up buyer time by removing 'noise' and unproductive activity from the current order-placement processes. Second, save time and money by holding suppliers more accountable for the promises they make. Third, invest time to improve supplier performance, which in turn saves more time and costs. Finally, develop procurement strategies for those expenditure categories that are sufficiently important to need them. All this indicates what abilities to look for in the job applicants.

I launch these gems of wisdom into cyberspace. Ed is obviously up there waiting for them as he's soon back and questioning what exactly these skills are. They include possessing the credibility and interpersonal skills to reach across functional boundaries. This is to challenge unjustified demands and gain agreement to new ideas. Then there's analytical ability to probe symptoms for the underlying causes of problems, creativity to seek new solutions, and project management disciplines to design improvement plans and relentlessly follow up on actions. These attributes are not procurement specific. Buyers usually possess the task know-how required to manage their expenditure categories, but they also need someone who can create the environment in which their time and talent can make best impact and who can make procurement's voice heard in the business. Procurement's goals must also be sufficiently ambitious to qualify as being genuinely strategic.

The flight's now being called but there's just enough time to answer Ed's last question about what to ask candidates during interviews. I suggest they should be challenged to define 'strategic procurement'. A good answer would say that procurement is 'strategic' when its activities are directly linked to the company's goals, when it changes supply markets so they behave as the business needs them to both now and in future, and when there is a cross-company, commercially aware process with top-level advocacy and senior leadership.

I press 'send' and look forward to a flight insulated from further interrogation.

I'm staying at the usual hotel one hour east of LA proper. I request a room facing west, not because I want to see LA but because this direction provides a good view of the nightly firework display at adjacent Disneyland. But it's still early evening and a walk outside seems a good way of exercising off the aeroplane-induced lethargy. It's pleasantly warm outside and I stroll past gates proclaiming these notices: 1) You Can Use Us for your Personal Storage Needs; and 2) Children Must Not Be Left Unattended. I conclude that item 2) means children can be stored but only with a minder.

Further on, a massive metal recycling facility bludgeons used cars and soft drinks cans into submission. The sign on its gate invites passers-by to donate cars (running or not) in exchange for tax-relieving donor certificates. Now there's a good idea. Steam clouds, restless conveyor belts and ever-increasing hillocks of metal chippings all testify to the success of this scheme. A large doorway intriguingly says 'Drive Thru'. For those donating vehicles this presumably means, 'Drive in, park up and get the bus home.'

Only yards away in the other direction the conveyor belt that is the freeway streams with bright lights and the ozone-pummelling beat of as yet un-donated vehicles hurtling to who knows where. I'm struck by the profundity of what I see: the meaning of life in the age of the speeding auto. Dash to crash and rush to crush. Neither roadway nor recycler look as if they ever stop. Perpetual motion. I am not surprised America reached the moon. Listening to all the V8s thundering past, I can believe it must simply have been a question of drivin' drivin' until, dammit, you just got there.

Chapter 23

THE FOLLOWING DAY is Friday. Over at Gullmech's factory we're going to consider strategic plans. I meet the folk who were at the session last time I was here: Ed, Shirley and Elaine from the local team; Antony from his capital project downstairs; and John and Mike from the UK. Then there's the empty chair that was Scott's. Mishal has also come across. Diane is visiting from Seattle and Bryn from Kansas. I wonder if he's motored down here in his capacious limo. And a newcomer, Dillon from 'Quality', has joined us as well. The clan grows.

Ed has planned a two-day session. Today we deal with what strategies should look like. Monday will be about creating the time to make them in the first place. The weekend will be free.

'Jon, can we look at the benefits of having a strategy?' he asks. 'Once we're sure about this we can delve into its contents.'

'OK, the main benefit is that it provides a goal to work for. This is the "desired future state" of the supply market, which is the way the business wants it to be in future. Doing a deal "today" then achieves two things. First, you acquire what you need right now, and in doing so you can take the opportunity to change the market, even slightly. Thus you move a step closer towards the future state. Without this longer-term aim, today's deals don't do anything to improve the current position.'

Shirley has a question. 'What do you mean, "change the market"?'

'Doing things like developing new sources; persuading suppliers to operate differently, by expanding their product range, for example; getting a better understanding of cost drivers and changing the way suppliers price their offerings to you.'

Shirley seems happy with this. She's mellowed since we last met and wants to be a model participant in the meeting. She demurely apologises for interrupting me and invites me to carry on.

'Second, the strategy is a way of getting "buy-in" from others, assuming it's been developed by a cross-functional team. Too often strategies don't succeed because they are prepared in isolation and "selling it to the user" is left until last. The strategy will be the poorer because it lacks informed input and then has to overcome resistance because of the fait accompli effect.'

Shirley again. 'Why don't we just tell them this is the way it's going to be instead of pussyfooting about?'

'That might make you feel better at the time, but it'll also annoy people. We talked about that back at Bryn's place. However, sometimes you do need help to get disinterested users involved. This is where influence from the top brass comes in.'

'So is this the third benefit of strategy?' This is Dillon, and we welcome his question.

'Absolutely. If you have a strategy to review with the board, then it gets their understanding and backing. You might have to use a trick or two to catch their eye in the first place. I sent some stuff to Ed about this.'

Enquiring eyes turn in his direction.

''Deed he did.' Ed recalls the way a tender board was weaned off rubber stamping and invited to comment on strategy instead, how a profit and loss statement was reconstructed to emphasise the scale of external supply costs, how monthly reports to a board deliberately triggered questions from them, and how board members can be allowed to save face if the policies they previously created are now not suitable. This guy's got an infallible memory. He gestures me to carry on.

'Taking senior executives through the strategy opens their eyes to the complex and dynamic nature of supply markets and the risks that are involved. They'll also see what your future goal is. Subsequent board reviews of procurement's progress will then properly focus on, "What progress are we making in implementing the strategy?" If strategy is absent, then questions inevitably turn to, "What cost savings have you made?" This perpetuates the notion that procurement's job is only to do with saving costs, and leaves the team constantly having to report savings to justify its existence.'

Ed fidgets; he's been through this stuff before. 'Are we done with this bit yet?'

'Nearly, but there are three more things that strategy can do for you. It greatly increases the probability of achieving ambitious targets. This is partly because strategy preparation consciously looks for positive forces at work in the supply market and seeks to harness them. The targets are usually more ambitious because they're based on a thorough market analysis, and this greater knowledge increases the "can-do" factor. Also, because a cross-functional team is involved to develop and follow the plan, the players understand their roles in, and the sensitivities of, strategy implementation. This reduces the chance of commercially naïve behaviour towards suppliers.'

This appeals to Ed's 'can-do' ethos.

'Second, the strategy stimulates actions beyond those concerned with "doing the deal" – for example, using technical specialists' visits to suppliers as an undercover means of establishing supplier cost information. Finally, it provides a framework within which to handle and respond to unsolicited or unexpected supplier behaviours or approaches.'

'Can you give us an example of this?'

'OK, here's one. A company was approached by a key supplier who suggested they opened the books and compared costs and margins. The customer didn't know where this would lead, was suspicious of the supplier's motives, and indeed wasn't even sure they wanted to use this supplier in future. So they refused and kept things as they were, losing the opportunity to get closer to an ally supplier to mount a joint war on wasted costs. Another example of reactive behaviour is where a supplier has quality problems so you look for an alternative source, find one and switch. Then the cycle repeats as the replacement supplier becomes complacent. Without strategy, market events are the tails that wag the dogs. Having strategy stops you flip-flopping all over the place reacting to events.'

We're all glad when Ed asserts that we've done enough on strategy. It's human nature to be action orientated so it's a real effort to stop and think beforehand. But that is exactly the characteristic that makes the best companies better than the norm. It's also time to make today's selection from Davina's Deli. Energy levels in the room rise in anticipation of food for real rather than strategic food for thought. I don't blame them. Anyway, noise levels in the outer office have risen as they're celebrating someone's birthday. A cardboard box the size of a shipping container is circulating with its contents of cream-laden pastries. We're invited to partake, and do.

We return, and I wonder if these task-orientated folk might prefer a production-line approach to making strategies. They like the idea and we sketch out a flow chart with five stages: define business need; get market intelligence and analyse what this says about the current situation, warts and all; define how you'd like the market to look in future; analyse the gap between 'the future' and 'now' and decide on gap-closing actions; do the deals that take care of today's needs but also move towards the future state.

Everyone's been writing furiously. Then they stop and look uncertain about what's coming next. It's Shirley. 'Jon, these are fine words, but can you give an actual example of what they look like when applied to a specific situation?'

Fortunately I can, thanks to the lately departed Scott, who was working on a strategy for 'forgings and castings'. Scott showed me what these things look like when they come in as raw material: fancily shaped lumps of metal produced by the supplier either by pouring liquid metal into moulds or by beating the hell out of hot ingots as they lay in templates. Once delivered to Gullmech they are machined to exacting specifications. The team agree to take 'castings' as an example. We also agree we don't have to revisit all the strategy steps, but just illustrate some of the less-obvious ones, such as 'business need'. This could be stated as, 'Gullmech needs fewer suppliers of castings in order to increase the influence we have over them to get shorter lead times.'

This is a poor statement because it illustrates a common failing: it includes all or part of the solution as well as the objective. What Gullmech really needs is a high-quality, cost-competitive supply of castings that can be depended on to keep up with the forecast sales of finished products. 'Understanding the current situation' is taken as read, since the questions are self-explanatory. We briefly look at how the data fits with the Kraljic analysis and Supplier Preference and conclude that castings are labelled as 'Bottleneck'. From a supplier's viewpoint, Gullmech is probably seen as a 'nuisance' by the larger foundries, and as 'frustrated develop' by smaller companies. Ouch. This is bad news seeing as the castings are essential raw materials. Without them an engineering company has nothing to engineer on.

'So what was your statement of the current situation?' Ed asks this just as I find the relevant piece of paper that Scott and I were working on. It says this: 'Gullmech does not attract the hearts and minds of the suppliers. We view suppliers as commodities and generally keep them at arm's length. We act tough, play the market and constantly change sources. The frequent switching incurs total costs which are greater than the initial cost savings achieved. This weakens our purchasing power and influence. It also reduces supplier commitment and they don't see our jobs as their top priority. The benefits of effective relationship management are not realised. If they were, then we would get preferential treatment with lead times and early engineering-out of quality or yield problems, both of which damage cost and lead times. We should in fact be treating these suppliers as extensions of our own production line.'

This sinks in as people think back to their previous buying jobs at Gullmech. They're possibly hoping they haven't had anything to do with castings and forgings procurement; if they have, they might feel guilty about not being too smart at it.

Ed comes to the rescue. 'Hey, guys, this isn't criticising past practice. The way we've operated up to now has been appropriate in a world that wasn't changing so fast new-product wise and where our expectations of supplier performance were more relaxed. But now we're facing new challenges and have new ambitions, hence we have to move up the performance curve.'

The team is reassured and we celebrate with a comfort break. These seem to come along as regularly as Davina's Deli does. Perhaps the two are related.

Chapter 24

REFRESHED BY THE break, we discuss restating the business need for castings. It comes out like this: 'Gullmech needs regular access to dependable, committed and cost-effective sources of castings who can also give us competitive advantage by responding to fluctuating demands faster than our competitors' supply chains can.'

Never one to be seduced by smooth talk, Shirley reckons many words in this statement need to be amplified. For example, how would we recognise 'regular access' if we saw it in practice? She's not wrong, but we decide to leave these details till later.

We then address specific needs. Some are obvious: lead time, cost, and accuracy of delivered quantities. Others, such as responsiveness to order variations and the supplier's ability to manage subcontractors, are less clear but still vital. All these aspects of supplier performance are important. They are used to assess supplier suitability, to evaluate the total cost of doing business, and periodically for reviewing supplier performance. In listing these needs we must think of all the different individuals whose lives are affected by the supplier's performance. This includes production, engineering, sales, finance... a lot of people, all of whom should be involved in drawing up the list.

'Right,' says Ed, 'it seems that a suitable supply market already basically exists, although many quality issues need fixing and we'd like suppliers to see us in a better light. We're also clearer about what's important to us performance-wise. So what did you and Scott envisage about the future supply market?'

'The main question is what is the best way for Gullmech to interact with that market? Then, as with all Kraljic bottleneck items, the main focus should be operational performance and supply security, not primarily cost. However, resolving operational problems often releases worthwhile cost savings as a bonus. Finally, we thought a phased reduction in the number of active suppliers would be better than one step-change from nearly twenty to, say, three. The first step could be to slim down to six suppliers, with a next step going from six to three or fewer. This avoids change overload.'

Mishal builds on this. 'I guess the way the six respond after step one will also provide more information about who should be in the final selection.'

'Good point,' says Ed. 'But Jon, what you've just said focuses on the steps you think we should take rather than defining what the end of the journey looks like. Did you envisage how we'd like things to be in future?'

'We did. It's like a nine-piece jigsaw. One part of the picture on the box is about being confident we have supply capacity available even if a current source has problems or disappears, or if there's a big uplift in the volumes we need. Another component says we have mini strategies in play to maintain each supplier's interest in wanting or keeping our business.'

On cue, Shirley provides the reality check. 'So how does that happen?'

'Give one or two suppliers a large slice of business but feed smaller volumes to the others, especially if they're pilot runs or trying something new. Above all, keep talking to them even if they're not getting any orders at the moment. Take an interest in their company progress and goals, especially any new developments they have under way.'

Mishal's making notes again and is hungry for more. 'Right, Jon, we have two of the nine pieces. What else?'

'Gullmech will be using a small number of tried and tested, motivated suppliers who value our business, and suppliers' technical experts are in regular contact with our engineers to optimise new-product development and implement continual improvements to casting processes.'

'This is like extracting teeth, Jon,' Mike observes with a wry grin. 'It's painful but we've got to do it!'

'OK, let's speed up. Here are three more pieces of the puzzle: first, we use clear criteria to decide which supplier gets which portion of the business going; second, we know exactly where all the tooling is at any time…'

'Excuse me,' Mishal interjects, 'but what's that about?'

'The tooling is the mould or template that's used to make the casting or forging. There are a lot of them, they're expensive and Gullmech owns them. So we need to know where they all are so we can account for them and also get them back before switching suppliers. And the next piece is about achieving ambitious cost targets, not by switching to cheaper suppliers or by squeezing supplier profitability, but by working jointly with supplier "partners" to eliminate wasted costs.'

Ed, ever vigilant, has been counting and wants to know what the last two pieces of the future picture look like. I check Scott's list and am sorry he's not around to take credit for it.

'OK, the final two. First, regular performance reviews take place with suppliers to cover a wider range of issues than currently, and finally, relationships are "personality proofed" so that our sourcing plans won't fall apart when new personnel arrive on the scene.'

Shirley again. 'Personality proofed?'

'Well, without some sort of written strategy it's all in someone's head. So when that person moves on or leaves, the game plan goes with them. But if you have a strategy in place and your management team has reviewed it and wants regular updates, then you're less reliant on whoever happens to be executing it at the time.'

Ed muses over the nine-part picture, which clearly appeals to his tidy mind. 'I guess we now compare this list with the way things are at the moment and then work out what we have to do to close the gaps…'

He stops as people glance pointedly at watches, signalling that there's not enough time in the day to dig into another layer of detail. While it's only four in the afternoon, a lot of the guys have been at work since six this morning, some even earlier. It seems to be the way things are done out here in California. Starting early avoids peak traffic and also leaves enough time at the end of the day to get home and fire up the BBQ.

Ed picks up on this and concludes '… but we'll put that on the back burner.'

We all welcome its reappearance.

'Guys, let's adjourn for the day and meet again on Monday – same time, same place. Have a great weekend. Jon, can I have a word?'

Ed wants to talk a little more about the day's discussion. We agree to do this back at the hotel so I get to ride again in the Star Trek SUV. It definitely feels like we're on a mission but we arrive intact. We're in time for the Manager's Reception. I've seen plenty of these but never the manager. We order beers and select sprigs of raw broccoli and cauliflower to chew over, lubricated by any dip of choice. There are vats of the stuff so no one's going to go short.

Ed tells me more about why Scott was fired and also that he's started the recruitment process to replace him. We enjoy both the discussion and the manager's largesse until it's time for Ed to head home.

I have the rest of the evening to myself. Another beer is tempting but, since the manager's reception is out of time, I have to buy one. The same surly bartender is on duty as on my first visit, but this time I remember to 'tottleitup' before he starts shouting.

Tomorrow is Saturday and I wonder how to spend the weekend. Actually, it's a no-brainer as it's time for the National Football League Super Bowl, equivalent to a football Cup Final in the UK. That settles it: I'll split the weekend between writing stuff, watching the game and everything that goes with it, while occasionally stepping outside to check on progress at the scrap metal yard.

Chapter 25

I T'S SATURDAY AND early-February sunshine streams through the hotel window. I'm back from a quick walk after breakfast among young families bent on spending their day at Disneyland. It's also the NFL Super Bowl weekend.

Coming from the airport two days ago involved an hour with a sports-savvy driver of the 'ground transportation'. He, too, planned to devote his weekend to Super Bowl and decided I needed wising up about the rules. Each team has twenty-eight players, though not all of them are on the field simultaneously. I assume this is because there's insufficient room for all that testosterone-charged, V-shaped padded musculature at the same time. On the sidelines are coaches for this and trainers for that, bringing the total headcount per team to around sixty. As the driver intones them, the rules begin to make sense of the frenetic rushes and collisions I recall from previous chance encounters with the game during idle channel surfing. It sounds like high-speed chess and I resolve to watch the game. It will start at 3.28pm. Four quarters, sixty minutes, and the previews have started.

Relentless preliminaries cover all the bases, if I may mix sports, including a report surveying the habits of TV viewers. Apparently only ninety per cent watch the TV for the game, and five per cent watch the adverts. What the remaining five per cent do is not divulged. The pre-match show features, among other luminaries, Presidents George Bush Snr and Bill Clinton. Intriguingly, they are not called ex-Presidents. They speak well about each other, sincerely talk about their soldiers fighting overseas and predict the game's final scores. Mr Bush comes straight out with his forecast while Mr Clinton precedes his with a presidential address. Anthems are sung, tension builds and precisely on time the game is on. And off. And so on. A brief move, a clash of titans, a speeding ball, then the referee blows and the clock stops. I realise this could take a little longer than the allotted hour, even allowing for the break-time oranges – or, more likely, raw meat.

I have one eye on the game and the other on writing. I appreciate this doesn't help those compiling the viewing statistics. But the adverts command attention, as indeed they should for the three million dollars it costs per thirty seconds of exposure. One shows a bright red auto, top-down convertible, waiting at traffic lights in the middle of a frozen snowy landscape. It carries on waiting. A traffic cop comes alongside, 'Excuse me, sir, you have a green.' Nothing moves. The cop taps the driver's cheek with his biro and there's a chinking sound, like a knife tapping a wine glass. Nothing moves. The cop lifts the driver's sunglasses: he's frozen solid with a 'watch-this-baby-go' look of anticipation ice-carved on his face. A voice intones, 'You just don't introduce a convertible this irresistible in the middle of winter. Coming this spring, the Ford Mustang.' So there's three million well spent. I remember every word.

Next is a hot, stuffy, drab courtroom scene. On the stand a curvaceous, full-breasted young lady wears a low-cut white top barely able to contain its excitement. It spells out the company she's advertising. The judge asks what she does for employment. She stands, bobs around a bit and says who she works for. A strap breaks but swift reflexes save her – and the viewing millions – from a repeat of Janet Jackson's 'wardrobe malfunction' during a previous Super Bowl half-time show. Our strap-clutching heroine does a twirl but is brought to order by the dusty grey judge who complains that she's disturbing things. I'll say. 'I'm sorry', she replies, 'I didn't mean to upset the committee.' The picture pans to an elderly, white-faced committee member taking oxygen.

Interestingly, a day or two later the TV runs a news story about the young lady's company complaining that the sports channel only ran the ad once. Twice had been promised, but presumably time was wasted fixing the girl's strap before the rerun. Or maybe they needed more oxygen. Anyway, the sports channel had received some calls and decided it would drop a 'repeat airing'. Who thinks up these sound bites, and do they know they're doing it? But the ad company is jubilant. They got free extra publicity from the news item.

Not all the ads are so good, though, and occasionally we return to the ball game. Little wonder it takes four hours before it's over. The New England Patriots seal a narrow victory over their Philadelphian adversaries. It's their third win in the last four Super Bowls.

And then, of course, comes the post-game show. It's been a so-so game. Moves are dissected, substitutions debated and dodgy decisions challenged. This country just loves analysis. Even the ads are pulled apart, and I see it wasn't just me who liked the driver out in the cold and the young lady nearly coming out in the warm.

Monday

But now the weekend's over and we reconvene at Gullmech. Having dealt with what strategies look like, we're going to see how we can create the time to be strategic in the first place. With luck we'll be through by lunchtime. Ed welcomes us, hoping we'd had a nice weekend. Sure did.

Ed acknowledges the difficulties arising from Scott's departure: the business is facing huge challenges owing to ERP implementation, production is behind plan, and relentless efforts go into expediting materials deliveries. Consequently, no management time remains to make the changes needed to increase procurement effectiveness. We decide to focus on the buyers on the front line and work out how they can make incremental changes on a daily basis.

Shirley pipes up. 'It's a treadmill out there. How do you expect us to change things when we hardly have time to breathe?'

Ed reassures her. 'Don't worry, Shirley, we're not asking you to do the impossible. Jon's convinced me we can only change so much by our own efforts. Beyond that we have to engage with other people in the company, and we need the board to be with us. So for the moment we're looking for any practical things we can do, doesn't matter how small, that will free up time to make changes.'

'We need to be clear about exactly where we're starting from,' observes Elaine. 'Let's describe what we buyers actually do right now.' She then obliges by taking us through it step by step. Sorting out Davina's Deli supply lines first thing is taken as read.

'First we look at the day's materials' schedule…'

'… or any other urgent needs, which, of course, there are …' Shirley chips in.

Elaine continues with a 'look, I'm doing this' expression on her face. 'Then we assess requirements versus current lead times. We decide which requirements must be acted on today because there'll be delays if we don't. Everything else can be handled "tomorrow".'

Unsportingly, we wait for Shirley to mutter, 'If it comes,' but she doesn't oblige.

'We then check whether we have internal stock which isn't yet logged into the scheduling system. If we don't have what we need we review possible sources and decide who to approach. That done, we invite bids from suppliers and chase them for replies. When we get them, we evaluate.'

'And do they respond quickly?'

'Usually, yes. Sometimes we do all this over the telephone. Then we put the bid data into a spreadsheet and compare prices, weights, total costs, etc.'

'We used to involve Scott at this stage,' adds Shirley, 'but for now I'm doing it.'

Ed looks at her with an enquiring look.

'And no, I don't want his job! I prefer to do buying.'

Elaine continues. 'This analysis helps us select the best source for the job, though sometimes we "cherry pick". It's unusual for one supplier to offer best prices for everything so we select what's best from that supplier, and the other items from other suppliers who are giving the best prices for them.'

'OK, sounds sensible,' says Ed. 'So are we there yet?'

'Not quite. We then place purchase orders depending on whether we're going to source from one or more suppliers, although, if it's appropriate, we first have a negotiation to squeeze out more costs if we can.'

'Are we done now?' Boy, this man's impatient!

'No, because we usually have to follow up, expedite and reprioritise if needed. We also have to go trouble-shooting if there are quality or other performance issues.'

'And maybe have to pacify suppliers over late payment for previous orders.' Shirley isn't having a good day.

Elaine has a last thought. 'Oh, and by the way, at the same time as doing all this we might undertake additional sourcing efforts to find suppliers for "new project requests".'

Ed thanks Elaine and Shirley. 'You've made it very clear. So, just supposing we have a bit of extra time available, what's the next thing we could do with it?'

Shirley decides it's time to stop sniping and help a little more. 'We already do it to some extent. We look at what market intelligence we have about item availability and prices, and our knowledge of the product, and may decide to place a proactive purchase order before the production plan tells us to. So we capture better prices than we'd get if we waited and we don't have delays.'

Shirley sees that Ed looks doubtful and gets in first. 'But Ed, let's assure you that this isn't speculative buying. We stay within the total forecast volumes so we're never buying anything that isn't eventually used.'

Ed has been busy writing this down, and rightly so. Neither of us thinks this portrayal of life in the buyers' office is understood by others in the company.

'OK. If all this goes exactly as you say, then we can put hand on heart and say we're satisfying today's need. Right?' Ed scans round the table looking for feedback.

Shirley obliges. 'Right.'

'That's fine. So what's the next step we can take, even if it's a small one, to start streamlining things? If we can do just one different thing today to make even the smallest improvement then it'll be paid back tomorrow because there'll be one less problem to worry about.'

Shirley's perked up and is on a roll, momentum-wise, that is. 'What we do, when we get the chance, is assess future volume requirements and decide where an LTA…'

Mishal, quiet for some time but taking everything in, interjects. 'LTA, what's that?'

Shirley patiently explains. 'Stands for long-term agreement, or call-off contract. So we decide whether one of these could replace all these purchase orders. We then target three or four suppliers and invite bids, or have one-on-one discussions, as appropriate. We then receive offers from them, evaluate prices and total costs, work out which bid is best, select it and haggle some more on various aspects of the deal, and then set the agreement in place.'

'Just like that!' murmurs Antony, but we ignore him.

Ed absorbs this information like a sponge. 'And is there anything more we can do that links to this?'

'Sure is,' says Shirley with an air of frustration which suggests that she doesn't often, if ever, get the chance. 'We can watch current and future company requirements and market trends…'

'Trends?'

'Yeah, things like market capacities, price movements, supplier news, and then play the market accordingly, mainly using the LTAs but also doing spot purchases where a good price pops up or we want to try a different source.'

'And,' Elaine chimes in, 'all the while keeping three balls in the air — namely, meeting the schedule, ensuring supply security and keeping costs competitive.'

Ed is enjoying this as the conversation is, surprisingly, upbeat and promising. 'I see where you're going with this. Doing what you say will improve performance because you're more in control of your destiny and have better mechanisms in place for doing business with suppliers.'

Shirley delivers the reality check. 'Just so, Ed, but hold your horses. This is what we could do, not what we normally do. We just don't have the time.'

'Understand that. And what one thing do you think we could do to create more time, which doesn't require recruiting more people?' Persistence is his middle name. There's a pause while people ponder this and glance at each other with a 'who's going first' look on their faces.

Shirley speaks for them. 'Increasing the dollar value below which we don't have to seek competitive quotes before placing an order would free up a lot of time.'

Ed is cautious. 'But won't we end up spending more on something because we've missed the cheaper alternative?'

I haven't said much so far, and perhaps I should if I'm to justify being here. 'Not necessarily. In any case, two things are going on here. One is what your rule book says about the subject. I've had a look at it. Apparently buyers have to seek competitive quotes for any purchase order costing more than 820 dollars. They call it the formal enquiry process.'

Mishal stops writing. 'Eight hundred and twenty? Where does that weird number come from?'

Ed feels he might know the answer. 'I think it was originally a lower number but it's been increased over the years in line with inflation. Anyway, 820 is the number at the moment. What's the second thing, Jon?'

'Some buyers are extra cautious and use the enquiry process for every purchase order.'

'That's crazy,' observes Shirley. 'If they make any saving at all, it won't pay for the effort involved.'

'Who's doing that, anyway?' Ed is on the hunt.

'One of the buyers at our Seattle plant,' volunteers Diane. 'But don't gun for them as their heart's in the right place and it's quite likely no one's explained the rules to them. Anyway, I looked at the category they call "shop supplies and small tools". They spend almost three-quarters of a million dollars on them each year.'

'How many purchase orders does it take to do that?' John likes numbers.

'Around 5,300. It costs most companies about a hundred dollars to raise and process a purchase order, so the admin cost alone is more than half a million. You can see the incentive to reduce the number of them.'

'Right,' says action man, 'we can do this, but first we must ensure all buyers know the rules and don't waste time seeking formal enquiries for everything. Any idea what it costs to do that bit of the process?'

We discuss this and also estimate how many of the purchase orders are below the 820-dollar threshold. It works out at seventy-seven per cent. If the threshold is raised to a thousand dollars, then something like ninety per cent of transactions won't need a formal enquiry. Shirley asserts that extra costs will be incurred if the thirteen per cent of orders which won't now be competitively sourced do not obtain the cheapest prices available. We discuss this and most of us conclude that any additional costs will be outweighed by the time saved through not having to pursue formal enquiries. Shirley's not convinced this is a good idea.

Mishal comes to the rescue and takes Shirley through the maths again. She's happier now. 'That's good, Shirley. We've proved that the time saved is the bigger prize, and we can then do more important stuff...'

'Like developing those LTAs that reduce purchase orders in the first place.'

Mishal bears John's interruption as he joins in the debate and crowds round the table with the rest of them.

Ed sees the logic in all this. 'Look, guys, I need to talk to our CFO about this, but we should be able to do something here. We'll take a break in a few minutes, but first let's chart up the time-saving things we've discussed.'

People rise, grateful for the opportunity to stretch legs and limber up for the light refreshments to be delivered soon. We chart how we'll create time and spend it more effectively.

The story goes as follows. Buyers will decide the size and timing of purchase orders based on what makes best commercial sense rather than knee-jerk reactions to the schedules. Orders will be larger to reduce order frequency. This also allows suppliers to buy better, locks in prices if it's felt they're going to rise further, and reduces the admin costs of placing orders, checking invoices and making payment transactions. We'll develop some LTAs but also make spot purchases when appropriate to check the market. Time-saving ideas include raising the order value below which formal enquiries aren't required and, with the boss's support, reducing the time spent unproductively on 'internal stuff' like meetings and reports. We'll also ensure buyers aren't being too cautious by seeking formal enquiries for everything. Finally, we'll brush up negotiating skills in order to reach better conclusions faster. All these ideas relate to the way the buyers do their job.

Then there are other actions which affect the way buyers interact with other people. We'll challenge (as diplomatically as we can, Shirley) requests from other colleagues for follow-up data. Do they really need it? What happens if they don't get it? They need to realise the time taken to provide this information is time not spent on other important tasks. This can also be said to anyone asking for revisions to an order after it's been placed.

We stand back and admire our work. It might be a small step for mankind but it's a big step for the procurement team. We're beginning to influence our future, and it's a heady feeling. Or is it a lack of sugar and carbohydrate? Davina's Deli is in attendance with coffees for now and a menu for later. Interestingly, people don't rush back to their desks to check things but want to stay in the conference room. Some laptops are deployed just to check emails, but this is done with the team and not in isolation elsewhere. It's as though they know they're making a breakthrough and don't want to miss the next step.

Now is also a good time to see what's arrived from cyberspace into my own inbox. It's the usual stuff, apart from an eye-catching news item. A small but entrepreneurial company is canvassing for votes which it hopes will enable it to win an industrial award. They're in the livestock feed business and blame farting farm animals for making greenhouse gas and causing global warming. They've invented a food additive based on garlic which, their tests show, greatly reduces the volume of methane vented to atmosphere by cows and the like. Bovine halitosis might be one side effect but, hey, it's a small price to pay for saving the world. What's more, this company has persuaded an airline to sponsor its work and they're going to feed the garlic stuff to all the animals on farms under the flight path of one of its London to USA services. How imaginative is that?! I'll certainly support them. I'll be doing my bit to save the planet by helping cows lead a fart-free existence. I feel good about that, and perhaps the cows will as well.

Chapter 26

W E'RE STILL ONLY halfway through Monday morning but the number crunching has made it seem longer.

Ed calls us to order. 'Right guys, we've looked at practical things we can do to free up extra time. Now, how do we use it, apart from getting more strategic, as we discussed on Friday?' He looks at me.

'I think the team already have some answers as they've tried some new ideas already,' I reply. 'Let's hear what they are and we'll list them so we can share them with the other businesses.'

People are again out of their seats, eager and conspiratorial. Bryn announces he's taken raw-material purchases away from his subcontractors. He now buys it directly and then issues it to them when needed. This has eliminated time wasted by contractors waiting for raw material. It has also bypassed cost inefficiencies in the procurement process. Bryn's purchases cover the stuff needed by several contractors so he's also got extra discounts from being able to do a bigger deal.

Folks like this idea, but Ed wants a reality check. 'Hey, guys, don't get too carried away with this. Try it by all means, but I don't want you buying so much material that it screws up our cash flow, or piles up if we don't use it.'

Shirley wants to get another, albeit legitimate, moan off her ample chest. 'I've been telling the finance people here to stop delaying paying the bills. It's infuriating and it's me, not them, who gets the flak from the suppliers. If you want to destroy goodwill then this works just fine, and you can forget getting any help from them when we need it.'

Ed isn't happy to hear this. 'I agree, Shirley, we shouldn't do that. I think any supplier whose yearly sales turnover is below five million dollars absolutely cannot withstand the "stopping payment" treatment. For small suppliers it's going to hurt like hell. That said, we do sometimes have to massage cash flow, so if payments have to be delayed, we should decide with finance which suppliers should be put on hold and which others should get prompt settlement as per the agreement. We should also talk to the suppliers affected.'

Shirley hasn't quite finished.' You'll have to tell finance, though, Ed, or they'll just carry on in the same old way.'

'They've come to the top of my to-do list,' smiles Ed. 'I'll tell 'em. Depend on it. Anyone got another example of doing things differently?'

John has. 'Yes, and it builds on what Shirley said about supplier relationships. I'm making more regular contact with key suppliers, especially when there isn't a problem to nag them about. This generates goodwill and we're getting some preferential treatment.'

'Such as?' Mishal enquires.

'Like jumping queues to give our orders a higher priority. I do checks on their free capacity and their ability to handle urgent changes if needed. I'm also disciplining myself to spend time, even if it's only ten minutes, before a supplier meeting to get my thoughts clear about what we want the meeting to achieve and how we'd recognise a successful outcome.'

All this sounds good. When we sat round the table in Kansas we compared notes on specific money-saving actions, but now it's different because it's more about the way people are approaching their job. We could be starting a virtuous circle.

The proactive approach is clearly in favour and Bryn takes a completely new tack. 'Another thing I'm doing is anticipating price increase requests and then using conditioning messages to head them off. Also I'm conditioning suppliers before meetings, especially if they are price reviews.'

'Why do you do that?'

'To get them thinking and behaving the way I want them to.'

Several eyebrows are raised at this, but it's Dillon who poses the question that is on all our minds: 'Hey Bryn, what's this conditioning thing you're on about?'

Bryn's in his element, and I recall he does part-time lecturing on the business course at his local college. 'It's a sort of mind game. Sellers do it to us so we have to do it back. Children do it to their parents, wives to husbands and so on. We're "conditioning" someone when we prepare their minds for something we're going to say or we want them to do. The word comes from the Russian psychologist Pavlov's work on creating conditioned reflexes in animals.'

Elaine's already on Bryn's wavelength. 'Wasn't that about bells and dogs?'

The team look interested but puzzled, perhaps wondering how they've stumbled into this parallel universe.

'Yeah,' agrees Bryn. 'Pavlov observed dogs making saliva when they heard a bell which they associated with feeding time. Salivating is a reflex reaction the body makes when it thinks of food. And Pavlov's dogs still salivated when they heard the bell, even if he didn't feed them.'

So Bryn's a psychologist as well. Hidden talent.

Ed glances round to see what people think, or maybe who's started dribbling at the thought of Davina's Deli. 'OK, I'm catching on. If my daughter wants a new bike she doesn't just come out and demand it. She starts a conditioning campaign.'

Elaine agrees. 'And they start with, "Dad, Casey over the road's got a new bike." And then later, it's more of the same. Next day it's, "Dad, my bike isn't working very well." Then they bring on the market intelligence. "Dad, the shop in town is selling bikes at sale prices. But for this week only."'

The daughter is clearly a grand master!

Dillon gets it too. 'So, when she actually asks for the new bike she's already planted the idea in Dad's mind well before she makes the request. So if Dad knows it's coming and hasn't done anything to head it off, then he's more likely to agree. The daughter gets the reaction she wants.'

'She does indeed,' sighs Elaine, suggesting she's just seen this plot played out in her own house.

'Actually, the "sale price for this week only" is also a conditioning tactic,' adds Bryn. 'The shop owner wants to push sales so reduces prices, but only for a limited time, and the knee-jerk reaction sees folks coming and buying before the price goes back up.'

Ed wants to get back to business rather than dwell on domestic realities. 'So if a seller wants a price increase, they'll plant messages in phone calls, emails and meetings saying, "Raw material prices are going up." Then, "We can't hold prices for much longer." Then, "We've already increased prices to some other customers by seven per cent." Then when they actually request the price increase it's less. How am I doing, Jon?'

'Spot on. What they might request is a 4.7 per cent increase.'

'Why that, for heaven's sake?' Shirley wants to know.

'Four per cent is what they think they can get and the 0.7 bit makes it look like it's been carefully worked out. So 4.7 per cent is great news because it's less than the seven we'd been expecting and so we agree before we can stop ourselves. Nice work if you can get it.'

'Thanks everyone,' concludes Bryn. 'That, in a nutshell, is what conditioning is all about.'

'So how do we cope with it?' It's a good question from Mishal, who waits, pen poised in delicate long fingers and looking at me.

'First, always ask yourself if you're being conditioned when you hear these messages. This neutralises the tactic because, for conditioning to work, you have to be unaware it's being done to you. Then, when you hear it starting, don't let it pass. You have to counter immediately.'

'And how do you do that?'

Bryn helps me out. 'For example, come back with, "So what are your plans for dealing with rising raw material prices, as we're not going to work with suppliers who simply pass them on?" And when they mention seven per cent, you can say, "Actually, we're looking to reduce costs by at least that much. I realise suppliers have to make a profit so we're looking for partners who can work with us to take out wasted costs. If jointly we can reduce underlying costs then we benefit from lower prices and the supplier's margin is sustained.'

Bryn's also a thespian! He's learned his lines well.

But Shirley wants results. 'So how does this help?'

'Well, it shows you're not a walkover and reduces their aspirations of what they hope they can get out of you. They might even give up the price-increase idea and work on other customers who are softer targets. If they give the right response to your conditioning, though, it can open the door to a more collaborative relationship.'

As usual, Ed has been committing this to paper, but he looks thoughtful. 'A lot of this stuff is about relating differently to suppliers. It suggests we're moving on from event-driven contacts with them – for example, when we have a problem or when they want a price increase. We're now contemplating an ongoing relationship scenario. But we're also going to play the market when it suits. So what information do we need to do this properly?'

Mishal's done her homework. 'For a start, we need general data on the dollars spent with suppliers and their performance on key issues over the past twelve months. This'll make it easier to compare suppliers, strengthen our negotiating position and point to critical areas where we need improvements.'

'Surely we have this?' Ed asks.

Bryn helps out. 'Not necessarily. What data we do have comes out of our accounts payable database, and it's rarely in a form that helps us to manage suppliers. And the only performance data we have is a list of problems we've experienced. We need to sit down with each key supplier, agree what performance areas matter to us both and regularly measure them: the good, the bad and the ugly.'

'This all sounds doable,' asserts Ed. 'Mishal, what else?'

'Dependable data on recent and forecast lead times and a means of inputting realistic and current lead time data into the scheduling system. At the moment we're not sure whose responsibility this is.'

Ed shakes his head in pained wonder. These are symptoms of a company so focused on the planning system and the daily tasks dictated by it that people have forgotten how they should be working together.

'We also need better forecasts of upcoming volume requirements,' says Shirley, becoming more involved, 'and data on price movements of key raw materials and dependable forecasts of where these prices are heading.'

Elaine's also been thinking. 'This'll put us in a much better position for price negotiations and so on. Why don't we also make a calendar of when regular price reviews are timed to take place in our LTAs so we can take the initiative first and not just wait for the supplier to start brainwashing us about how tough things are and they need a price increase? The performance track record will strengthen our negotiating position as well.'

'Excellent work,' applauds Ed. 'I feel we're getting somewhere now. None of this is rocket science and we can do a lot of it ourselves.'

'If time permits,' adds the ever-vigilant Shirley.

'Guys, I think we're about through here. It's been a long two sessions. Let's just recap.'

He is interrupted by Davina's Deli doing a food drop of our lunch choices. No problem: we can eat at the same time as listening to Ed. That's multi-tasking.

'OK, the recap. On Friday we looked at the benefits of having a strategy for making key purchases as opposed to raising orders only when we need them. Two things sticking in my mind are that strategies help us change supply markets, and they also look good in the boardroom, thus raising procurement's credibility and profile. We then defined a five-step process for producing a strategic plan, illustrating this with extracts from the work done by Scott and Jon. Then today we've laid out exactly what our current *modus operandi* is, especially what wastes time, and then decided how to create more time and what we'd do with it.'

No one disagrees as they're too busy downloading carbs and calories.

'So that's it. Thanks for your time. Looking ahead, I think next time we meet as a team we ought to include more guys from the other businesses. Meanwhile I've got some persuading to do upstairs with the boss, and I'd also like to spend more time with Jon and Mishal, possibly in London in a month's time if you can both make it? And an invitation to you all: Mishal and Jon are available by email or phone if you need help. Meanwhile, everyone, thanks again.'

Outside the office it's a clear-skied early afternoon and the ground transportation is waiting to head for the airport. The driver's a quiet, moustached, short-sleeved-white-shirted senior sort of guy who probably won't share his woes with me en route. A pity in a way as I'd like to have met Ray again to hear whether he's making progress with his friendly salutations to Californian folk. But it's been an intense few days and I welcome the personal space now being given to me by driver Don.

Chapter 27

London – April

I'M *EN ROUTE* to meet Ed again, this time at AeroCorp's London HQ. As usual, I drive seventy miles east to board the fast train to Paddington from a station near Swansea. It's due soon. Meanwhile I'm entertained by intercom announcements which, since this is Wales, are bilingual. Usually it's Welsh first, then English. Both versions end at the same destinations in England, but the Welsh one starts differently. It's a roll call of station names which, initially unintelligible to unaccustomed ears, gradually morph into more familiar sounds. The transformation is complete from Craven Arms onwards. Where is that? Possibly up North as Manchester Piccadilly and Crewe are neighbours. Apparently the Welsh for Crewe is Cree-yewe.

AeroCorp's office suite is as swish as Penserin's a few floors up. There's plenty of marble but no oasis. Instead there's a coffee station and water cooler, artfully concealed behind potted palms and, intriguingly, a couple of sculptures. I'm shown into an airy conference room where glass, steel and leather create a sophisticated ambience. Mishal looks at home and greets me, just as Ed appears. They are in great form, buoyed by the company's latest quarterly results and the positive impact made by procurement initiatives on them. We're on the two journeys – getting better deals in parallel with Route 42 – and getting traction. It's time to stop for a while and look back at where we've come from.

I start a summary. 'Ed, all our work to date fits into two categories, each representing one of the parallel journeys. First there's all the task stuff.'

'Meaning what?'

'Meaning the things buyers do to get better deals. There's pushing harder and probing further. The first one makes sure we don't leave money on the table, and the second is about being better at playing markets, negotiating, and developing closer relationships with selected suppliers.'

Mishal adds the intellectual bit. 'And, to make sure we're pulling the right levers, we use the Kraljic matrix to carve the supply market into four distinct segments.'

'Yeah, a great tool,' enthuses Ed. 'I used it in my presentation to the company Presidents and it hooked them immediately.'

'It also worked for me in Ireland,' adds Mishal.

'You guys and many others! Lots of CPOs round the world have made their names at board presentations using that analysis. Peter Kraljic said he wished he'd patented it!'

'Right, remind me what else we covered task-wise.'

'We distinguished between what many people call strategic activity but which is really only tactical muscle power, and genuinely strategic procurement which is directly linked to the company strategy and changes the world to our advantage. We then identified three different approaches to deliver cost savings and other benefits.'

Mishal consults her notes. 'Correct. These were to use leverage to get cost savings, collaborate with suppliers to remove wasted costs and get other advantages, and be smart at circumventing market distortions like monopolies and cartels. Right?'

'Right.'

'We haven't talked about monopolies and cartels yet, have we?' Ed detects a missing link.

'No, but we'll do it soon. Coming back to the tasks, you also gave Mishal the job of coordinating stuff across the Division to aggregate deals, increase leverage and ensure consistency. We then looked at tactical things to do during economic hard times, how to handle price increases, and the pros and cons of LTAs.'

'Long-term agreements?' Mishal checks. But she knows I know that she knows.

'Exactly.'

'Is that all task-wise?'

'No, because we discussed how to evaluate deals using lifetime costs rather than today's price. Then we saw how to improve negotiations by increasing the number of negotiable variables, and also by alerting ourselves to the subliminal effect of conditioning tactics and how we can do them back.'

'Hey, we've certainly covered some ground, especially as we've been putting it into practice as well.'

'Sure have. Then there's the process side, the other part of the parallel journeys.'

Ed grimaces. 'My brain hurts. Explain it again.'

Mishal obliges and clarifies further. 'Let me check I've got this right. If task is the deal-making done by buyers, then process describes the way it's done and how we engage with other people in the company, even if they're not directly part of the procurement team.'

'That's my take on it as well,' confirms Ed, 'but is this just theory or does it really work?'

'Even if you don't like so-called mission statements it's vital to define procurement's role. It sets the tone and not only strengthens the buying team's sense of purpose but also flags up to others what it's all about and why it's important. Remember, "We buy, we transform and we sell"? Procurement's not a service function but a core part of that business model.'

'Yeah, that also went into my presentation for the Presidents,' recalls Ed.

Knowing him, I guess that not a lot was left out. He's a details man but also sees the big picture. Like Kraljic, I wish I'd patented the phrase, but it isn't really mine as it belongs to the VP who opened the meeting in Kananaskis country.

'Then we saw why procurement can only go so far down the task road by itself, after which it needs to collaborate with others to make more progress. So we looked at tactics for getting users and budget holders involved, and how psychology can overcome resistance to new ideas.'

Ed's eyes gleam with new interest. 'And we also need the pincer movement to work on budget holders, among others, so they get pressured by procurement at the same time as getting heat from top management.' Ed's brain is now functioning perfectly.

'Correct. There's no hiding place. But top execs don't just fall in line after being fed a bit of profit-and-cost logic. That's where some CPOs have been very subtle at catching the CEO eye and hooking interest. We discussed what some of them had done.'

'I remember the tactics,' Ed chuckles, 'and we're doing the same. That way we'll get more user collaboration and also the approval to change the rules and policies that are stopping buyers from being as effective as they could be.'

'Exactly. It'll massively improve your buyers' effectiveness. It's like you've recruited more procurement people, except you haven't. But you don't have to wait for the CEO to give the green light. We talked about a number of smaller things buyers can do to free up time to be more strategic. It's like a snowball. Once you start rolling the impact gets bigger. Then we looked at why it's good to have strategy and what its five components look like.'

As if on cue, refreshments arrive borne by Tasmin and an acolyte. They have left their oasis on a higher floor in the office building. I guess she just wanted a change of scenery and maybe a chance to do her eyebrow thing again. If so, we're a willing audience.

Suitably refreshed, Ed returns to the previous conversation. He thinks this comprehensively summarises what we've done in regard to task and Route 42. But Mishal wants to dig a little deeper. 'Guys, you're forgetting you're on a trip that started before I got on board. Route 42 was referred to when we met the Irish team but we didn't go into depth, and I want to understand more about it. Can we do this now?'

Action man explains. 'It's about assessing seven aspects of procurement practice to see how good you are, six being top marks. Seven times six is forty-two.'

Mishal gives Ed a look that says she too can do the maths, thank you.

'So take me through the seven.'

Ed hands over to me with a gesture that suggests he's done the hard bit.

'First comes "image and influence". This measures where procurement sits in the company, ranging from a score of one, where it's simply an isolated drudge-type clerical activity, through to six. Here it's positioned as one of the company's core activities, fundamental to achieving corporate objectives and hard-wired into its day-to-day *modus operandi*.'

'So what's our score there, Ed?' Mishal again.

'About 3.5.'

'What do you mean, about 3.5? It sounds like you've measured it quite accurately.'

'In a way we have, Ed confirms. 'We asked all the businesses to assess where they thought they were vis-à-vis the seven dimensions, and that's what they came up with for procurement's influence.'

To me this seems high, but then self-assessments always are. That said, it's still a long way from six.

We go on to talk about the 'operating framework'. This is the system of management controls found in any well-run company. It includes the policies and principles that are the DNA of procurement behaviour and decision-making, and how the CEO delegates commitment authority to the CPO. Buyers' activities are guided by principles rather than dictated by procedures which are often unworkable. In a top-scoring team, buyers have considerable authority to spend money and also have the flexibility to negotiate, ask for bids or go single tender. Poor companies insist on getting three bids, even if there's only one suitable supplier available.

'Organisation' is the third component in the best-practice procurement mix. Smart companies realise there's no one-size-fits-all organisation and structures should be flexible. This allows procurement teams to change shape as appropriate to the prevailing challenges. In a dispersed company like Ed's, a centre-led network works best. This is better than taking strategic buying away from the businesses and giving it to a centralised team which can be remote from the action.

'Infrastructure', the fourth aspect, includes information technology and the analytical and decision-making tools used by buyers, the strategic planning process, and measurement and reporting disciplines. All these support and focus organisational activity and make it effective.

I continue. 'Then we have 'relationships'. This refers to external and internal relationships, but mainly the latter. A low score is when the procurement team is marginalised as a back-office function, avoided by users and budget holders until the last minute.'

'Why so?' Mishal is bent on maximising learning from this session.

'Because the popular impression is that buyers spend their time quoting rules about what can't be done and are little more than clerks. Also, people don't really understand the nature of commitment authority.'

'Remind me about that.'

'It's the powerful authority a buyer has to commit the company to a legally binding contract. Budget holders don't have it but they think they do.'

Mishal again. 'OK, so what about a top score?'

'That's when buyers are seen by colleagues as valuable allies in achieving operational and financial objectives, and are involved very early in decision-making.'

'And our score here, Ed?' This lady has class.

'Three.' This isn't a feat of memory on Ed's part as the numbers are programmed into his phone. That's dedication.

Again I think this is high. Mind you, it helps when buyers are involved in the daily routines of others, especially when food supplies are circulating in the engineering office back at the factory.

Chapter 28

WE TAKE A short walk outside for some fresh air and grab a takeaway lunch, consuming it on the hoof. That's bad practice but we're deep in conversation and don't really notice it's happening. At least the pigeons can enjoy the crumbs.

We return to the office, where Ed scans what we've covered so far with the components of Route 42. 'What about people? We haven't mentioned them yet.'

'They're the penultimate piece of the jigsaw: the quality and numbers of staff, their professionalism and the training and personal development you give them to improve skills.'

Mishal raises a finely shaped eyebrow and it's my turn to be interrogated. 'Seems odd to leave them till last. Surely people should have a higher place in the pecking order?'

'Well, firstly, there isn't a pecking order. All seven aspects of best practice are important. Get them all in place and you've set the scene for highly effective procurement.'

'I know, but it still looks like people are the afterthought.'

'Not so – they're vital. But you must sort out all the other things, especially the roles and authorities you give people. Then you're clear about what you want the team to do and you know what skills they require.'

'Hmm. I'm not sure we have too many people of the required calibre.'

'Probably not, but at least you'll know what capabilities need developing. Most companies discover that people have hidden talents, and the process of change – Route 42 in this case – discovers them for you.'

Ed's been assembling the pieces of the best practice jigsaw and finds one missing. 'Jon, we haven't talked about "agility and ability to change", although you've mentioned it before. Can you explain?'

'OK. A low score reflects an organisation stuck in a rut. It may be doing a reasonable job, but it's complacent and has no appetite to do things differently. A high-scoring team is always searching to do better and is agile when dealing with unexpected events. Also, it uses various techniques for managing change and, importantly, once a new performance level is reached, underpins it to stop backsliding. Such a team is good at "making change permanent."'

'Hang on,' says Ed. 'How does being agile fit with making change permanent? Seems contradictory.'

'No. When the team makes a change, it does things to sustain its impact. But it doesn't mean you have to stick with the changes made. If new circumstances arise, especially unexpected ones, then we're looking for agile responses and then secondary actions to support the new responses until further change is deemed necessary in future.'

'Interesting. It's like a ratchet,' observes Mishal. 'Ed, where do we score on this, then?'

'This one is 3.4.'

Mishal seems surprised. It reflects Gullmech's 'can do' mentality but the company is somewhat disorganised when making changes. Brown eyes glance down at notes and then focus on Ed. 'OK, so what's the total score you all came up with?'

'23.7.'

Again, the engineer's precision. But it feels about right.

Both Mishal and Ed have been getting all this down: one in the burgundy book and the other on a laptop.

Ed looks up. 'That's really useful. If we can fill in the gaps between one and six in each category then we'll have a great tool for assessing procurement's effectiveness in the different businesses.'

'And for clarifying how to improve it,' adds Mishal. 'It'll also test what the CEO or President of each business thinks the role of procurement is. I mean, in AeroCorp we have some guys for whom procurement is merely about controlling the order-placement process, while others regard it as the way to acquire value from critical resources outside the business.'

'Most large companies have this range of mindsets but it's slowly changing. Increasingly, top executives view supply markets as sources of competitive advantage and as means of achieving strategic objectives. This isn't just about managing costs but also includes attracting other forms of value.'

'And we've already said the CPO's job is to influence company strategy, interpret it and implement it,' Ed recalls.

'You have a good memory.'

'No, I have a good filing system!'

For a change we chat generally until afternoon coffee appears. Tasmin and team have materialised again from their oasis elsewhere.

'OK,' says Ed, 'do you think all the above arguments are sufficient to convince the business world at large about procurement's potential? Mind you, so long as they don't get it then we'll have the competitive advantage, but I'm interested in the bigger picture. '

'Having laid out all the incentives for taking procurement seriously as we've done, my view is that it's up to CEOs, business schools and other commentators on business practice to justify why it shouldn't be given the priority it needs.'

Ed looks dubious. 'I understand what you're saying, but is there a more direct way of putting them on the spot?'

'Yes, I'd challenge them with some key questions.'

'Such as?'

'Does your search for new customers benefit from understanding where their procurement process is on the road to best practice, does this influence your decision-making, and is your sales approach tailored accordingly?'

'OK, that's a good one. Got another?'

'Are the company's financial plans vulnerable to supply-price volatility and unexpected increases, or are they protected by cost-management programmes you have in place? Are supplier payments synchronised proactively with the company's cash flow requirements?'

Ed observes that a third question has slipped in under the radar, but he notes it anyway.

Mishal has a question. 'On the financial one, what do you mean by "proactively synchronising payments"?'

'Simply that the procurement people are in the know about how much cash the company has and therefore what's available to pay suppliers. But they know it ahead of the game so they're not forced suddenly to stop payments to cope with a cash flow crisis. Similarly, finance knows in advance what contractual commitments govern future payments so they can build these into their cash flow planning. The left hand knows what the right is doing.'

'OK, got that,' says Ed. 'Now, coming back to the questions, I like the way they hardwire procurement activity directly into the ongoing job of managing the company and addressing its priorities.'

'That's the intention. We have to get CEOs who are facing a business challenge to say, 'How can procurement help us solve this?' rather than only expecting a reaction when supply costs or problems occur.'

'Isn't this just semantics?'

'No, because sustaining high performance depends on the culture and values of a company rather than its mechanisms, as well as its ability to form effective linkages both internally and externally. This is very appropriate in an era where managing knowledge, and the people who possess it both inside and outside the company, is the emerging challenge once the IT revolution, not to mention the economic crisis, have shaken down.'

Ed muses for a short while. 'Hmm, heady stuff. This is important. We'll need to keep referring back so we don't lose sight of why we're changing things, and also stay true to the values and beliefs guiding us on the journey.'

Mishal agrees and adds, 'But as always we need to keep things grounded in today's reality. Don't worry, I sure am going to be banging all this into people's heads as time goes on.' She has an idea for doing this. 'Why don't we organise a video conference to look at where we've got to procurement-wise for the whole Division, while also emphasising what we're doing differently to improve things?'

Ed likes this and we decide to schedule this for a month's time.

It's getting late and I glance at the time. 'I need to get to the train station and you need to prepare for your meetings tomorrow, so I suggest we all keep email dialogues going once you're back at base.'

'Sounds good,' agrees Ed. 'It's a plan. Meanwhile have a safe trip home.'

'And you enjoy the rest of your time in London. Don't forget to buy souvenirs for the family. We need export-generated income!'

Ed grimaces. The thought of 'shopping' does that to a guy.

I set out for home and descend into London's underground system where I'll take two different trains. The first one is fine, but the second one isn't going anywhere. So I disembark and return to the first line which I left only fifteen minutes ago. A train comes along but is massively overcrowded on account of the other delay. But at least it moves, bumping and grinding its way to Paddington station.

The first suitable west-bound train is for Cardiff, but there's a long queue at the ticket office. However, there's plenty of time because this train, too, is delayed. So there's time to evaluate options. I can either get this train when it's available, or wait another thirty minutes and board the train for Swansea, which is nearer to where I need to go. I decide on the first train. Getting beyond Cardiff will require another, but that's for later.

The Cardiff train finally leaves but goes slower and slower, apparently because it's running on only one engine. Ninety minutes later I realise the Swansea service might be catching up and could overtake us. Bristol Parkway provides the opportunity to switch trains. I alight, only to discover that the Swansea flyer is now also delayed. So I re-board the Cardiff train, whose single engine has not yet hauled it out of reach.

We actually reach Cardiff. Here I move to platform four to await the Swansea train. We'll call it train two. I have time to enquire whether it's a good idea to wait a bit longer for train three which will also stop at Cardiff but go beyond Swansea. Station staff scratch heads and mutter, 'How should we know, we're only the workers,' but eventually assure me that train three is the one I will need after finishing with train two. It's not exactly new information.

The PA system crackles into life with an urgent message. Depending on whether or not you're affected, its content is either confusing or entertaining. It says, 'Train three will arrive on platform four while train two will arrive, possibly, on platform five.' I wonder if 'possibly' signifies uncertainty about train two's exact point of arrival or whether it will appear at all.

What does arrive is another announcement. A smooth-talking, pre-recorded lady comes on with the news that train two is on time. But she doesn't finish, being elbowed aside by a heavily accented man who says train two is now delayed. The smooth lady tries again but gets even shorter shrift before her man friend barges in. He reaches new levels of incoherence as microphone distortion strangles his words. Is it 'leaves on platforms' or 'leaves on lines'? 'Crossed wires or delayed connections'? God knows, because the train company certainly doesn't.

Train two arrives. Confusingly, train three does as well. I decide to go with train three which leaves on time and with an agreeable sense of purpose. A retired-looking man with a tired looking trolley comes by. My asking for a sandwich reveals they were all sold this morning. If he tells me they might still have some on train two I'll probably do him harm.

Night has fallen, and it's a crisp, clear, chilly one in the West Wales countryside. At last I'm home and outside on the deck, fortified by a shot of whisky and uplifted by the firmament above in which countless stars shine brightly in their velvet-black setting. Some of them arc swiftly across the sky and are satellites. There's also a slower one. It's probably only running on one engine.

Chapter 29

Seattle – May, Friday

A FEW WEEKS pass before we can line everyone up for the video conference, but time has not been wasted and the parallel journeys have gained momentum.

Now I'm freshly arrived in the USA again and present myself and my fingerprints at Immigration for the photo opportunity. Smile, you're on Homeland Security's candid camera. My biometrics are in order and I'm allowed in, this time to Seattle. Yet again the reception has been courteous and swiftly conducted. Thank you.

Ground transportation takes me northwards. There's plenty of waterside here lapping at the feet of impressive mountains: the Olympics to the left and others, whose name I don't catch, further away to the right. A very large icing-sugared peak over there looks volcanic but is, I'm assured, harmless. By contrast, Mount St Helen is about three hours' drive further away, but when it last smoked in 1984 it still managed to drop ash on nearby Spokane's carpet. Apparently people made souvenirs out of it. Ashtrays would've been appropriate.

Dusk gathers as the cab driver pulls up in front of the hotel. The lobby is crowded with what appears to be an old folks' convention. A group of four guys suddenly burst into song and do a barbershop routine. I don't know what brought it on but, whether or not it was drug-induced, it was brilliant. I say this to another guy who's been applauding vigorously. He agrees and immediately offers details of a heart operation he's just survived. He describes the medication that has been prescribed to keep him going. It's a cocktail of anabolic steroids and thalidomide. Down this little lot with root beer and he'd be flying.

As the songbirds drift away I make it to the reception desk and eventually the room. Windows look out over the car park. Other attractions include the freeway, a major road and a small business estate. So it's… convenient.

North Seattle is home to Duvall Components. It's where Diane is based, and the next day she arrives to take me to the factory and company's

HQ. It's on an airfield which houses an aviation museum around which are parked some fabulous old aeroplanes. Butch O'Hare would have been totally at home. He probably flew some of them.

In Duvall's building I'm introduced to a big genial guy. It's General Manager Sydney who is anxious to meet me as he wants me to join in a tricky conference call with a UK customer.

We gather in Sydney's office, which features the 'regulation' set up: big desk, lots of trophies, a golf bag and clubs in the corner, and a conference table strewn with papers relevant to the upcoming phone call. The main exhibit is the customer's letter demanding price reductions on the kits of parts that Duvall sell them. Although it's a simple price demand there is so much legalese in it that I have to read the letter twice to realise the customer is not suing Duvall for something. It is adorned with phrases that reflect the worst vocabulary of muscle-bound traditional procurement. The customer is a large one for Duvall. The kits sold were specially developed for this customer, so it's not as though they have the luxury to stop buying if they don't like the prices.

We spend time hatching out a response to the letter and then grab a coffee. The conference call is scheduled for when it'll be around the end of play in the UK.

In due course the phone rings and we go live. With a minimum of pleasantries the buyer guy launches into his repertoire of strong-arm tactics, despite the fact that Duvall is the monopoly supplier. He makes several ethically questionable comments, such as, 'When we said in the contract we would review prices we had no intention of doing it … and we're not reviewing them now, just demanding reductions.'

Sydney plays it cool and isn't drawn into an argument. He insists prices will remain where they are, with a whiff of 'take it or leave it' to be read between the lines. Eventually the buyer grudgingly signs off, having achieved nothing other than to blight the relationship.

All this occupies Friday morning. I spend the afternoon looking at various supply agreements that Diane wants critiqued. Later she and Sydney suggest we quit for the day and eat at a local steak house. Cold beer helps us celebrate the successful outcome to the conference call and we muse over the way it went. Duvall came out of it winning handsomely. Quite possibly, the buyer never knew.

'That buyer certainly behaved like the big gorilla,' I remark.

Sydney chuckled, 'Yes, but he'd forgotten we were the only ones with the bananas!'

Next day brings one of those early mornings when nature's feeling good with itself. Everything is in bright, sharp focus. The sun is strong but hasn't yet begun to bleach out the colours, and the air is so clear that distant objects seem close enough to touch. This is Seattle on a Saturday morning. I decide to take the Washington State Ferry from nearby Edmonds to Kingston, thirty minutes away across Puget Sound. It's blissful. A few fishing boats and a container ship go about their business, while gulls do theirs on the ship's railings. Across the water are low-lying islands, covered with pine trees erupting from them like exuberant green geysers. Off left, downtown Seattle distantly extrudes high-rise buildings to add to nature's profile.

It's just out of the holiday season and only a few passengers are aboard. Several seize this half-hour cruise as the opportunity to phone loved ones to tell them where they are. I can't help but hear. 'You can probably see me as we're just passing behind a small container ship.' 'Guess where we are... we're on a ferry.' 'Hey, you guys back in Texas would just love this cool breeze.' Other more surreal conversations are also in pro. 'I'm trying to move my mother-in-law to Alaska,' and '... maybe they all want to go over there and strip off naked.' So what's that about?

The ferry nudges into its berth at Kingston. It's a small community rising gently away from behind the dock. I explore, encountering signs admonishing 'Wrong Way' once you're already committed to it, and without indications of where 'Right' is. Maybe the answer lies with the Kingston Christian Community building. Signage outside counsels, 'Can't sleep? Count your blessings.'

I recall a similar dictum on a mug in a hotel lobby shop. 'Can't sleep? Tell God your problems. He's going to be up all night anyway.' But the Kingston Christian Community hasn't finished yet. 'What do we do to earn your gift? Nothing. We accept it.' Thank you, and goodnight, then.

But here's something more tangible. 'Paradise Found' says the notice. However, subtitles promising 4,000 square feet, five bedrooms and four bathrooms confirm that this is about a piece of real estate rather than the everlasting peace promised next door. I walk on and sense that spirituality is strong in Kingston. A native church, '100% native and 100% Christian', eclectically offers 'Drumming and Community Soup at 5pm'. This notice is outside a shop selling used books. Although the shop is closed, the window displays offer more enlightenment. *Meeting Angels: 101 Real Life Encounters'* and, here's a beauty: *'100 Years of Invention in the Pacific Northwest: Sexless Oysters, and the Self-Tipping Hat'*.

All this in the country that put men on the moon. A nearby notice proclaims, 'Discover the Pacific Northwest and Discover Yourself.' Perhaps it's more about discovering how weird other folk are. Or maybe I've just led a sheltered life.

I spend the rest of the weekend preparing for the video conference when we'll be beamed down to the audience gathering at Gullmech.

It's Monday, and Diane collects me from the hotel. We head for the factory, where we join Sydney in the conference room. This is smaller than its Kansas cousin, albeit sporting the same size seats. There's just enough room for us to congregate at the far end of the table in order to be properly positioned for the TV screen and camera.

The screen flickers into life and we see folk gathering before the camera at Gullmech. The assembly includes Ed, Mishal and an assortment of Presidents from the various US businesses who have come together for a quarterly review. Carol and Peter from the UK are also there. People have brought along food supplies in various quantities. The top brass seem happy enough to settle for cups of newly vended coffee but their junior colleagues seek more sustenance in the form of bagels, crisps and as yet unrevealed food offerings concealed in large brown bags. It's obviously an 'executive' thing to appear not to need food.

The purpose of the discussion is to make procurement plans for the next financial year. I want to engage senior people in the effort, to up the energy levels and to heighten expectations about what can be achieved.

We start with the usual round of welcomes and joshing before it's eyes down on the few charts I sent round earlier. The first is an overview of current AeroCorp supply expenditure noting that, so far, about half of it has been treated to new-look procurement medicine. The first year cost saving of ten per cent across the board has been sustained, largely by the individual efforts of the separate businesses. I introduce the idea of 'black', 'dark grey' and 'light grey' spend.

A figure lurking in the shadows at the back of Gullmech's conference room turns out to be Dora from Kansas. 'Hey, Jon, how ya doin'? Now what's this about black spend and so on?'

'OK, black spend covers purchases that directly affect the cost of sales…'

'Like raw materials and outside processing?' suggests Elaine, whose presence and big hair come into focus stage left.

'You've got it. And you regularly report those costs as "materials cost of sales". Then "dark grey" covers what's spent on other operational needs such as plant maintenance, utilities and tooling.'

'We haven't really looked at that yet, have we?' muses Ed, whose lanky frame near the front of the room means his head is only just in shot on the screen.

'So what about the light grey category?' This time it's Antony who's on air.

'This is ancillary stuff like professional services and office operations.'

Ed again: 'Right, that's sorted out the colour code, but why do it in the first place?'

'Firstly to make sure we capture all the money you spend. Those costs not included in "materials cost of sales" are out of sight and therefore out of mind. Then the dark and light greys simply reflect the different impact of those costs on your operations.'

Mishal makes an important observation: 'Saving money or acquiring better value in all these areas will help profitability, and I'm sure an effective procurement process works for all of them.'

The next charts look at the big ticket items identifying where we can combine purchases currently made individually by specific businesses. Everyone's now up to speed about the tactics for improving individual deals so the new emphasis is how AeroCorp as a whole gets its act together, connecting up similar activities within the Division. We're clearly moving into more strategic territory. This means creating, inside and outside the company, the conditions needed to achieve business objectives as distinct from doing sharper deals. We identify possibilities for the next year: developing and bringing new sources on line, increasing market competition, overcoming monopolies and cartels, changing specifications, and getting earlier involvement in new product development. The parallel journey of Route 42 hasn't been forgotten either, and people throughout the company are becoming more commercially aware and collaborative as they realise they're part of the whole procurement process. More discussion ensues about who's going to do what to continue the good work.

Carol, as ever, has her eye on the bottom line. 'Jon, what I'd like now is an overview of AeroCorp's total expenditure with an analysis showing the specific areas we'll target, what we'll do there and what the potential cost saving will be. Can you do that?'

Fortunately I can as we did the 'planning basis' exercise a while back. I retrieve the chart and explain how it works. The planning basis represents reality without being an exact financial forecast, which I could never get the individual businesses to come off the fence about anyway. It also provides a framework for adjusting figures if actual expenditures are higher or lower. Psychology must be at work here as the CFOs were happy to agree the planning basis if not the actual forecast. Perhaps they thought it was just a theoretical exercise, but at least we have a good basis for next year's budgets.

However, we haven't quite finished.

'Jon,' it's Carol again, 'you've included some numbers about "probability". Can you say a bit more about this?'

'It's a judgement about how easy or not it'll be to get the cost saving. It includes what we know about a supplier's willingness to collaborate and how attractive they view us as a customer. Or it can reflect the degree to which the supplier won't budge because they have a monopoly or, we suspect, may be a cartel member. Most of the probabilities are in the eighty to hundred per cent range, while the lowest is fifty. That's a fifty-fifty chance of being successful.'

'I hope we'll be more ambitious than that,' urges Carol, 'but I accept we have to be credible about the numbers put into the budgets otherwise our financial planning will be flaky.'

People have had enough of the numbers by now so we decide to pull the plug on the video link. We've decided what new opportunities exist in each business to deliver more cost savings, and where we can orchestrate cross-business deals as well. With cameras and screens off we welcome catering supplies into the conference room for a quick working lunch. I've come to the conclusion there aren't any other types of lunch in the USA, or at least not in this dynamic company.

The afternoon disappears while looking at some of Diane's other supply issues. It's late when I get back to the hotel but there's enough time to pack bags and get ready for an early flight to LA in the morning. I wonder why we didn't host the video conference from there, but it's too late now to be asking.

Chapter 30

California

IT'S TUESDAY'S DOMESTIC flight to Los Angeles so I miss the customary banter associated with immigration processes and am quickly on the plane. Reading matter is stuffed into the back of the seat in front.

Sky Mall magazine is particularly gripping. 'White wedding chapel birdhouse fashioned in wood with its own wedding bells and white picket fence.' Sounds nice, but should you purchase and not think so, then complaining is not a problem: 'Don't be frustrated. Use our WhingeMaster letters of complaint with pre-drafted beginnings and ends leaving you only to insert the subject of your complaint.'

Then there's 'The Complete Solution for Nose and Ear Hair. TurboGroomer 2 with powerful new motor and dual LED headlamps ensures nothing is missed.' And there's more stuff for, I assume, the older person. 'Let the UpEasy automatic lifting cushion gently seat you and then help you back on to your feet.' It includes machine-washable blue cushions. Good, that's a relief then.

Sky Mall helps seniors by putting related items next to each other. 'Send your painful swollen feet on a permanent vacation' comes alongside the 'Pet Ramp' which 'makes it easier for the old dog to get into the car'. Then there's a Smith & Wesson Rifle (remember we're flying in the USA here) alongside another advert promoting 'The safe and effective way to solve your barking old dog problem.' Finally, 'These digestion tablets deal effectively with flatulence and trapped wind', right by a device that enables you to 'Enjoy the therapeutic benefits of low-pressure air massage.' How convenient. I love this crazy country.

Soon we descend into LAX. Ground transportation awaits, heads east towards the hills, and in a little while rolls into the car park at Gullmech. The timing is good as Ed simultaneously arrives from a supplier visit downtown. He eases out of the SUV while a stranger emerges from the passenger side. Ed introduces him. It's Rich, the new Procurement Manager.

Ed announces he has good news and bad news. We hurry through reception and into his office.

'So what's the good news?' I ask, ever the optimist.

'It's getting on for two years now since we started our journey towards better procurement. Remember the big profit improvement we ascribed to procurement a year ago? Well, we've sustained that impact and everyone in the company wants more. They love cost savings!'

'So what's the problem?'

'Cost savings,' grins Ed.

'Meaning?'

'Well, everyone thinks doing procurement differently is only about saving money. It's caught on like wildfire. But you and I know there's much more to it, don't we?!'

I never thought I'd hear Ed say this, but here we are. It's out.

'So,' he continues, 'we must tell a more strategic story. Trouble is, I'm not sure how to put it. We don't want to assault them with mission and vision statements, although I know they have their place. I'm looking for something more directly connected to the hot buttons of the business.'

We spend most of the morning working on a new message. It focuses on five key aspects of business which depend on high-performance procurement.

First is Sales Growth. This can be driven by supplier innovation with new product development and also shortening the time to get new products to market. Having a better understanding of customers' procurement game plans also wins new orders and helps sales growth. Ed cites AeroCorp's UK company which successfully won a big order by working with a key supplier to prepare a bid for an important customer. They judged this wouldn't have succeeded had they adopted the old process of putting a bid together without supplier input. Then there's the willingness to field test new ideas and enjoying supplier innovations shared by being a 'preferred customer'. Favoured treatment also reduces lost revenue by shortening equipment downtimes.

Engaging with suppliers in a more strategic way leads to procurement's second impact: Secure Supplies and Relationships. Here the company benefits from dependable and agile relationships with key suppliers. Supply chains respond quickly to up-cycles in time and volume while helping to develop a presence in new markets and geographic regions. I tell Ed about one company where procurement said they'd 'discovered South America'. This was a bit of in-house marketing. The company wished to create a first manufacturing base there and had commissioned the Procurement VP to establish local supply lines, not just for routine operations but also for building the manufacturing facility in the first place.

Gullmech's CFO, Jeff, looks in at this point and asks what we're discussing. 'Surely it's all about making costs savings?'

Ed puts him right. 'Yup, that's where we started, but that's the traditional view.' He explains the buy/transform/sell equation, advocating procurement as a core business process and not an order-fulfilment service justifying itself with cost-reduction prizes. The three of us talk a little more and end up defining procurement's impact on two more business priorities. Improving Costs and Margins means establishing and managing a highly competitive external cost base for the company, aligning costs with the company's sales prices. And the fourth of the five is labelled Optimising Cash and Working Capital, with cash available in any period equalling or exceeding cash requirements.

This is the time to tell Jeff that delaying supplier payments isn't smart, it being better to discuss cash flows with suppliers rather than arbitrarily cut them off. Jeff begins to protest but thinks better of it. Perhaps he's still hurting as he remembers his accounts-payable folk recently paid a supplier twice for the same invoice.

Jeff remembers why he's looked in on Ed in the first place, deals with it and then rushes to the next meeting for which he's now late. He's made a useful contribution.

We're left to come up with the fifth and final area of procurement impact: Better Productivity and Processes. This is where internal processes and productivity benefit from the application of superior equipment and supplier support, as applied to ongoing operations as well as capex projects.

Ed thinks he can tell a good story with this new material. The five impact areas explain how procurement is a business player essential to the success of the whole company, over and above saving money.

We consume an early sandwich lunch, after which Rich looks in. He's decided we should hit the road and visit a couple of suppliers. We're going to a suburb not far from downtown LA and 'it's, er, a rough area... not the place you'd want to be alone in'. I pause only to question Rich's motives: am I here to help his negotiations or am I riding shotgun?

Our first call is to a supplier making metal castings. Wax and alcohol are both involved in the process and their fragrance hangs heavy in the air as we enter the workshops. It smells like a pub after they've blown out the candles.

Next is a forging foundry, where small bars of red-hot metal are pummelled in a massive edifice called a drop hammer. We alight from Rich's car to the sound of heavy blows being dealt out the back. The ground shakes in sympathy. A well-used, once-painted door opens into the firm's reception area. It's an intimate space about the size of a small sauna, with sides and ceiling panelled with wood-effect wallpaper. But instead of heat we have beat. I think of Rich's engineers and finance people back in their air-conditioned ivory-towered offices, cushioned from this reality and ready with their fastidious requirements and petulant complaints about supplier quality. Once in a while they need to visit places like this for a reality check.

As is the custom in small spaces, Rich and I do not speak, but our presence has nevertheless been detected. A small sliding hatch in the wall opens to reveal a gentleman who offers a cordial welcome. The entire wall in which the hatch slides is then swung open and we are invited into an adjacent office. Our receptionist introduces himself as Fred. He turns out to be the company President. We talk. He understands our need for urgent delivery and promises to help. Right in my line of vision is an interesting contraption suspended on two twelve-inch wires on Fred's desk. Imagine, if you will, the bottom part of a teardrop but without the pointy bit on top, and about the size of a generous ice bucket. It's made of thick hirsute leathery stuff, and its outer surface is covered with close-cropped wiry hair. President Fred uses this interesting receptacle to put his pens in. I begin to form an idea as to what it might be but can't really believe what I'm thinking.

Rich leaves us to go and beat up another supplier so Fred invites me to see the facility out the back. En route he says, 'Jon, what I'm about to show you is a museum.'

He's not wrong, and I stand in awe of equipment of almost biblical proportions: a massive, towering, very solid iron monolith. It wouldn't be out of place on an epic film set with Charlton Heston doing a stint on it. This machine, and its companions, have pounded away for thirty-five years and I can see them stamping on well into the future. Heavily-visored leather-aproned attendants deftly tong and turn red-hot metal as it assumes its intended shape. Two other acolytes pass the metal to and fro. It's a close-knit team where communication happens by nods and winks since no words can be heard above the thunderous blows raining from above. The drop hammer has spoken, the metal submits, the ground has shaken and everything is in order in this fiery firmament.

Fred leads me further into an open yard basking in hot LA sunshine and explains some more about the process we've just witnessed. After a while we return to his office and the thing on his desk. I need transport to the hotel as it's too late to get back to Gullmech, so we try calling a cab, unsuccessfully.

'I tell you what, Jon, it'll be my pleasure to drive you back. I'm about through here, so let's go.' I offer grateful thanks and ask what exactly his capacious pen-holder had been in a previous life.

'Ah yes, my son sent this from Texas.' He swings the thing gently and the meaning is clear. 'It used to belong to a bull.'

So what we have here, then, is a large scrotum. Where its owner once had lead in his pencil, he now has biros where his balls were. Ignominious, or what?

Back-stage the hammers thunder their goodbyes as Fred ushers me out to the presidential truck. I notice another smaller scrotum – more a scrotette – dangling from the truck's gear stick. 'You ain't seen nothin' yet,' says Fred, and he steers me to the back of the truck where a couple of plastic testicles dangle from the appropriately named ball hitch. These are more gifts from Fred's son, who clearly has a one-track mind. Or perhaps he runs a knackers' yard. Whatever, it is kind of Fred to drive me back and I enjoy the ride.

It's a quiet evening and tomorrow I'll return to the UK. The journey will give me a chance to start work on the subject of Procurement Transformation as requested by Ed.

.

Chapter 31

June – Wales, UK

MISHAL, ED AND I have kept up email contact since the LA meeting, and they regularly remind me I owe them something on Procurement Transformation.

Now I'm at home base and must commit thoughts to paper. But there are many distractions as it's a gloriously sunny day. There's a panoramic view from the office. To the left is open sea, calm now after recent winds produced pounding waves and white horses in the bay. Then, straight ahead, the headland drops steeply into the sea on the one hand and connects up to the Preseli Hills on the other. Over there is the highest pinnacle, called Hill of the Eagles. That's where the River Gwaun is born at the start of its eight-mile journey through a melt-water valley where time stands still. In 1752 no one told the valley folk to put their clocks forward by thirteen days to catch up with a mainland Europe already on Gregorian time. So they still celebrate New Year in mid January. It's a festival fuelled with prodigious quantities of home brew, singing and house visits. No one exactly recalls when it's time to stop partying. Potent drinks paralyse the senses and still the passage of time.

The Gwaun winds its way through river meadows, home to prize-winning Welsh black cattle, before entering woodland glades full of bluebells and wild garlic – in season that is. Journey's end is the little harbour of Fishguard Lower Town. Boats shelter behind the stone quay lined with quaint cottages and the newly painted yacht club. All this, too, is visible from the office so it takes an effort to focus on transformation.

I start with a message for Ed. 'Ed, here's the complete story about transformation. You've heard bits of it before but it's worth assembling it again all in one place. Hopefully that'll help you and others to tell the story as well. So, read on.

'Today's fast-moving business world requires company teams to be agile, focused and demonstrating every characteristic of high-performing organisations. However, few display these attributes. High performance can be created by applying organisational transformation techniques, and procurement provides the most fertile business area in which to apply them. Typically, the journey towards excellence starts by making cost savings. This is good and necessary, but also potentially dangerous if nothing else is done over and above exerting purchasing power. A limit is soon reached when purchasing muscle ceases to prise more savings from supply costs. Beyond this point, the procurement process has to undergo more fundamental change. This is procurement transformation. Success delivers significant reductions in supply costs and also repositions procurement as a core player in the business. Recalling the words of the CEO of a large Asia–Pacific company, "The procurement process is a microcosm of the company. Transforming the effectiveness of this process achieves direct cost reductions and, more powerfully, benefits the culture and performance of the business overall. But because procurement starts from such a low point in many companies, making change is tough. It's the pain involved that makes the change such a positive and lasting one."

'No company is an island: it needs suppliers as well as customers. Conventional wisdom puts great emphasis on managing certain aspects of business such as customers, operations, strategy and finances. Typically, however, much less regard is paid to external suppliers and the risks and opportunites present in dealing with them. The object of transformation is to correct this imbalance.

'Such change programmes are examples of projects that span the company. The role and capability of procurement is enhanced through the priority given to it plus changes in culture, processes and technology. But, for the potential benefits to be fully realised, stakeholders as well as the procurement team need to change behaviours. It's an all-embracing change and the business as a whole must be involved, not just the buyers.

'There are several reasons why procurement can't transform itself in isolation, but we'll deal with these when looking at the process of managing change. Things will start moving in the right direction if there's a clear statement about the future goal. As one unusually clear-sighted politician said, "Do we have a clear picture of where we want to end up?"

'Earlier we asked, "Are we doing our procurement intelligently?" This will be part of the "clear picture". It will also feature a CPO or equivalent positioned at a high level in the company. She or he will have two roles. One is a "business" role, helping to frame corporate strategy and contributing to the running of the company, distilling out the strategy's supply implications and then managing the resources to deal with subsequent actions. Second, there's the "task" role, which is to create and sustain the supply markets the business needs for it to succeed now and in future.'

The phone rings. It's Ed, wanting to know how things are going.

I explain about needing to define the future goal, as in, 'How will we recognise success when we eventually see it?'

'And how would we?' he probes.

'Procurement would be permanently and equally engaged at the top of the company in running the business overall while also having specific responsibility for managing its external sources of supply and orchestrating the company's dealings with them.'

'Shouldn't it be more task-oriented than that? For example, I heard a speaker the other day saying that "procurement's number one priority is to remove cost while protecting the business from risk".'

'That's alright as far as it goes, but there's no reference to shaping the company's future or challenging why costs are so excessive for there to be a big cost-saving potential in the first place. Those costs don't only reflect what's specified but also what information has leaked out of the company regarding budgets, urgency and sourcing preferences. All this affects what prices the suppliers think they can get.'

'Which presumably are higher than they need to be?'

'Yes. It's not exactly smart to let a whole lot of unnecessary costs build up in the first place and then task a procurement team with getting them down.'

'OK,' concedes Ed. 'I understand why you define the goal as you have. I think I'd better let you carry on working on it. But actually the other reason I called is to alert you to some big changes that may happen in the company. Nothing certain yet, but potentially worrying. I can't say more over the phone. You need to come over to the USA again.'

And then he was gone.

It takes a while, and a breath of sea air, to clear my mind again and refocus on transformation.

'Achieving the future goal requires "primary changes" which directly increase procurement's impact. A new approach to the supply market is needed. This means being less predictable in setting up deals, and projecting a "tough but fair" image. There will be deeper knowledge of suppliers' situations, their plans and how they view us as a customer. In some cases there will be much closer collaboration with them and new sources will be developed.

'There will be new relationships with budget holders and operational colleagues, requiring closer and earlier collaboration to define needs and optimise the timing of purchase orders and contracts. Unjustified specifications will be challenged and alternatives jointly developed.

'Flexible procurement methods will allow a buyer's approach to the supply market to reflect its competitiveness (or not) and also the aim of the supply strategy. The effect will be to remove barriers and commercially inappropriate actions which are dictated by rigid procurement approaches.

'New techniques will bring more "science" and structure into decision-making when looking for profit opportunities, targeting prices and understanding risk.

'Finally, buyers will be given more authority: to choose from an approved suite of alternative ways of inviting supplier offers rather than struggling with a "one approach fits all" procedure, and they will be able to place higher-value orders. Empowering buyers in these ways must go hand in hand with personal assessment and skills training beforehand.

'All this is good and will make tangible impact. The big question, though, is how long primary changes will remain effective once those championing change have moved on. "Supporting changes" are therefore needed to sustain procurement's impact and embed it in the business as the normal *modus operandi*.

'The keystone in the supporting foundation will be the new statement of procurement's role and purpose, along with new policies and company-wide principles governing the procurement process.' I can hear Shirley saying this is only bureaucracy, but it actually represents the DNA of high-performance procurement.

I continue. 'I was once involved in some Europe-wide benchmarking of procurement best practice. Several high-class companies joined in to compare how procurement contributed to financial results. Among many, one correlation was particularly intriguing: the companies having the greater number of procurement policies also made the biggest impact on costs, in a good way.

'Eventually we figured out why. All participants had policies in place that controlled basic business practice. For example: business ethics; social responsibility; confidentiality; and separation of authorities to requisition, legally commit and pay. Then there was the control of procurement practice within the business overall. This covered the use of approved suppliers, enquiry types and formality, terms and conditions, and supplier performance. Again, all participants had policies like these.

'We then moved to a smaller group where additional policies ensured an intelligent approach to searching for best value. These encouraged flexibility when inviting offers from supply markets, and ensured that competing bids were evaluated on a "best overall lifetime" basis rather than just comparing the offered price. A "face value" concept was also described, which allowed buyers to ignore searching for best value when conditions warranted it.'

These are dry topics and my gaze wanders over to Lower Town, which is also dry. The tide is out and boats are grounded, some perched on bilge keels. Others teeter at acute angles, hoping they can hold on there until the incoming tide picks them up again.

Back with the benchmarking. 'The best-in-class participants still had a few more policies up their sleeves. Subjects included supplier relationships, dealing with supplier visitors, who did what at the buyer–seller interface during contract administration, and early involvement of procurement personnel in major items. Now I understood why procurement in these companies, seemingly overloaded with policy, actually made a bigger impact. It was because these latter policies involved others in the procurement process. And they were mandatory, not just helpful guidelines. They would be the reference points for audit.

'Which brings up another issue: the "procedures manual". One company proudly showed me theirs: ten centimetres thick and full of good stuff. But this tome doubled as the reference bible for audit, so any minor transgression from procedural detail was frowned on. A closer look revealed three different types of content: fundamental policy, procedures and helpful hints for buyers. We decided to separate these components. The policies, just like the ones described above, were published in a small booklet about the size of an iPhone.

'Procedures deserved their own manual, but the preface was all important. It said, "These procedures will help buyers and prevent reinventing the wheel. They govern most common situations encountered and adhere to the procurement policies. However, if a buyer encounters a situation where these procedures do not sensibly apply, then she or he has the authority to develop a customised approach so long as it, too, reflects the relevant procurement policies and principles."

'What of the material left over? This was incorporated in a buyers' reference handbook, simply presented as a fund of knowledge which was neither procedural nor mandatory.

'One client was undergoing a quality assessment and the auditor wanted to see procurement's quality manual. Not wishing to produce more paper, the CPO gave the auditor the small booklet on policy and principles.

'A short time passed. "That's fine," said the auditor. "This is your quality manual. I wish more people expressed things so succinctly." Relief all round.

'Other things support the primary changes of transformation. There'll be comprehensive development of new skills and knowledge, commercial awareness training for non-procurement folk, improved systems to aid data analysis and decision-making, organisational changes and recruitment. But get the policies and principles right, get the auditors used to them, and best-practice procurement will become ingrained in the company as normal behaviour.

Outside the sun still shines and invites a coffee break, during which I relax on the balcony and catch up with business reading. It's an article about brands, starting with references to some of China's hilariously inappropriate export brand names. These include Front Gate men's underwear, Long March luggage and Great Leap Forward floor polish. This is only a short step away from nonsense labelling – as on a bottle of Sleeping Aid medicine: 'Warning: may cause drowsiness.' Or the US airline helpfully advising passengers how to enjoy a packet of nuts: 'Instructions: open packet, eat nuts.'

I resume writing. 'The next thing about change is how to make it happen. *Making It Happen* is the title of the late Sir John Harvey-Jones' book about how to galvanise a company from top to bottom to gear up for success. His tenure as CEO of a large chemical company proved how good he was at this. He said, "Why is there such a total myopia in business about the things which release human energy and talent? We have estimated that in industry we get about thirty or forty per cent of what people are actually capable of. Probably the absolute optimum would be sixty to seventy per cent, so there is plenty of scope for improvement."

'People have to want to make change. A Sourcing VP of a large pharma company said, "We need a burning platform." If a company's in obvious distress then the need for change is self-evident. But if it's doing well, then the "ain't broke, don't fix it" mentality leads to complacency. So there must be a compelling reason for change. The day a company stops trying to do better is the day it'll start going backwards, because other competitors who are still trying harder will creep up and overtake. In Gullmech's case the motive is to take advantage of the economic down-cycle to gear up and beat the rest of the world when the good times come again.

'If there isn't a clear reason for change, then dissatisfaction with the status quo has to be created. One boss was candid and, as I knew from behind the scenes, genuinely sincere. To the entire workforce she said, "This company is doing well but I believe we can do even better. The fact that we're not doing better is my fault, not yours. So I'm asking you to help identify what are the barriers holding us back, and what we can do to remove them." Initial cynicism gave way to positive involvement. The benefits of change were described in terms of people's own jobs and how they would be different. The changes would help them be more successful, especially if they were involved in diagnosing what the improvements should be. This helped reduce fear of the unknown.

'As Sir John put it, "The engine of change is dissatisfaction with the present and the brakes of change are fear of the unknown and fear of the future." The notion of engines and brakes echoes the technique called

Force Field Analysis, where the status quo is represented as an equilibrium point where positive forces acting in the direction of change are countered by opposite forces resisting it. But you only have to increase one positive force, or reduce one restraining one, and the current status shifts in the direction you want to go.

'Another way of looking at opposing forces is to identify them as barriers standing in the way of change. These stop the desired future goal from being a reality today. This in turn requires a very clear picture of what the future goal looks like: "How will we recognise success when we see it?"

'All this is helped by widespread communications to achieve full understanding of the new approaches, a fresh appreciation by buyers and non-buyers about their respective roles, buyer–user workshops to identify profit-contribution opportunities, and skills training.

'One company set up a week-long "training academy" for buyers. The agenda included negotiation, time value of money, legal aspects of purchasing, and strategic selling. Company lawyers, finance people and marketers were involved in presenting their specialist subjects. Participants included a few non-buyers as well – at least for the first event, because several more followed, driven by the increasing interest of non-buying folk in what their procurement colleagues were up to. The enormous impact of these events was partly a result of upskilling the buyers, but even more a result of non-buying colleagues recognising how a new involvement with procurement could help them be more successful too.

'Another bonus of procurement transformation is to change culture. We live in a digital world where transparency and accountability are mandatory. This requires following the rules, working through checklists and providing evidence for decisions made. None of this is inherently bad, but procedures are often dictated by people who don't understand the real world. That's why, a few years ago, an eminent head teacher resigned his post after giving his reasons: "We have been overtaken by a culture of box-ticking geeks who seem to think you can fatten a pig just by measuring it."

'Procurement transformation turns "can't be done box-ticking" mindsets into "can do". It lifts people out of functional silos and unites them around a common goal. And it makes every individual in the company realise they're part of a cross-business process where the connected "whole" is greater than the sum of the parts – where personal agendas and myopic actions give way to thoughtful, even-handed, joined-up behaviour.

'These stories highlight the two prerequisites for successful transformation: a clear view of where you want to get to and the changes needed to get there; and the deliberate use of change-management techniques, plus the pincer effect of the two journeys. Sir John has the last word: "It is only when you work with rather than against people that achievement and lasting success is possible.'"

Chapter 32

FOR A CHANGE I'm in the USA on other business, but Ed finds out. How does he do this? He asks if I can extend my trip by a day or so and call by. I agree, fly to his part of the country and check in at the usual hotel.

Next day a small group gathers in the conference room. The usual suspects are there from the LA business, and Mishal has arrived as well. We're going to discuss monopolies and cartels.

Monopolies first. 'Many of these are self-imposed by users insisting on non-standard specifications available from only one source,' I begin. 'Or maybe the requirement has been defined by its brand name.'

'Like, "Buy me a Xerox copier"?' suggests Elaine.

'Yeah, rather than saying, "I need the means of copying documents",' adds Rich.

'Exactly. And then sometimes a possible alternative supplier is rejected because of bad experiences in the past, maybe with poor quality or late deliveries. But sellers and buyers can work together to improve performance and thus introduce choice and competition where none currently exists.'

'I'm thinking of the trucking story you told us a while back,' recalls Shirley. 'You know, the one where the customer wanted a better supplier for delivering liquids and helped the "new" trucking company modify its dry-powder wagons to do it. So there was no need to trouble the poorly performing monopoly supplier with more business.'

Other options include establishing new relationships with buyers in other companies using the same product or service, thus increasing bargaining power. We recall the paint company teaming up with a paper business so they could jointly do a better deal purchasing titanium dioxide from a sole supplier.

There's also the remarkable story of a drinks company purchasing bottles from an aggressive supplier insisting on massive price increases. The buyer spent time gleaning market intelligence. They found out who were the other key customers for the bottles, discovered these customers were also suffering price-increase pain, learned the supplier had embarked on an ambitious investment programme, and that their cash flow was tight.

Ed now ponders what he'd do, as a customer, given these facts. 'Y'know, I'm thinking I'd contact the other customers and see if they'd hold back on their orders to exert a cash flow squeeze on the supplier. Then they might be more ready to talk sensibly about pricing.'

Let's just say something like that happened and the supplier yielded. A great example of 'knowledge is power', coupled with concerted action to exert it.

Antony joins the meeting and quickly catches up with where we've got to. He tells a story from his previous life where his company was totally dependent on a well-run family company supplying an expensive rare-metal raw material for his engineering workshops. The metal wasn't widely available elsewhere. The supplier played hardball on price but otherwise offered an excellent service. Pushing for price reductions was a waste of time. Based on previous quality visits to the supplier, Antony's team became convinced the high price was partly a result of wasteful aspects of the supplier's process. Also, money generated from recycling scrap metal was not being credited to the customer's account.

Mishal quickly worked this out. 'So your team was paying for the metal actually shipped to them and also for the scrap the supplier was selling to someone else?'

'That's what we thought, but couldn't prove it,' responds Antony, 'but sharing this opinion with the supplier actually made them defensive and angry, and even more determined not to concede on price.'

'So what did you do?'

'We tried to persuade them we didn't want to reduce their profit margin but we wanted to work with them to eliminate wasted costs...'

'... which would reduce the price you paid because the underlying costs would be less.'

'Just so, but they got even angrier, saying they wouldn't reveal their costings to us.'

We're glad Antony has joined us as everyone is now absorbed in this story and wondering where it's going next.

'We said we didn't want them to open their books; all we wanted was to collaborate on looking for ways of removing wasted costs. By now they'd really worked themselves up.'

Ed again. 'So did you feel they were hiding something given all the fuss they were making?'

'We certainly did, but by then we knew they'd walk away if we kept pressing on price. So we changed tack and looked for other things they could do that would be a cost benefit to us without reducing the price we paid.'

'Such as?'

'They agreed to provide consignment stock with invoicing only upon use, and longer payment terms. We actually saved a lot of money.'

Antony's story is a great example of knowing when to stop pushing on an issue the supplier is sticking on and to start teasing out concessions on other aspects of the deal. These are the negotiation variables. I think it's a good time to show how creative and devastatingly effective these can be.

'A great example recently surfaced in the business press about a CEO negotiating his "golden goodbye" when it was time to leave his company after it was acquired by another,' I tease. 'Want to hear about it?'

Ed looks doubtful.' Sounds like a good after-dinner story but surely nothing to do with monopolies?'

'Agreed, it's not a typical buyer–seller scenario, but the new owners were effectively the monopoly supplier of the leaving package. The outgoing chairman demonstrated stunning creativity in assembling a deal of great value to him, even though the "supplier" had a fixed view about the maximum single payment they'd part with.'

I call up the news item and read it verbatim. '"The chairman has options on 200,000 shares, but he, of course, is already blessed with a unique retirement package awarded by a grateful board. The deal includes four Wimbledon Centre Court and Covent Garden tickets each year, an annual consultancy payment of £150,000, a daily lunch allowance of £100, £60,000 annually for office and other services, a car and chauffeur, travel and hotel expenses and private health cover."'

'Wow, now there's a guy who'd really worked out what he wanted. It was probably worth much more than a single golden-goodbye payment.'

'Most likely, and the lesson is this: some of these variables were of great value to the outgoing chairman but didn't cost the new company much to provide.'

'Like the downtown office and the car ride to work?'

'Those are good examples.'

Ed brings us back to earth. 'So is that the end of the story?'

'Not quite. The deal hung together for a few months, by which time the new company had worked out what it was really costing them. This led to another announcement in the press, along the lines that "the company has renegotiated the chairman's package and has paid a lump sum. There are now no further ongoing payments."'

'I wonder if they did a time value of money calculation,' Ed muses.

'I'm not sure they were up to that, but you can bet the chairman did. How else would he know whether the final pay-off was good or bad? And it was probably more than the sum originally tabled.'

To prove we're taking monopolies seriously, today's provider of lunch is not Davina's Deli but a local competitor. Reassuringly, portion control is as generous as Davina's.

Having comprehensively dealt with the carbs on offer, we return to the topic of non-competitive markets, this time cartels. Recent research shows they're on the increase and getting better at concealing their existence.

Ed interjects. 'Just one point before we move on. You've given plenty of examples of tactics to get better value from monopolies, but no actual figures. Any relevant data?'

'Remember the thirteen, fifteen and twenty-five per cent figures we mentioned a while ago?'

'I do,' Elaine responds. 'They are, in order, the typical cost savings resulting from consolidating fragmented deals, collaborating with suppliers and outmanoeuvring non-competitive markets. Right?'

'Right. So we're talking at least twenty-five per cent savings from better deals in monopoly and cartel situations, and sometimes a lot more. There's also the reduction of supply risk, which is tricky to put money on but worth having.'

'OK,' says Ed, 'so moving to cartels... What's your definition, by the way?'

'It's when different companies collude to inflate prices and to act in concert rather than in competition with each other.'

'How do they know when to do that?' queries Antony.

'They have to be certain they're looking at the same bit of possible business. Imagine a smoke-filled room where the cartel members secretly meet to share info about what their customers have recently asked them to quote for. When they're certain they're quoting for the same job, they can decide whose turn it is to win the contract. Then this company will put in a price and the other suppliers will also send in quotes, but these will be higher. So supplier number one gets the order.'

'Why smoke-filled room?'

'OK, that's dramatic colour, but the cartel members do have to meet in secret partly because collusion is illegal and partly because they don't want to be seen together in public.'

We discuss what can be done to stop cartels kicking off in the first place. The key is to sow seeds of doubt, either making cartel members suspicious of each other or creating uncertainty about whether or not they're looking at the same prospective deal. The tragedy – idiocy even – is that many companies' procedures require buyers to obtain three or more competitive bids before placing a contract. This is commercially naïve as the cartel members compare notes and know they're looking at the same deal. The three-bid approach works fine in genuinely competitive markets but is dangerous when they are not.

'It helps to know what market sectors are tainted by cartel activity,' I continue. 'Useful pointers come from occasional reports in the business press about investigations into cartel activity and the resulting law suits. International fraud and "transparency" surveys also pinpoint countries and cultures where corruption and cartels are normal practice. Past history can help too, when you look at which suppliers or contractors have "won" previous bidding rounds. Be suspicious if last year's successful bidder is now coming in with the highest price. What's changed – other than it's not their turn to win this year's contract? Forensic analysis of price quotes can also reveal murky behaviour.'

Ed again. 'What's this about forensic analysis? Never heard of it!'

Possibly not, as the term has only just occurred to me as another eye-catching idea.

We decide to take a break to clear up the debris from lunch and also to allow emails and calls to be dealt with. It's going to be a busy afternoon dealing with cartels and how detective work uncovers them.

Chapter 33

MISHAL IS FIRST back in the conference room. We join her as she is posting new wall charts headed 'Cartels.' She's clearly expecting to fill them with wisdom hard earned from forays into the supply market jungle.

She takes the lead. 'Right, Jon, take us through forensic analysis.'

I admit to the phrase being another attempt to grab people's interest. 'It's about subjecting an array of prices quoted by different suppliers to a mathematical treatment to see if there are underlying patterns which reveal links between what look like independent bids.'

I recall an oil company investing in offshore exploration and needing vast quantities of steel piping to line the holes they're drilling in the sea bed. The pipe is called 'casing'.

'I'm meeting with procurement director, Lora, when her phone rings, announcing a call from the guy managing the project and wanting an immediate meeting.

'We oblige and find him in aggressive project-manager mode, demanding why the prices he's been quoted for casing are so high and well beyond his budget. His team of buyers had invited bids from five suppliers. Steel piping and casing is a cartel-ridden market, we tell him. He says he knows this, implying that smart arses like us can't tell him anything new. But he reckons he's an important customer so where's the evidence the cartel kicked in this time?

'We're looking at a spreadsheet comparing the prices he's been quoted. Across the top are the names of suppliers who've submitted bids, and down left are listed the different sizes of casing being sourced. Within the grid the prices all look different, but far too high for him. His idea is to cherry pick and buy casing "size one" from the supplier offering the best price, casing "size two" from whichever supplier is best for that one, and so on. But still the total price exceeds his budget. So what can we (smart arses) do about it?

'We'd love to have a conversation about how he's got himself into this mess in the first place and why. If he knows so much about procurement, why did he go competitive bidding in the first place? The suppliers are calling the tune and steering the buyer towards the supplier offering the best price for a particular item. Each supplier then gets the piece of the cake suiting them best, and at the price they want.

'Lora and I exchange glances, wondering how best to respond. And then… a brainwave. I recall a mathematical technique learnt from an excellent CPO in an oil company where I once worked. We hold our breath and apply the maths to the spreadsheet prices. It's like developing a photo in a tray of chemicals. Gradually a picture of clear collusion emerges as we see a consistent item-by-item ratio-relationship appearing between the prices from different suppliers. Each time we do the calculation, the "answer" is 1.03. It's like peeling an onion. On the surface the prices look independent of one another, but the next layer down reveals consistent correlations between them that weren't accidental. Stark evidence of collusion.

'This takes the wind from the project manager's sails and, although it's gratifying, it's mean of us to see how desperate he is for new ideas. The first thing is to cancel this round of bidding and inform the suppliers accordingly. Seeing as it's late in the afternoon we'll start a round of phone calls tomorrow to do this. We stress the need for absolute secrecy as we have to catch the suppliers by surprise.

'Next day certainly brings a surprise, but it's not what we were expecting. Lora takes an early call from one of the suppliers who's angry and wants explanations about why we're cancelling the bidding round. We've no idea how the hell he knows this. Maybe walls do have ears. Or perhaps the cleaning contractor who tidied the project manager's office also inspected the contents of his waste bin. Whatever. Lora wisely says she's not going to discuss this on the phone and invites him in to meet this afternoon. We have the rest of the morning to work out a plan. Importantly, we get the CEO and the project manager on board as we don't want them to be caught out by irate phone calls from the steel suppliers.

'The steel sales director appears after lunch with a backup team. There are terse welcomes and then he's straight in demanding explanations. Why aren't we going ahead and placing orders? What we'd like to say, but don't, is that it's because we think he's part of a cartel. An accusation like that carries the risk of landing us in court, and in any case there's no mileage in letting this get personal. So we recite our pre-planned response: "We're cancelling this bidding round because we have reason to believe we haven't received competitive offers from the marketplace."

'Pressure is piled on by the sales team wanting more information about our reasons, but we sidestep the questions and stick to the party line until they get tired of hearing it. After a while they leave, muttering dark threats which we know won't materialise. The only thing left is to contact the suppliers formally, thanking them for their quotations but announcing cancellation of the bidding round. They won't need an explanation as the guy we've just met will already have seen to it.'

Folks have been quiet while this saga has unfolded and there's a trance-like silence in the room. Ed breaks it, asking 'OK, so that's stuffed the cartel but won't get the steel in. What happened next?'

'A crack sourcing team was urgently put together to search worldwide for an alternative supplier. Incidentally, that's one of the options for dealing with a cartel: if you can't pick off the weakest, look outside and further afield. They found one with a good track record of supplying southern-hemisphere customers and who coincidentally wanted to break into the market up north. Highly competitive prices showed how keen they were to win the order. Negotiable variables came into the equation with the supplier agreeing that the casing would not be paid for until it had been delivered and actually connected to other pipes in the drilling "string" as it disappeared underwater. At that time, one length of casing was joined to the next by screw threads, and any weakness in the steel led to the pipe cracking as the connections were made. Also, the customer would bear the cost of failure. In the new arrangement the pain would be borne by the new supplier, not the drillers.

'Supplies commenced and the learning curve kicked in. Before long, casing was delivered to site so fast that the drillers were being pushed to use it. This was a big change from hanging about waiting for pipe to turn up. Drilling crews love making holes in the sea as fast as possible, and the supplier helped them achieve new performance levels. Sounds nerdish, but worth oh so much money.'

It's been a heavy session so we take a walk outside in the Californian sun. We leave the factory and go round the corner to a fast-food joint for some late-afternoon sustenance. Ed says he'll be along momentarily. People relax and chat about the day's discussion.

'So,' says Mishal, 'have you another cartel story?'

'Yes, and we can talk while we're here. This concerns a company with a manufacturing plant needing regular painting for weather protection. A lot of money is involved and it's a rolling annual programme. So the bids are in from the painting contractors and already something seems fishy.'

'Which is?' Ed has caught up with us, though his question is barely decipherable as it comes through a submarine-sized baguette he's devouring.

'Two things. Firstly, last year's lowest bidder now comes in with the highest bid...'

Elaine pounces. 'Which suggests that this year it's not their turn to win the business?'

'Seems so. Also, one bid is much lower than the others, and even then it's a lot higher than the budget, which was based on last year's actual cost.'

Ed agrees. 'Yep, this is looking suspicious.'

'And the cartel was able to kick in because the customer was predictable with its purchasing and always sought several bids. So all the contractors knew they were looking at the same job.' Shirley's now on the case as well!

As in the previous story, the customer cancelled the bidding round and then worked on a new approach. Market intelligence was gathered, revealing that the contractors bought paint from three suppliers, all of whom were in the clear cartel-wise. An idea germinated: why not ask one of the paint suppliers to take on the painting project? Of the three, one showed at least some interest in this idea, although the company wasn't experienced in supervising contract work. 'No problem,' said the customer, 'we can help you there, so all you need to do is get labour prices from the painting contactors to apply the paint. Further, let's disguise the approaches we make to them. In one case, let's specify the total job and ask for a lump sum quote. For another contractor, just ask for the unit rate for labour without saying where the job is. In another case, a subsidiary of the paint company was asked to make the approach, again not mentioning where the job was.

'So what happened next?' checks Shirley.

'It introduced too much uncertainty and doubt into the situation for the cartel members to be sure they were looking at the same job. They decided they weren't and proceeded to make independent bids instead of concocting artificially inflated ones.'

Ed again: 'And was there a cost saving?'

'The painting project came in thirty per cent lower than the initial bids and, pro rata, also lower than the previous year.'

'So the learning is …?'

'Don't be predictable in the way you approach the supply market, be on the lookout for tell-tale signs that a cartel is operating, and create confusion and doubt to prevent the cartel activating in the first place.'

Cartels turned out to require more discussion than we'd expected, but it's time well spent, and all the more pleasant for being in a place with windows and fresh air. We decide we've had enough 'distorted market' excitement for one day and I'm free to return to the hotel. I'm not to know I'll only be coming back to Ed's place one more time in the future.

Chapter 34

September – England

I'VE BEEN INVITED to a meeting at one of the UK's northern universities to imagine how procurement might look in future. It's a gorgeous late-summer day. Approaching the university, I'm struck by how the architecture of the buildings reflects what goes on inside them. The space technology building is dominated by a huge clock tower reaching skywards, like a Saturn rocket poised for lift-off. Sharply pointed steeples on the medical school suggest hypodermic procedures going on inside. The students' union building looks like an old pub. And the business school, where I'm headed, has lots of hot-air ventilation grilles. Enough said.

The long, narrow meeting room is just big enough to accommodate us eight invitees. It's hot in there. Heat input from the sun is controlled by light-grey and yellow roller blinds all in the 'down' position. Heat out is achieved by keeping the door open. Not exactly high-tech. The ceiling is assembled from what appear to be inverted washing-up bowls creating an effect like an egg-box. Not pretty, but probably cost effective.

Apparently, 'the future' starts in two hours' time, when we're invited to stay for dinner. So we focus on making menu choices. This done, we're asked to look further ahead, namely fifteen years. Our host, the senior lecturer who's running the project, wants to produce several possible scenarios of the future. Companies can then choose which one they prefer and start planning accordingly. Right now we discuss the supply-management scenario where 'everything changes'. But the research assumes that everything else in the business world continues to operate 'as now'. What if there are fundamental changes to corporate structures, ownership and financial accounting conventions? Will we see the end of 'functions'? Will robots and artificial intelligence rule the roost? This is good kite-flying stuff, but we're asked to behave ourselves and concentrate on supply management.

The general opinion is that the structure and behaviours of supply markets for what might be called primary sources, such as raw materials, will continue to operate much as now, warts and all. But significant change will occur in the space between these sources and the ultimate customers. For example, new technologies have the power to transform distribution arrangements. Drones and 3D printing are frequently mentioned. Capital projects get larger and happen more quickly, in turn making greater demands on contractors and others who turn drawing-board dreams into reality. We believe the gap between customers and primary sources could diminish as companies do more vertical integration.

We examine how these possible changes will affect supply-management activities. The need to make good deals and execute ambitious supply strategies will remain, but there'll be increasing emphasis on almost continual surveillance of supply markets in order to detect opportunities or threats to the buyer's company. This will require procurement teams to be directly involved in developing company strategy and constantly relating their work to it.

Procurement folk will live more in the future than they do now – at least, some will. I mention a company CPO who told me where he spent most of his thinking and planning time. At that time it was one year ahead while the materials controllers were occupied with hourly and daily events. The average time horizon across his whole team was one month. The plan was to bring this average up to one year, and his time would then be focused on issues three to five years ahead. In contrast, a European survey found some senior managers spending only three to four per cent of their time thinking about the future, whereas the CPO mentioned is already at the thirty to forty per cent level. And somehow his company goes along just fine while achieving ever higher levels of performance. What a change from the fire-fighting atmosphere in many companies where, never mind tomorrow, the challenge is more to do with finding out what happened yesterday.

We discuss the dangers of procurement positioning itself as a profession to be followed only by the qualified few. I remember a procurement head saying that a 'professional fence has to be erected to stop other people coming in and taking over our job'. Fortunately, other, wiser, heads were present and saw this line of argument as a recipe for eventual extinction. But they totally advocated the need for professionalism in procurement practice. So here we have the stark contrast between those who see procurement as a closed shop and those who see it as a cross-business process which needs inspiring leadership promulgating the values and principles of best practice to make strategic impact.

My neighbour at the table hasn't said much so far but now comes alive, suggesting that, to survive in future, procurement has to get a lot better at explaining its *raison d'être*. We need to bust many of the myths that lead people to believe that buying is simple, and hammer home the realities of the supply market and its workings where only commercially savvy buyers can survive.

Two hours pass swiftly and harmlessly before our host says it's time to stop. She says the meeting has been helpful, and invites closing comments. We observe that the emphasis has been on 'where are we going to?', but there's little mention of 'where are we starting from?' A statement on this would be useful to define the gap between now and the future and so define the challenges for procurement and its preparedness to surmount them. It will also help to understand what have been the major changes in procurement over recent years and what has driven them. There's no guarantee that these drivers of change will continue, but the analysis will shed light on what influences procurement's impact and, conversely, how it has influenced business in general. All this will 'ground' the study in reality.

Dinner awaits, and we adjourn to the business school bar, which would not look out of place in a five-star hotel. Two professors join us to help consume the liquid hospitality for which they have given prior approval. I choose a bottle of real ale from the fridge. This prompts technical input from one of our discussion group who comes from the food and drinks business. He asserts that if the drinks fridge is constantly illuminated and the drink is in a clear glass bottle, then the light will slowly degrade it and it won't be worth drinking after a month. Apparently the sub-zero temperatures at which some drinks are stored serves to hide how bad they taste once they've gone off.

At last we're summoned to the restaurant, our seats being identified by place-name tent cards stating what we chose from the menu only two hours ago. The guy next to me selected the aubergine and courgette bake but instead gets free range chicken wrapped in Parma ham which, the waiter insists, is what he ordered. So a minor delivery issue here demonstrates how, even in supply chain academia, the unexpected crops up.

That's actually going to be a defining quality in the future: the ability to handle the unexpected. Crazy things do happen, and the daily press faithfully reports them. What else but a tabloid newspaper would carry the headline, 'Holy Moly! Nuns on the run caught speeding at 120 miles per hour as they dash to see injured Pope.' The Sister driving the much-used car told the Italian police, 'We heard the Pope had fallen over and we were on our way to make sure he was OK.' The paper said the police 'chose not to side with the Lord' and instead ticketed the nun with a large fine and a one-month suspension. Perhaps even more surprising is that the nuns actually got such a high speed out of an old car well past its 'sell-by' date.

And then there's the zealous traffic warden who was sent for 'retraining' after ticketing a bus as it picked up passengers at a bus stop. The driver thought it was a practical joke as the warden emerged from the queue and booked him. 'He told me the bus had been booked because it had parked in a restricted area,' said the driver. 'I said, "Restricted to who?", and he said, "Buses." Then he said I shouldn't be parked there while the passengers were still getting on.'

Worryingly, the French appear to favour blowing things up as a quick way to settle industrial disputes. Not long ago, workers at a factory in France, which was up for sale, threatened to blow up the building unless they were paid severance compensation. The employees said they would detonate bottles of gas in the factory unless a new owner could come up with the funds. 'The gas bottles are in the factory. Everything is ready for it to blow up,' said a union rep.

Presumably this succeeded in releasing the necessary funds, as the stunt was copied some months later by striking French factory workers who threatened to destroy their place of employment in the latest round of hostile industrial actions aimed at stalling economic reforms. The idea was to light a trail of wooden pallets which would act as a fuse leading to a propane gas tank near the main building of the factory.

Meanwhile in Essex, England, an attempt to set a new world record for the number of women being photographed wearing bikinis in one place failed after only forty-two of the required 1,094 turned up.

You couldn't make this stuff up, but it is out there. Truth is stranger than fiction, and the 'unexpected' is always ready to become reality.

In the bar again after dinner my fellow diners have departed and the academics have returned to their think tanks. Now alone, I order another clear-bottled beer in order to stop it going off, and muse on crazy happenings and how to manage uncertainty. The point is that we can't predict what the future holds, and extrapolating trends from the past only provides a base line that shows how wrong we can be. In fact, working from past history can be downright dangerous because we humans instinctively reject data that doesn't fit our preconceived ideas of what is credible. While it's vital to envisage future scenarios and make strategies to deal with them, it's also necessary to be as good at possible at handling unexpected events while hoping we can get lucky in the process.

There will be many such situations. The tectonic plates that support the way we customarily do things around politics, finance, social behaviour, law and order are shifting and creaking under pressure from social unrest, wars and natural disasters. Meanwhile, technology races ahead, hopefully for the common good but, in the process, shows just how creative humans can be in finding new ways of circumventing the rules, committing crime and enforcing religious extremism.

Free-flowing scenario planning helps us to think about the unthinkable, especially if creativity techniques are employed to expand the realm of, albeit unlikely, possibilities. This makes 'the unexpected' smaller, but it's still there and it's where the so-called 'black swan' events come from. Once upon a time people thought swans were only coloured white. Black ones were impossible, but they did actually exist in Western Australia. So the 'unexpected' consists of events that we just haven't thought of. If we had thought of them, they would have been assigned some sort of probability. This would label them 'unlikely' rather than 'unexpected'.

So how do we handle what the future throws at us? Having active strategies helps, since momentum is created as they are put into practice. If the unexpected happens it is easier to respond if we're already on the move rather than cranking up from a standing start. Also, the goal of the strategy continues to provide direction, although the path to the goal may now be different.

Sport offers useful anecdotes. Before an important qualifying match, one football manager asserted, 'We can't predict the future, but if we're in control of ourselves and our performance then we'll be OK.' As it happened, his team won the match against the odds. The post-match interview found him in celebratory mood: 'Look what happens when you have a plan in place!'

My Keep-Beer-Fresh campaign needs topping up and, while I wait for the drink to be poured, my mind wanders back to past travels across Hong Kong's Victoria Harbour. Dinky little Star Ferries ceaselessly ply its murky waters and I was on one going to the eastern shore's magnificent Convention and Exhibition Centre. The journey wasn't long but there was time to scan various notices on board. One said, 'No Spitting', while another below warned, 'Wet Floor'. I'm not sure which notice came first. And then there was the Kowloon-side travel agency promoting holidays with straight-talking candour: 'If you look anything like your passport photo then you definitely need a break.'

However, this wasn't a holiday, but a conference in the Convention Centre. I listened to a highly accomplished Chinese businessman attributing his success to luck. It didn't seem credible, and he and I analysed things over coffee during the break. He reckoned that seventy-five per cent of his success came from hard work, ten per cent from charity work which gave him peace of mind, and ten per cent from listening to the Feng Shui fortune man. That's ninety-five per cent of what we decided to call 'planned luck', leaving five per cent for 'pure luck'. This seemed more reasonable.

Another Hong Kong business lady joined our discussion and contributed her own definition of planned luck: 'Luck is where preparation meets opportunity.' The Asians know a thing or two about what they see as three types of luck, but perhaps it was Louis Pasteur who also hinted at 'planned luck' by noting that 'chance favours only the prepared mind'.

Penicillin pioneer Alexander Fleming came up with something similar. He said, 'The unprepared mind cannot see the outstretched hand of opportunity.' He went on to say, 'One sometimes finds what one is not looking for. When I woke up just after dawn on Sept. 28, 1928, I certainly didn't plan to revolutionise all medicine by discovering the world's first antibiotic, or bacteria killer. But I guess that was exactly what I did.'

Perhaps there's another less-publicised benefit of having a strategy: that we're consciously looking at ways of achieving it without knowing precisely 'how'. But the fact that the strategy radar is active increases the chance of finding what we weren't looking for.

Despite the consistent theme that being prepared helps us handle the unexpected, the right attitude is also useful. UK psychology research examined why some people get all the luck while others never get the breaks they deserve. The research identified four characteristics of the 'lucky' mindset. People who have this can imagine success, which helps them create self-fulfilling prophecies. They are resilient, think positively in the face of adversity, and are skilled at creating and noticing chance opportunities. And, perhaps most powerfully, they listen to intuition.

There is a plausible, albeit untested, connection between these observations and those of the Chinese tycoon: doing charity work involves doing something different with different people (increasing the likelihood of chance opportunities), and acting on the advice of the Feng Shui man must depend more on gut feel and intuition than on logic.

While the bad news is that intuition can't be audited, the good news says it comes from a lifetime of experience.

In 2009, a plane carrying 155 passengers and crew suffered a bird strike just after leaving New York's La Guardia airport. Split second decisions were needed and, deciding not to head back to the airport, pilot Chesley B Sullenberger, ('Sully', with forty years' experience and 20,000 flying hours behind him) heroically 'landed' in the Hudson River. Only 208 seconds elapsed between bird-struck engine failure and splash down. No one lost their life, although they did get wet.

In due course, the film Sully came out. This was a riveting account of the follow-up to the incident rather than the event itself. We saw the sneering behaviour of the investigators trying to blame the pilot for making the wrong decision, their reasoning based on what turned out to be a flawed simulation of actual events. In describing the investigating board's task, a film critic unwittingly provided a superb definition of 'instinct': 'The big question the board has to answer is this: are Sully and his co-pilot heroes, or did they in fact impulsively risk 155 lives on instinct? To the board, instinct is nothing more than a twitch of the gut. But for Sully, it is expertise, ingrained by decades of quietly doing things well, the patterns of which run deeper than knowledge or habit.'

Sully was proved to be right. Instinct? Intuition? It ain't what you say, it's the way that you feel it.

In an uncertain future where actions need to be rapid, dependable, imaginative and effective, forecasting can scope out the risks and possibilities, but human commitment and resourcefulness is what counts when dealing with whatever actually turns up. The future belongs not to those who seek to predict it or to repeat the past, but to those who have the capability to deal with whatever the future will throw at them, and especially to those having the ability to make planned luck.

The uni bar is now empty and I'm tapped on the shoulder by the barman who says it's time to go. He wants to close up and turn off the lights, probably to help the beer degrade more slowly. It's been an interesting day about a thought-provoking future where speeding nuns, traffic wardens, propane tanks and bikinis have all proved they have the potential to surprise us.

Chapter 35

THE PLANE TOUCHES down in the country of the speeding nuns, although this is the island refuge of Sardinia. CEO Carol has called the AeroCorp business chiefs together at this secluded location to discuss 'the future'. It's an attempt to expect the unexpected, to prepare the businesses to be in great shape just in case the whole company is sold in the coming months. This must be what Ed alluded to.

The venue is a boutique seaside hotel at the top of the north-east coast. When I arrive it's early evening, with the setting sun illuminating offshore islands in stunning golds and reds. Fancy yachts sail homewards, reefing their sails as they motor to no-doubt expensive moorings. It's still and warm, and the AeroCorp folk have settled down to sunset cocktails on the terrace overlooking a swimming pool. Since most of them have come in from the USA, I wonder why they've been asked to fly to Europe for this session. Sardinia seems a way-out location for this meeting as it's only the Italians who are on home ground, but I guess it's because they're on the margins of the Division and this location will make them feel more involved. Perhaps it's Carol's cunning plan to lull the feisty Americans into jet-lagged acquiescence. On the other hand, their journey provided the opportunity to see how the aircraft bits they make actually perform in practice.

Ed is hiding behind a large potted fern and emerges to introduce me to his colleagues, among whom I sense some tension. In fact, I've already heard that this group got together only two weeks ago in the USA and there was 'a lot of venting'. Although AeroCorp is making good progress under Carol's leadership, it seems there's still a lot of baggage left behind by her predecessor. Apparently one President vented particularly spectacularly, saying, 'AeroCorp's management process was forty years behind the times and, based on every screw-up they'd experienced, operating like a cottage industry throughout.'

Another colleague at the blood-letting observed that 'the previous leadership team in the UK did an excellent job of cost control, but didn't know a damn thing about growing the company'.

So they're a hot-headed bunch and not afraid to say it as they feel it.

Two of the hotheads are included in the group now. They're all from varied backgrounds and I've met some before. 'Hi,' say Dora, Sydney, Nick and Tara. New to me are Sylvio, who is CEO of the Italian company, and two more Presidents from the US companies: Byron, a former fighter pilot, and Rex, who served in submarines. None of them suffers fools lightly and Ed hints I've been invited along to provide mediation and soothing words should things get too lively. After all, their livelihoods and their businesses are possibly at stake. If it doesn't go well there'll be more venting.

However, conversation is amiable enough and Paulo the maître-d' calls us into dinner. We're getting the tasting menu so don't have to pore over the à la carte. That said, Sydney spots a number of no-nos on the list – clams, cuttlefish and tentacles – so he goes instead for real food in the form of spaghetti carbonara followed by steak. The rest of us negotiate our way through the tasting menu, which consists of appetising but small delicacies served on huge plates. Space not occupied by food is decorated with smears of jus or dobs of something else so the whole effect is picturesque if not filling. However, the whole turns out to be greater than the sum of the parts and we leave the table quite satisfied.

The following day we convene in a glass-walled meeting room with views of tree-planted lawns sloping gently to the sea. We wonder why much of the grass has been indiscriminately dug up. Apparently the wild boar, which overrun the island, have been in overnight foraging for their own tasting menu.

Carol kicks things off by going through AeroCorp's core values. She uses an acronym to tie these down. I'm not sure anyone's seen these core values before and I suspect it's Carol's ploy to lay the ground rules for this meeting. Anyway, it seems to work, although there's some restlessness in the room as these action-oriented types want something more practical to work on.

Next, Ed gives a quick round-up of recent and forecast performance across AeroCorp. Significant cost savings have been secured by doing procurement differently. He cites better contracts aimed at improving supply security and increasing collaboration. Further cost-saving opportunities for the forthcoming year have been identified, equivalent to six per cent of annual spend. This is not a ball-park figure but is based on an item-by-item assessment of what cost-reduction approach will be used with which suppliers. So the target is credible.

Carol points out that, despite the emphasis on cost savings, the targets are more to do with sustaining ongoing financial performance and are not the end game.

196

Other facets of the business are put under the spotlight, leading to the consensus that AeroCorp is in good health but still possesses the potential to improve its appeal to a future buyer. This is the first time I've heard it directly said that the sale of AeroCorp might be in the offing. In fact, this is the cue for Carol to say we'll be using a different approach to strategic planning. Rather than looking at how supply markets can be raided for more savings she wants us specifically to determine how the various driving forces in the business, procurement being one of them, can contribute to what she calls 'maximum enterprise value' in future. And so the concept of EVmax is born. We agree this will encourage a more fundamental look at how the business creates wealth.

And then there's the 'multiple'. Nick explains how enterprise value is calculated by multiplying earnings, before interest and tax, by the 'multiple'. The price eventually paid for the business will equate to enterprise value minus debt. Working out the multiple seems something of a black art as there's no precise calculation available. It depends on things like the outlook for the sector in which the business operates, the market position (dominance) of the company, the security of future cash flows and, reassuringly, human talent. It's all very subjective.

This takes up most of the morning, hastened along by regular deliveries of coffee and amaretti biscuits made, it says on the packet, to 'our grandmother's secret recipe'. Davina's Deli and giant muffins seem a million calories and a long way away.

As architect of the meeting, and concerned to head off any venting, Ed insists lunch will be taken together in a different location. 'Together,' he says, 'means no phones, no messages and no surreptitious contacts with the home office.'

A small bus awaits at the hotel's stylish entrance on the small, tree-lined road leading to the beach. We're heading for another location just eight kilometres up the coast where there's a beach restaurant.

After a light lunch we venture on to a pink-granite promontory thrusting out into azure sea. This was where the Romans used to quarry stone for shipment to wherever in the Mediterranean was the site of their latest building project.

We're intrigued to stumble upon rough-hewn columns still lying there and cubes of rock awaiting splitting. We see lines of small holes driven into granite slabs into which they hammered metal wedges until the rock split. Another method involved inserting dry wooden pegs which, on being soaked with water, expanded and split the rock. A great example of mind over matter.

And what the Roman slaves didn't fashion, nature did. Wind and water has shaped massive boulders into fantastical smooth, rounded forms, any of which could be exhibited as modern art. It's a special place.

Back at the hotel we resume our assault on EVmax. Carol produces another acronym: CHIP.

Byron thinks this is appropriate since we've just got back from seeing how the Romans chipped away at old blocks, but he gets a cool look from Carol.

'Byron, we're not looking to chip away at our performance but to deliver significant improvements. If anyone's got a better idea for an acronym then just let me know.'

It looks like Carol's been quietly generating acronyms and is pissed off because her efforts aren't being taken seriously.

Rex intervenes. 'OK, take us through it, letter by letter.'

Carol obliges. 'The whole word basically captures the components of EVmax. C, for example, represents the Commercial assets of the business.'

'Like…?'

'Like earnings and overall financial performance, especially relative to our competitors; debts and borrowings; the position AeroCorp occupies in its market and the attractiveness of that market in general, especially to a prospective buyer of the company.'

Ed spots an omission. 'Carol, should it also include the customer and supply contracts we have in place which ensure attractive revenues and cash flows in future?'

'Absolutely. Then there's H for Human capital. I've already talked to Sydney about this to benefit from his background in HR. Sydney?'

Sydney snaps to attention, looking up from the notepad upon which he's been toying with alternative acronyms alongside the odd doodle. 'Er, yes. What we're looking at here is the value of the people in the company: their expertise, motivation, loyalty, creativity and professionalism. There's also their flexibility in terms of managing change and dealing with the unexpected.'

Happy to have Sydney's attention again, Carol continues with I: 'This covers the Intangible aspects of the company, especially as seen through the eyes of a prospective new owner. Let's go round the table for your suggestions.'

Dora kicks off. 'OK, things that fit in with a buyer's game plan, like our business strategy being consistent with theirs?'

Others join in.

'Our markets, and our relationships with key suppliers and customers.'

'Our company brand.'

'And our image in the public eye, with our trading partners, the finance community and with the regulatory authorities.'

Carol's pleased with this response, proving she's successfully awoken people from post-lunch torpor.

'Let me guess,' offers Ed, 'P represents the one thing we haven't included so far, namely the Physical assets of the Group.'

Carol concurs. 'It does indeed – not just the equipment and inventories we have, but also our properties, operating systems and IT infrastructure.'

There's some debate about whether or not CHIP refers to EV or the multiple. This looks like it could go on indefinitely so Carol says if we focus on what puts the 'max' into EV then we won't go far wrong.

There's a momentary lull in the room, with people seemingly thinking, 'OK, that's done, then. Can we go home now?'

Carol suggests a short comfort break, after which she initiates general discussion on what might be the relative importance to a buyer of each part of CHIP. 'Rex, you've had a previous life as a takeover specialist. What's your view?

'Well, each purchaser will have a different weighting, depending on their individual priorities and timelines.'

'Your mission was turnarounds rather than long-term ownership, wasn't it?'

'Correct. Our hold period was generally three to five years. We looked for fundamentally strong businesses with exceptional brand recognition in their particular niche of business, but which, for one reason or another, were performing sub-optimally.'

We all agree we need to position AeroCorp as an attractive takeover prospect, but the weightings would probably be similar if a new owner was instead looking for long-term ownership.

Coffee and biscuits put in a timely appearance. The label on the amaretti packet tells Byron it's OK to dunk them in his coffee. This produces an intriguing liquid–solid sensation and overcomes the tooth-breaking risk of biting too vigorously into the biscuit. The downside is that the practice leaves a dodgy-looking sludge in the bottom of the cup. Timing is everything, though. Dunk for too short a time and the biscuit merely gets wet; too long and only the bit left above water-level remains intact and dentally dangerous. Give them half a chance and the engineers round the table would start writing equations to calculate optimum dunk time, but Carol returns to the weightings.

Discussions continue late into the afternoon, concluding that the CHIP recipe is forty per cent Commercial, fifteen per cent Human, thirty per cent Intangibles, and fifteen per cent Physical assets. Rex believes his old takeover colleagues would agree with these numbers. The numbers point to where we should spend most of our time tomorrow getting EVmax-ready.

We adjourn for more cocktails around the pool prior to dinner and another encounter with the tasting menu. This evening's offerings feature swordfish and beautifully herbed bits of lamb. But they've managed to smuggle cuttlefish on to the menu again in the form of ground-up black bits. Sydney plays safe and sticks with carbonara and steak again.

The next day we divide our resources according to the 'we buy, we transform, we sell' formula. Rex and Sylvio have 'sell' hats on; Sydney, Tara and Byron will look at the internal 'transform' operations; Ed and Dora the 'buy'; while Carol and Nick join forces to address finances and investor attractiveness. I'm invited to join the 'buy' group.

We make a matrix with CHIP written across the top and, as we're the 'buy' team, the five key components of procurement's contribution to business performance written down the side.

'Remind me what the five are?' says Dora.

Ed obliges. 'Sales Growth, Improved Costs and Margins, Optimised Cash and Working Capital, Secure Supplies and Relationships and …' after a short pause for thought, '… Better Productivity and Processes.'

The man has total recall.

'What do we do next?' asks Dora.

I suggest we fill in the cells in the matrix and, for example, determine what procurement can do to help grow sales, which is part of the 'C' in CHIP, the commercial assets of the business.

Ed agrees and quickly we have some ideas. For example, we need to get better at evaluating target customers' procurement strategies and assessing AeroCorp's position relative to them.

Looking at me, Dora asks, 'This is fine in general, but are there some specifics?'

'OK, we have to learn more about their company strategy and then decide how we can complement it. How do they view us as a supplier? Then, what are their bid evaluation methods and their decision-making processes? Also, what can we offer that will give their procurement team a "win" in the eyes of their colleagues. Things like that.'

We continue in this mode for some time and the cells in the matrix are quickly populated. Ed suggests we try something less obvious. For example, we've included 'brand' as part of the Intangible value of the company. How could, say, 'Secure Supplies and Relationships' connect with 'brand'? This turns out to be easier than we thought as 'reputation' quickly emerges as a top priority – for example, having a reputation for dealing only with ethical supply chains.

All this prompts discussion about what AeroCorp's own brand is and we decide the Division has these attributes: innovation, responsiveness, agility, technical excellence, ethics, market leadership, and being where the action and the new thinking is. These values need to be mirrored by our key suppliers and be the primary tests of supplier assessment when we're looking for close collaboration. Where we don't have these measures in place, then part of the EVmax strategy will be to implant them.

Discussion is intense and, judging by the level hum of conversation in the room, productive. Time passes quickly and the comments in each cell of the matrix add up to a comprehensive list of procurement actions that will help to put the 'max' into EV.

The 'transform' and 'sell' teams have also produced lists. One common theme is the plan to develop markets and production facilities in new territories. This will need a lot of procurement work as well in order to establish supply lines and, not least, set up supply bases for the Capex projects to build new factories.

The feeling in the room is that we've done enough on this. Someone now needs to collate all the output. Ed volunteers and earns Carol's thanks.

Although the time for another crack at the tasting menu draws near, some venting is apparently necessary before everyone can feel satisfied with their day. Byron thinks AeroCorp has grown big on the back of its constituent businesses which, back in the past, were quite small.

'A lot of small-time MDs have failed to grow in the process and are incapable of seeing any vision of the future,' asserts Byron. So he feels strongly about this. Carol looks a bit pained, although it's not clear whether she's thinking a day's good team-building is about to go down the pan, or whether AeroCorp's legacy is about to jump out and bite them.

Ed gets the discussion back on track with ideas about how the EVmax plans can be upward sold to the Penserin board. The reminder that Penserin is a class act effectively defuses things and conversation turns to lighter topics. This sort of free-wheeling discussion works well over drinks, so these are ordered and Carol calls business to a close.

Chapter 36

London

IT'S AUTUMN IN London and I approach the conference centre along pavements thick with fallen leaves. A frisky wind swirls and successfully sweeps them up. I haven't heard much from AeroCorp since we met in Sardinia, so I don't know if they're still venting about Group or busy maximising EV. However, regular contact with Ed and Mishal says they're getting along just fine.

Conference registration is quick and efficient. I'm directed to elevators heading for the fifteenth floor and spectacular views of some of London's iconic buildings. Conference staff signal where people should go. Much thought and experience has gone into making things happen smoothly. The whole floor is used as a mingling area, with several coffee stations spaced around so queuing is not an issue.

I talk to some of the folk manning stands exhibiting the wares of conference sponsors, most of whom are offering technical solutions to procurement problems One keen-eyed salesman persuades me to be the first to enter his prize draw, promising that winning is a dead cert if no one else puts their business card in the jar. His company offers a purchasing card service and he invites an opinion on how important the 'pay process' is to the supplier. Bit of a no-brainer, I would have thought.

It's like a trick question, so the consultant's standard fence-sitting answer seems appropriate while thinking how to respond. 'It depends what the situation is …' and I realise this actually is the right line to take. 'If the supplier's strapped for cash then getting the money is all important. But if cash flow isn't a problem then they'll be more interested in 'certainty'. They want confidence the money will arrive when promised. This avoids the hassle of last-minute borrowing or debt renegotiation and they can plan for other cash outflows.

He returns to quizzing me more, like how the bank-card sales pitch needs to be tuned to where a customer is on their procurement-maturity journey. This stretches from 'silo-service' right through to 'intelligent organism', I

203

tell him. But I'm saved by the bell. An airport-type tannoy message invites delegates to go to the main conference arena, next floor up. Some 400 of us move obediently to a spacious hall softly lit by blue spotlights and the glow from large screens on stage. We settle down for the show.

Opening comments from the chairperson are brisk and business-like, and the first speaker is introduced. He's an economist surveying the global economy. We're treated to a plethora of spreadsheets with a sleep-inducing voice-over. It's performances like this that have labelled economics the 'dismal science', so it's not the best start to the day. It's a shame, as this science can, in the right hands, be stimulating. I would rather have heard about behavioural economics and the recent Nobel prize-winning research into how irrational choices affect buyer–seller behaviour.

It's around spreadsheet number three when my mind drifts back a few years to an excellent discourse from the senior economist at one of the major banks. He was blind and, as conference chair, I could see his hands clasped behind his back, fingers skating over braille-imprinted cue-cards. This was just before the financial markets went pear-shaped. The problem, in his view, was the huge amount of debt in the world and no one knew where it was. But we weren't to worry as economists were on the case, their credibility ensured by the fact they'd correctly predicted seven out of the last five recessions! He went on to talk about finance ministers he'd met, referring to one especially dour character who could be relied upon to 'brighten a room just by leaving it'. We applauded his efforts with gusto, and it is applause now, albeit lukewarm, that brings me back to the current proceedings.

The next topic is the state of the European Union which, as a conference tonic, does not hit the spot. I'm wondering how these subjects relate at all to the conference theme of 'Unlocking Competitive Advantage'.

Mid-morning refreshments provide the opportunity to meet fellow delegates while avoiding the man selling purchasing cards. I make a covert inspection of the prize draw jar. Two more entries have arrived so I'm still in with a chance of winning a prize, even if it's only third.

Back in the main hall, the topics for the rest of the morning more obviously connect with the conference theme. Proceedings get off to a cracking start with a ten-minute input from a sales/procurement expert whose insights entirely justify that label. He starts by expressing his amazement as to why so few CPOs read books about sales techniques. We've all been issued with handsets allowing us to vote on things, and his amazement is justified as only thirty per cent of the people in the hall have done so. That leaves seventy per cent who either can't read or prefer other subjects. Further probing reveals only twenty-one per cent of those present do deep research into the salesperson. He then gives, at high speed, a spellbinding summary of how he researches a buyer: starting with a look at their LinkedIn page, personal data, links, what groups they're in and who else is in them. Then he looks at Twitter feeds, and what annoys them. Then Facebook and Instagram surveys. Then a Google search for any mentions in trade magazines or press releases. All this is aimed at creating rapport when he meets them, and gaining access to the decision-influencing part of the brain that's not rational.

We'd like to hear much more of this, especially as time could've been freed up had the economics chap been forced into a ten-minute slot instead.

The rest of the morning is reasonably interesting, with 'inclusivity' and 'collaboration' being on trend. Collaboration between company departments is advocated, although most delegates would have known for a long time that this was a Good Thing.

Some on-stage collaboration is exhibited by a CPO and an HR chief who share some case histories. But I'm riled by the CPO when he declares that 'procurement and HR have much in common as we're both cost centres to the business supplying services to it'. This reflects the mindset of a company split into silo functions, where top management is more concerned with managing what the company has become rather than with managing what it was set up to do in the first place.

The folk at Gullmech would be riled as well. Defining procurement's *raison d'être* in terms of providing service, making cost savings, even adding value, all suggest an activity feeling the need to prove why it should exist. But if you're in business then you're in procurement. It's not discretionary. The real choice is to decide how good you're going to be at it. That guy in the Rockies – 'we buy, we transform and we sell' – was absolutely certain about what drove his business and where talents and time should be focused.

Lunch is a demonstration of high-performance catering. Little dishes of starters and desserts are provided on tables strategically located around the fifteenth floor gathering-space. Then there's a long counter with several choices of mains, also served in small bowls. This approach permits eating and networking on the hoof in a free-flowing way which wouldn't be possible were we seated at table.

We've been told that a CPO-profiling survey report can be found on one of the stands. I track this down and flip through it. It looks interesting and could be a useful diversion if an afternoon session fails to engage. It's a first-of-its-kind psychometric study into the core characteristics of successful procurement leaders.

The afternoon programme starts with a choice of breakout sessions. These avoid the risk of a conference hall full of slumbering delegates with the hapless speaker on the so-called 'graveyard shift' trying to waken them from post-lunch slumber. Physical activity also sharpens the brain as we walk to different floors to find the venues. I choose the session on procurement risk. This is a sensible presentation, one takeaway being that the least expected things can happen as well as the most expected. I think of French saboteurs and speeding nuns. The speaker reckons a risk strategy should focus twenty per cent on risk mitigation and eighty per cent on risk management, the emphasis not being on 'if it happens' but more on 'what to do when it does'.

We return to the main hall and listen to a well-structured talk on government procurement. In itself this is good but, as a taxpayer, I'm irritated to hear about yet another attempt to bring government spending up to date. More than thirty years ago the UK government set out to do this by forming the Central Unit on Purchasing (CUP). They did good things, made lots of savings and enabled its head honcho to sail into the sunset clutching a New Year honour. Ditto at least two times again in subsequent years but still not good enough to prevent, some twenty-five years after the CUP's formation, what a British MP called a 'gold standard cock-up' in military procurement. That was about helicopters.

Frustratingly, success is always judged by how many cost savings were made. All this does is allow a new initiative to show how many savings were left on the table by the previous one. Improvements would be more permanent and far-reaching if profound change had been on the agenda rather than cutting sharper deals.

But the current speaker seems to get this and is bent on making organic change in government procurement. This is heartening. Procurement transformation not only moves company performance to a new level but also embeds a new culture and agile organisational dynamics, equipping the organisation superbly to handle tomorrow's world and its 'black swan' surprises. It can also change people's lives and tap into human motivation and resourcefulness not evident hitherto.

There's a brief tea break, after which the speaker from an international pharma company insists that inclusive practices are no longer nice to have but are essential for competitive advantage. I assume he's referring to collaborative relationships both inside and outside the company. This is an old story but it needs continual retelling since senior procurement people still refer to their work as a 'function' serving the business rather than having a direct involvement in making business happen. Business doesn't work unless there's a supply base, and innovation often comes better from outside when customers realise they don't always know best.

He concludes with a warning: the procurement profession has to evolve or it may not exist in twenty to thirty years' time. I think this is a dead cert if procurement seeks immortality by ring-fencing itself in as a profession which only the qualified few may pursue. Certainly professionalism and knowledge is vital, and highly developed procurement specialists will always have their place. But business entities, public and private, will only achieve and deliver anything like EVmax if procurement is positioned as a key business-management activity that can be headed up by any senior executive with the right leadership qualities, and possibly CEO potential.

Remember the maxim: 'Procurement is like managing a large part of our company, which we cannot see and which is staffed by people we don't employ. That's a lot more challenging than just placing orders.' Maybe this perception of procurement's role, unequivocally accepted right across the business world and in academia, is what the pharma man was thinking we should evolve into, but he didn't say.

I return from this reverie to find the pharma speaker has finished, replaced by someone less interesting describing new techniques for managing 'tail spend', the ninety per cent of transactions consuming only ten per cent of spend. These technologies certainly help to release time for more strategic stuff, but it's not the most riveting subject at this stage of the conference. So I take a sneak view at the survey report on psychometrics.

The survey invited forty-five CPOs from large, global organisations to do a psychometric test, measuring the dimensions widely considered as most relevant to a senior job in an organisation. The results showed the ideal CPO to be someone great with numbers, brilliant at understanding and expressing ideas, as extrovert as a salesperson, better with words than a marketer, and with an artistic bent. Apparently this profile most closely mirrors that of a CFO, with CPOs to CEOs not being an obvious comparison.

'CEOs are more entrepreneurial and prepared to act more intuitively,' says one of the authors of the report. 'Procurement must evolve to help businesses deal with future uncertainty, and the need for transformation that comes with it.'

This is exactly what's taking place in AeroCorp.

The pace of the afternoon quickens upon the return of the buyer–seller guru who'd made such an impact in the morning. The voting technology is out again and he asks, 'How important is the way you come across to getting a good deal?'

Ninety-six per cent of us think it is.

He then asks, 'How many of you try to create rapport with the seller at the beginning of a meeting?'

Only half admit to doing so. Such is the gap between good intentions and good practice.

The final speaker is billed as 'motivational'. All the ones I've heard before are either pumped up with their own ego or have somehow heroically survived a life-threatening ordeal which, unfortunately, doesn't necessarily make them a good speaker.

But this time it's different. The speaker is a young Scottish chap who's set up a jam-making business. It's a homely narrative since the jam is made to his gran's recipe. We're hooked by the articulate yet self-effacing way in which he speaks, and how his restless optimism refused to take 'no' for an answer when encountering early setbacks.

He's gone on to set up a beer company and also a registered Scottish charity. But what makes the jam story stick is that, although they sell hundreds of thousands of jars of the stuff to major supermarkets around the world, his team comprises only fifteen people, none of whom actually makes jam. All this is done by a contracted jam factory – a very large part of his company that he doesn't own and which is staffed by people he doesn't employ. Magic.

And so to the post-conference reception. Canapés appear and drinks flow. I'm in animated conversation with a young chap employed by one of the conference sponsors, a PR agency. He's recently graduated with an MPhil in Judaism and Christianity in the Greco–Roman World. I suspect he's good at his job, which, if so, suggests that success in business doesn't necessarily depend on arcane academic qualifications. I don't think our motivational speaker needed to graduate in jam studies.

Journeying back to the hotel I reflect on a good day and, perhaps, the end of a longer chapter. The gut feel proves to be correct as, when I look at emails again, there's the letter I'd half-guessed Penserin have been working towards in recent weeks.

It's from Ed.

'Dear Jon, I am pleased to be able to write to you today further to the announcement this morning that Morag PLC intends to acquire the AeroCorp group of companies which, in combination with two other acquisitions, will create an industrial group with annual sales of more than £650 million.

'There is no doubt the procurement journey we've been on over the past two years has helped enormously to position AeroCorp as a highly attractive enterprise, especially as Morag's due diligence has confirmed our strong trading relationships, robust supply contracts, competitive costs and effective supply risk management. Perhaps key, as we navigate into the future, is the role procurement transformation has played in creating a collaborative and commercially aware culture in the company which is not afraid of change and constantly pursues organisational high performance. Morag has noted this and, I believe, intends to use AeroCorp's change-management model as the catalyst to create change in its other acquisitions.

'We firmly believe the proposed acquisition of AeroCorp is good news for all our stakeholders and, in particular, our suppliers. The acquisition is dependent upon the approval of Morag's shareholders, but in the meantime, it's very much business as usual.'

I suspect this is a cut-and-pasted letter, as procurement wasn't the only aspect of AeroCorp's business they were transforming. But Ed's words about procurement are founded in fact and I appreciate them. It may mean 'business as usual' for the AeroCorp folk, but I guess my work there is done.

While I am reading this my phone announces an incoming message. It's Ed. He asks if I've seen the letter. I say I have and it isn't a surprise, although I'm sorry our paths may now divert.

'Not just yet, Jon. I want you to come over to LA again so we can have an AeroCorp wrap-up procurement-wise and also identify aspects of our transformation that could be transferable to Morag.'

It sounds like the end of one chapter and the beginning of another. Although it's been a long day in London, Ed's invitation has stirred many thoughts which will probably germinate better in the hotel bar downstairs. Single malt whisky stimulates this process but doesn't stop the mind from wandering to a nearby newspaper headline: 'Lost in Translation: Litter Sign Ruder Than Intended'. Apparently a country park on England's south coast has apologised after an internet translation of the Hindi text on a sign gave it a different meaning written below in English. The sign was asking visitors not to drop rubbish on the beach. However, the Hindi translation of the word 'rubbish' was wrong. Instead of being asked not to litter, Indian visitors are being told 'not to drop bullshit' on the beach. A spokesperson added, 'It's a good lesson not to use any kind of computerised translation.'

Chapter 37

California

THREE WEEKS LATER I'm jetting west again to visit the folk where it all started. Inside the arrivals hall in LA's iconic airport the tannoys still advise that 'soliciting is illegal and we should have nothing to do with solicitors'. This probably reflects many people's feeling about the profession.

A quirk of fate finds driver Ray waiting outside with the ground transportation. I look forward to another comparative analysis between the nice folk of the mid-west and the salutation-hostile Californians. But this time he's more subdued. It's many months since I first met him and maybe he's realised he can't change them. We ease into the traffic on the eastbound Freeway while Ray fiddles with the radio, tuning in to the day's news. It's about industrial strife at some place where the workers are holding management to ransom. The story triggers more observational wisdom from Ray along the lines that it's the firm's management who are responsible for the mess, not the employees. 'Trouble is, these firms treat people like they don't have feelings and aren't interested in anything but the pay. Now, here's the thing. People only have one life and most of them don't want to waste it. They have a lot to give to their jobs if only management give them the space to do so.'

I tell Ray about Sir John Harvey-Jones and his belief in people needing headroom.

'Not sure I've heard of him, but I'll tell you about an American who you may not have come across,' he replies.

'OK, who's that and what did he say?'

'Studs Terkel. He may have been pissed off by his boss when he said this, I dunno, but what he said was, "Working is about a search for daily meaning as well as daily bread, for recognition as well as cash, for astonishment rather than torpor; in short, for a sort of life rather than a Monday-through-Friday sort of dying."'

'How true.'

'Yeah. Now there'll be some bums out there who don't buy into that, but I'll guess the majority do.'

So… Ray's a philosopher as well as a student of salutations.

Checking in at the suites hotel reveals they have total recall of my previous stays. They confirm there's a room ready, facing the theme park. I ask for food to be sent up to the room as a precursor to retiring early in the hope of beating jet lag.

The following day, I take the now-familiar journey to Gullmech and we pull into the front parking area, still dominated by Ed's SUV. I enter the building and hot tarmac gives way to cool carpets as automatic glass doors seal off already-rising temperatures outside. As before, Donna is at reception. 'Why, good morning, Mr Walsh, it's great to see you again. How was your journey? Let me take you through. Most of the team are already here.'

Little has changed in the office zone, although pictures adorning the corridor depict Antony's one-time project now firmly installed and put to work producing high-spec aeroplane parts. Alongside are impressive photos of airborne aircraft using, somewhere inside them, said parts. In the conference room it's good to see the local team again. Folk from a couple of the other US businesses have also come for this final gathering, as have Mishal, Mike and John from the UK. Ten of them in all. It's no surprise to find them perusing Davina's menus ready for the first Deli drop later in the day.

There's some discussion about how best to spend this wrap-up session. We decide to break into four groups, each to summarise the key messages and effective practices that have liberated procurement's impact since the day I first met Ed … and Vince Lombardi. We regroup in four areas of the large conference room and set to work.

Mishal, Rich and Antony are the first to report back shortly before lunch. They've been looking at 'the making of cost savings'. That's appropriate, as Mishal has been responsible for coordinating AeroCorp's cost saving achievements since joining the project. She has excelled at exhorting the businesses to make faster progress. Their feedback to the rest of the group starts by recalling the three primary cost-saving levers: pushing harder and aggregation (thirteen per cent), collaboration (fifteen per cent plus) and outmanoeuvring hostile supply markets (twenty-five per cent plus). They've remembered some great case histories, including the oil company's forecourt rebuild contract, changing the sugar specification to 'sweetener', the hotel chef who succumbed to the CPO's persuasive psychology, the conversion of dry-goods haulage to liquid transport capability, and the company who beat the steel cartel. But there are plenty of good AeroCorp examples as well which, while perhaps not as headline grabbing, have delivered substantial profit contributions by pushing harder on existing and new deals and holding suppliers accountable for better performance. They also recall the tell-tale signs of a supplier who's being pushed too far and is either about to go under or stop supplying.

Interestingly, Mishal and co's feedback includes how to make space for buyers to use their time more fruitfully. For example, the creation of long-term agreements and call-off contracts. They're about to get into more strategic territory when Shirley interrupts.

'Guys, you've given a great summary there but I'll say two things. One is that we'll be covering strategy stuff in our feedback and, two, I'm hungry. How about a break?'

We've been engrossed in the cost-saving story and have lost track of time. Moreover, Davina has made a food drop but Donna has held it back because she saw we were busy. Now we're not, and we're hungry.

We resume after a quick lunch and give the floor to Shirley, Mike and Elaine. An interesting combination: Shirley, who used not to take prisoners but now takes a longer view and sees a business world holding more promise than simply repeating today's hassle tomorrow; Mike, who brings the UK perspective and wants to build better procurement on the foundation of good day-to-day practice in Lenwall's business; and Elaine, who has potential which wasn't, but now is, being realised. She's also cut her hair, which is no longer waist-length but short and chic. Self-belief is growing.

This team recalls how procurement needs to operate in different supply markets. Elaine leads by summarising the Kraljic matrix and I'm taken back to those earlier sessions when the lately departed Scott was trying to introduce us to four-box thinking but Ed kept putting it on the back burner. Even then, Elaine showed a good grasp of the tool's power. Mike echoes the previous team's comments when he reiterates some of the 'pushing and probing' successes achieved with 'leverage' items. Then Shirley comes in with the need for a different approach for the so-called strategic items. I never thought I'd hear her say this, given that my first impression was that she believed cracking the whip was the only way to keep suppliers jumping. But now she sketches out the five-stage approach to developing a procurement strategy and reminds us we used Scott's work on castings as a practical example. We agree that a major benefit of a strategy is defining how we want a particular supply market to look and behave in future. It provides a constant goal which maintains direction when dealing with unexpected events en route, and having strategic momentum enhances agility. Strategies also invite 'planned luck'.

Elaine makes concluding references to the need for relationship-management plans with key suppliers and also the use of negotiation variables to create better deals when suppliers won't move on price. There's light relief as she recalls the British CEO's retirement package.

Time presses but we agree that a quick walk outside will be good. We exit through the factory floor and into afternoon sunshine. Shirley knows her way around here and suggests that instead of an aimless stroll why don't we get refreshments at the nearby coffee shop and enjoy them outside. John begins to protest as he and Dora are up next to reprise procurement's role, but he changes tack as a new idea dawns. 'Let's do that, Shirley. And while we're at it, we'll address our topic in a different way.'

'Meaning what?' says Dora, who's clearly thinking that John's gone off piste.

'All the time we've been working with Jon he's come up with quotations he's either invented or picked up on his travels. A lot of those are about procurement's role. Let's see how many we can recall.'

Dora builds on this. 'Nice idea. It's like coming up with a so-called "elevator pitch".'

Mishal agrees. 'I once bought a book on communication which had a great title: *Can You Put It On A T-Shirt?*'

'And how was it?' asks a contemplative Shirley, who hasn't said much all day, although what she has said has been spot on.

'Very useful. A lot of good stuff inside, although not as punchy as the title.'

By now we've reached the coffee shop where, having ordered, we push a couple of tables together outside and get seated.

Ed kicks off. 'Right, Jon wants us to recall quotes that hammer home procurement's real job without lots of consultant words! And I'm going to break the rule right away with one of Jon's own: "Procurement is about managing a large part of our company which we do not own, cannot see and which is staffed by people we don't employ. That's a lot more challenging than placing orders."'

Ed looks pleased with himself but gets a 'look' from Dora in the process. Incidentally, it's great that Dora is here at all. She has a big job in AeroCorp's business in Kansas and yet she's now a real convert and sees procurement as an integral part of the business model.

Ed catches Dora's fleeting expression. 'You don't look pleased with me. What have I said, Dora?'

'Nothing terminal, Ed,' says Dora, now smiling. 'You took the words out of my mouth. What you said is my favourite quote too. But I've got a close second.'

'Which is?' Rich is writing furiously to get this stuff down, and I realise he hasn't heard some of these before.

Dora channels the VP in Kananaskis Country: "'Business is simple. We buy things, we transform them, and we sell things – and we have to be equally good at all of that to succeed as a company.'"

The pace hots up as folks chip in with other contributions.

"'If you're in business, you're in procurement. It's not discretionary. The only question is how well are we going to do it?'"

"'We don't measure savings to justify procurement's existence because we already accept it as a vital business process. We measure simply to check we're doing it as well as possible.'"

"'We make our business out of selling and our profit out of procurement.'"

Ed recalls these last two quotes as coming from the successful Scandinavian company, so he chips in with a third: "'Procurement exists to ensure we have access to the supply markets the company needs for it to succeed now and in future.'"

And finally, Diane ruefully observes that 'budget holders guard money like it's their own but spend it like it's someone else's'.

Ed comes in. 'That's a great note to finish on, Diane, because you and I need to tell the guys what we discussed around procurement transformation and handling the unexpected. Let's get back inside and finish the day on that note.'

We're back in the conference room for the last time.

'OK, says Ed,' let's remember what we learnt about transformation and managing change. First we have to measure what has to change and by how much. Any ideas how we do that?'

We know Ed's playing with us, so several people chant, 'Six times seven is forty-two!' There's an end-of-term feeling in the air.

Diane steps in, subtly reminding Ed he's not teaching high school. 'And that's Route 42 for you ... one of the two parallel journeys to the same destination.'

'Ah, yes, the pincer movement,' adds Elaine.

We go on to discuss the importance of enlightened policies and principles and the need for them to embrace the whole company, not just the procurement team.

'Which brings us back to what I said just before we came indoors,' says Diane. 'Our colleagues in other departments will behave like prima donnas unless we convince them they're part of the procurement process. If we get the process right it'll open up new opportunities for them...'

'And stop them wasting money,' Shirley is quick to add.

'Actually,' says Elaine,' that reminds me of another of Jon's quotes, the one about the Asia–Pacific CEO's unstinting support for what his company called their "Procurement Academy".'

For once, Ed doesn't have it at his fingertips. 'Elaine, remind us what he said.'

"'The procurement process is a microcosm of the whole company. Transforming the effectiveness of this process achieves direct cost reductions and, more powerfully, benefits the culture and performance of the business overall.'"

Mishal joins in, "'But because procurement starts from such a low point in many companies, making change is tough. It's the pain involved that makes the change such a positive and lasting one.'"

Excellent. These guys have learnt their lines well.

It seems like we're approaching the end of the show. We could go on to talk about barriers, primary and supporting changes, planned luck and handling the unexpected, but the team won't need reminding about these things, vital as they are.

It's time to conclude. Ed looks at me enquiringly.

I respond to my cue. 'Actually, I do have one more quote. It's the Vince Lombardi one I saw in Ed's office when we first met. The one about "winning is not a sometime thing". Mr Lombardi then went on to say, "You don't do things right once in a while; you do things right all the time." That's the real message for strategic procurement, and that's what Route 42 and procurement transformation help you achieve. And guys, you've got there.'

People fall silent as they realise just how different things are – and for the better – compared with where they'd started.

Back to Ed. He summarises that the day has been not so much about the results achieved but about the changes that have delivered them, and how the barriers and resistance have been overcome in the process. The main takeaway is how necessary it is to deliver cost savings that justify the change process and pay for it, and simultaneously to make underlying changes which transform procurement from being a service function into a key management activity that everyone buys into. Ed acknowledges Mishal's vital contribution over the past year, and this is greeted by an enthusiastic round of applause.

It looks like we're done, but Ed has another treat in store. He invites us to adjourn to the nearby hotel which by now feels like a second home and where he's organised a farewell reception. The SUV is deployed in that direction with a squad of cars following as backup.

And here we are again in the hotel with the big atrium. The same palm-fringed river runs into sandy-coloured pools where goldfish languidly feed off bagels and potato chips that have ended up in the 'sea'. They say you can never step into the same river twice, but in this case I suspect you can as this one's on recycle. Whether the fish food is the same is anyone's guess. The same little bridge leads to the thatched hut, but this time its purpose is clear. It's reserved for us and we gather for drinks and celebratory toasts.

Ed makes a speech about how thrilled he's been that Gullmech and the other AeroCorp teams have so completely taken on the challenge to transform procurement, with all the extra effort that implied.

We then line up for photos, during which we're all presented with a beautiful small glass pyramid, each of the five sides having a symbol engraved on it to represent procurement's five-fold role in business. That's a nice touch. Mine also has a special thank you engraved in the base, which can be seen through each window. Another nice touch.

It's clear there's something else to divulge, and Ed is coaxed into announcing he'll be moving to a special assignment in Morag, reporting directly to the CEO, to look for procurement synergies across the entire company and, more importantly, to roll out a culture-change programme similar to AeroCorp's. Maybe I'll see more of him, after all.

So that's it, and we return to mingling and making merry.

Shirley beckons me and confides that tomorrow it'll be announced she's seizing the change of company ownership as the opportunity to take early retirement.

'Ed already knows,' she says, and then breaks off as he joins us. This isn't because she doesn't want him to hear, but because she's naturally feeling emotional. We always knew she had a soft side but didn't often allow herself to reveal it.

Now she does. 'Ed, I want to wish you every success in your new job. You'll be making lots of changes, just like here, and it'll be so worthwhile not just for the business but at the human level as well. So,' she pauses to gather herself, 'I want to thank you for all you've done to make the last two years of my life here in the company so absolutely enjoyable and productive. You've made it possible for me to do the things I've always known to be right but the system wouldn't let me. It's been a joy to work with you.'

Ed and I look at each other as she leaves. We can't follow that and settle instead for a slightly embarrassed man-hug and fresh beer.